W9-CMR-889

Historical Dictionary of the "Dirty Wars"

David Kohut
Olga Vilella
Beatrice Julian

Historical Dictionaries of War, Revolution, and Civil Unrest, No. 24

The Scarecrow Press, Inc.
Lanham, Maryland, and Oxford
2003

SCARECROW PRESS, INC.

Published in the United States of America
by Scarecrow Press, Inc.
A wholly owned subsidiary of
The Rowman & Littlefield Publishing Group, Inc.
4501 Forbes Boulevard, Suite 200, Lanham, Maryland 20706
www.scarecrowpress.com

PO Box 317
Oxford
OX2 9RU, UK

Copyright © 2003 by David Kohut, Olga Vilella, and Beatrice Julian

All rights reserved. No part of this publication may be reproduced,
stored in a retrieval system, or transmitted in any form or by any
means, electronic, mechanical, photocopying, recording, or otherwise,
without the prior permission of the publisher.

British Library Cataloguing in Publication Information Available

Library of Congress Cataloging-in-Publication Data

Kohut, David R., 1953–
  Historical dictionary of the "dirty wars" / David Kohut, Olga Vilella, Beatrice
Julian.
      p. cm. — (Historical dictionaries of war, revolution, and civil unrest ; no. 24)
    Includes bibliographical references.
    ISBN 0-8108-4853-8 (alk. paper)
    1. Argentina—History—Dirty War, 1976–1983—Dictionaries. 2. Chile—
History—1973–1988—Dictionaries. 3. Uruguay—History—1904–1973—
Dictionaries. 4. Political violence—Chile—History—20th century—Dictionaries.
5. Political violence—Uruguay—History—20th century—Dictionaries. I. Vilella,
Olga, 1954– II. Julian, Beatrice, 1954– III. Title. IV. Series.
F2849.2 .K64 2003
303.6'098'03—dc21

                                                              2003010162

♾™ The paper used in this publication meets the minimum requirements of
American National Standard for Information Sciences—Permanence of Paper for
Printed Library Materials, ANSI/NISO Z39.48-1992.
Manufactured in the United States of America.

Contents

Editor's Foreword

Warfare can assume many forms other than the more classical wars between states and civil wars, which are generally recognized if imperfectly regulated by international law. There is a vast category that does not pit one state against another or even the state against armed force—instead, it is the state that engages in warfare against some of its own citizens for economic, social, ethnic, or ideological reasons. These are often horribly violent and implacable because the state, namely, the government and/or military establishment, has infinitely more power than its opponents and can crush them or just make them disappear with impunity. Such "dirty wars" have occurred on both sides of the communist-capitalist divide for much of the past century for sometimes rather specious reasons, and sometimes for no reason at all. And they have been around much longer in countless countries of mixed racial or religious composition through "ethnic cleansing" and other techniques. Only in South America, more specifically Argentina, Chile, and Uruguay, has the subject received serious attention, and where circumstances and events have been sufficiently elucidated to see just how this kind of warfare manifests itself and just how dirty it can be.

This *Historical Dictionary of the "Dirty Wars"* is, therefore, particularly welcome in expanding the scope of the war series and showing us what the future of warfare may hold in store if we are not careful. This is done, first, through a chronology of events, and more broadly, by putting these events in the overall context in the introduction. The dictionary includes more details, with entries on persons—those who ran the state and those who were crushed by it—some considerably more guilty than others and some who were pure victims. There are also entries on various political parties and other organizations that were involved in these events, again on both sides, and the methods they used, including torture and guerrilla warfare. Some entries, all too few, trace efforts to stop or at least restrain the excesses. The situation in each country is brought together in the three key entries on Argentina, Chile, and Uruguay. This book, while reasonably rounded and comprehensive, obviously cannot tell the whole story. The bibliography, therefore, refers readers to other sources of information.

This book was written by three persons with a keen interest in the situation of Latin America during the period of the "dirty wars." They are all close observers but with somewhat varied academic backgrounds and careers. Both David Kohut and Beatrice Julian are reference librarians at the Byrne Memorial Library of Saint Xavier University in Chicago. Olga Vilella is a professor at the same university with a specialization in Latin American literature. Between them they have done an excellent job of tracking down often elusive information and providing an overall picture of a period that is all too often seen only from one angle or another, missing those parts one does not want to see.

Jon Woronoff
Series Editor

Preface

The "dirty wars" waged in the Southern Cone of South America—Argentina, Chile, and Uruguay—during the 1970s and 1980s form the scope of the dictionary. The term "dirty war," originally associated with the dictatorship in Argentina from 1976 to 1983, is now regularly applied to the regime of General Augusto Pinochet Ugarte (1973–1990) in Chile and to the dictatorship in Uruguay (1973–1985). Indeed, the term has become a byword for state-sponsored repression anywhere in the world. These countries were selected for inclusion for three reasons. First, they were notorious offenders, their names synonymous with human rights violations, though Uruguay, overshadowed by its neighbors, received far less world attention. Second, they are often discussed together in the literature on the topic of military dictatorship and its aftermath. Third, the arrest and eventual release of Pinochet Ugarte in Great Britain have brought renewed attention to the period and the region.

Categories of entries include the countries themselves; guerrilla and political movements that provoked (though by no means exonerated) government reaction; leading guerrilla, human rights, military, and political figures; local, regional, and international human rights organizations; and major literary figures whose works reflect the period of repression. Other entries relevant to the story include the United States, the Catholic Church, and such terms as "dirty war," *desaparecidos*, and liberation theology. Words in boldface point the reader to additional entries.

The alphabetization of the dictionary entries follows the letter-by-letter system in which sorting ignores spaces, hyphens, and apostrophes. Commas and slashes, however, interrupt the sorting: FAMILIARES / RELATIVES precedes FAMILIARES DE DESAPARECIDOS Y DETENIDOS POR RAZONES POLÍTICAS, and PERÓN, JUAN precedes PERONISM. Dictionary entries for organizations formed in Spanish-speaking countries will be found under the Spanish version of the name; hence, readers looking for the Argentine human rights organization MOTHERS OF THE PLAZA DE MAYO will be referred to MADRES DE LA PLAZA DE MAYO. References to individuals will follow the Spanish-speaking model. If an individual has two surnames (the paternal followed by the maternal), both will be used; Salvador Allende Gossens, then, after the first reference in an entry, will be referred to as Allende Gossens, not simply as Allende.

The introduction attempts to compare and contrast the three countries as they descended into military dictatorship, experienced repression, and returned to civilian rule. The bibliography begins with a listing of general works (books and articles on at least two of the three countries), followed by sections on each country in turn. The country sections are divided into works examining the background to the "dirty wars," the "dirty war" period itself, and the aftermath. The subsections on the "dirty war" period are themselves subdivided into works of nonfiction and *testimonio* (a genre that blurs the line between nonfiction and literature), works of literature, and films and documentaries.

Thanks are extended to Saint Xavier University for granting David Kohut a sabbatical leave to work on the project; to Margaret Hoefferle, interlibrary loan technician at Byrne Memorial Library, SXU, for going to great lengths to obtain materials; and to Mary Krekelberg for offering helpful comments and suggestions.

Acronyms and Abbreviations

AAA	Alianza Anticomunista Argentina (La Triple-A)
AD	Alianza Democrática
AFDD	Agrupación de Familiares de Detenidos Desaparecidos
AFEP	Agrupación de Familiares de Ejecutados Políticos
AI	Amnesty International
AID	Agency for International Development
ANCLA	Agencia de Noticias Clandestinas
APDH	Asamblea Permanente por los Derechos Humanos
CADHU	Comisión Argentina por los Derechos Humanos
CC	Comando Conjunto
CELS	Centro de Estudios Legales y Sociales
CGT	Confederación General del Trabajo
CGTA	Confederación General del Trabajo de los Argentinos
CIA	Central Intelligence Agency
CNI	Centro Nacional de Información
CNT	Convención Nacional de Trabajadores
CNVR	Comisión Nacional de Verdad y Reconciliación
CODEPU	Comité de Defensa de los Derechos del Pueblo
CONADEP	Comisión Nacional sobre la Desaparición de Personas
CONAPRO	Concertación Nacional Programática
COPACHI	Comité de la Paz (Chile)
COSENA	Consejo de Seguridad Nacional
DICOMCAR	Dirección de Inteligencia y Comunicaciones de Carabineros
EAAF	Equipo Argentino de Antropología Forense
EGP	Ejército Guerrillero del Pueblo
ENR	Ejército Nacional Revolucionario
ERP	Ejército Revolucionario del Pueblo
ESMA	Escuela Mecánica de la Armada
FAP	Fuerzas Armadas Peronistas
FAR	Fuerzas Armadas Revolucionarias
FASIC	Fundación de Ayuda Social de las Iglesias Cristianas
FPMR	Frente Patriótico Manuel Rodríguez

FREJULI	Frente Justicialista de Liberación Nacional
FRIP	Frente Revolucionario Indoamericano Popular
GOU	Grupo de Oficiales Unidos
GT	Grupo de Tarea
HIJOS	Hijos por la Identidad y la Justicia, contra el Olvido y el Silencio
HRNGO	Human Rights Nongovernmental Organization
IACHR	Inter-American Commission on Human Rights
IADC	Inter-American Defense College
ICJ	International Commission of Jurists
IELSUR	Instituto de Estudios Legales y Sociales (Uruguay)
LASA	Latin American Studies Association
MAP	Military Assistance Program
MDP	Movimiento Democrático Popular
MEDH	Movimiento Ecuménico por los Derechos Humanos
MIR	Movimiento de la Izquierda Revolucionaria
MLN	Movement for National Liberation
MPL	Movimiento Peronista de Liberación
MTP	Movimiento Todos por la Patria (also known as Todos por la Patria, or TPP)
NGO	Nongovernmental Organization
OAS	Organization of American States
PC	Partido Comunista
PDC	Partido Demócrata Cristiano
PIDEE	Fundación para la Protección de la Infancia Dañada por los Estados de Emergencia
PIT	Plenario Intersindical de Trabajadores
PJ	Partido Justicialista
PL	Patria y Libertad
PO	Palabra Obrera
PRT	Partido Revolucionario de los Trabajadores
PS	Partido Socialista
SEDHU	Servicio Ecuménico por la Dignidad Humana
SER	Servicio Ecuménico de Reintegración
SERPAJ	Servicio Paz y Justicia
TPP	Todos por la Patria (an alternative acronym for the Movimiento Todos por la Patria, or MTP)
Triple A	La Triple-A (also Alianza Anticomunista Argentina)
UN	United Nations
UNHRC	United Nations Human Rights Commission
UP	Unidad Popular

VOP   Vanguardia Organizada del Pueblo

Chronology

Argentina

1912   The Sáenz Peña Law passes Congress, requiring
                        secret and compulsory voting for males over 18.

1916   Hipólito Yrigoyen, leader of the reformist
                        Unión Cívica Radical, or Radical Civic Union
                        party), becomes president in the country's first
                        popular election.

7–13 January 1919   The *porteñazo* uprising by workers in the port
                        city of Buenos Aires; the army is called in to
                        quell the rioting; also called *La Semana
                        Trágica*, or Tragic Week.

1921–1922   Patagonian rebellion of workers against British
                        and **Argentine** sheep ranchers; soldiers kill
                        1,500 workers.

1922–1928   The government of Marcelo T. de Alvear; not
                        until 1989 will another constitutionally elected
                        administration give way to another.

6 September 1930   President Yrigoyen, having been reelected in
                        1928, is deposed in a coup led by General José
                        Félix Uriburu.

1930   The Supreme Court rules that the armed forces
                        may legally oust an elected government.

17 April 1931   A palace coup forces General Uriburu to sched-
                        ule elections before the end of the year.

1932–1942   During the "infamous decade," General Agustín
                     P. Justo and Roberto M. Ortiz come to power in
                     fraudulent elections.

4 June 1943   The **military** overthrows President Ramón S.
                     Castillo; in the resulting military government,
                     Juan Perón becomes increasingly powerful as
                     secretary of labor and welfare, minister of war,
                     and vice president.

9 October 1945   The military arrests Perón and removes him
                     from government.

17 October 1945   Thousands of workers demonstrate in the **Plaza
                     de Mayo**, forcing Perón's release.

24 February 1946   Perón is elected president. In his first admini-
                     stration (1946–1952) he aggressively pursues
                     policies of nationalism and social reform. **Eva
                     Duarte "Evita" Perón**, his wife and political
                     partner, gains prominence as an advocate of the
                     working class.

1952–1955   The second Perón administration loses popular-
                     ity owing to economic crisis and the death of
                     Evita from cancer (1952). Perón angers the
                     Catholic Church by such acts as legalizing di-
                     vorce.

16 September 1955   General Eduardo Lonardi initiates a coup that
                     deposes Perón and sends him into **exile**.

13 November 1955   The "liberating revolution" of General Pedro
                     Aramburu, who overthrows Lonardi in a palace
                     coup.

1955–1958   The administration of General Aramburu, who
                     vigorously suppresses **Peronism**.

9 June 1956   Peronist generals Juan José Valle and Raúl
                     Tanco stage an ill-fated revolt against Aram-

buru. Valle and many supporters face the firing squad.

1958–1962   President Arturo Frondizi allows Peronists to participate in gubernatorial and congressional elections. Peronist candidates do so well that the military forces Frondizi from office.

1963–1966   President Arturo Illia allows Peronists to participate in gubernatorial and congressional elections. As in 1962, Peronist candidates do well, and the president is deposed in a coup.

1966–1970   The authoritarian regime of General Juan Carlos Onganía.

29 July 1966   "The Night of the Long Sticks": Police quell unrest at the University of Buenos Aires.

1967   The Argentine-born **guerrilla** Ernesto "Che" Guevara dies fomenting revolution in Bolivia, inspiring many young Argentines.

1968   Leftist **trade union** leaders, removed from the **Confederación General del Trabajo** (CGT, General Confederation of Labor), form the CGT de los Argentinos (CGTA, CGT of the Argentines).

29 May 1969   Students and workers in the city of Córdoba stage a weeklong rebellion (the "*Cordobazo*") against the government.

29 May 1970   Former president Pedro Aramburu is kidnapped and murdered, allegedly by a militant Peronist group called the **Montoneros**.

8 June 1970   The military ousts Onganía; General Roberto Marcelo Levingston becomes president.

24 October 1970	**Salvador Allende Gossens** is declared president of neighboring **Chile**, becoming the first democratically elected Marxist president in the world.
March 1971	A second uprising in Córdoba prompts the military to remove Levingston; General Alejandro A. Lanusse becomes president.
22 August 1972	Massacre at Trelew: The military executes 16 political prisoners held at a navy airbase.
November 1972	Perón briefly returns to Argentina, naming **Héctor José Cámpora** to represent him in the forthcoming presidential election.
March 1973	Héctor José Cámpora wins the presidential election as Perón's stand-in, clearing the way for Perón's return to power.
20 June 1973	Right-wing Peronists open fire on their leftwing counterparts at Ezeiza International Airport, where over a million people gather to welcome Perón on his return.
July 1973	President Cámpora is forced to resign in a right-wing palace coup.
11 September 1973	Chilean president Salvador Allende is overthrown in a military coup led by General **Augusto Pinochet Ugarte**.
23 September 1973	Perón is elected president in a special election; his third wife, **Isabel Perón**, becomes vice president.
October 1973	The Montoneros and the **Fuerzas Armadas Revolucionarias** (FAR, Revolutionary Armed Forces), merge under the name Montoneros.
1 May 1974	In a speech, Perón denounces leftist Peronists.

1 July 1974	Perón dies; Isabel becomes president.
November 1974	The military imposes a state of siege, escalating its war against guerrilla groups and other suspected subversives.
24 March 1976	A military coup overthrows Isabel and imposes a three-member junta led by General **Jorge Rafael Videla**, who becomes president.
January 1977	**Jimmy Carter** is inaugurated as president of the **United States**.
January 1981	**Ronald Reagan** is inaugurated as president of the United States.
March 1981	General Roberto Viola succeeds General Videla as president.
December 1981	Lieutenant-General **Leopoldo Fortunato Galtieri** replaces General Viola.
2 April 1982	Argentina invades the **Falkland Islands/Islas Malvinas**. The British, long holding claim to the islands, send troops to recover them.
18 June 1982	Argentina surrenders. General Galtieri is forced to resign in disgrace.
2 July 1982	General **Reynaldo Benito Bignone** becomes president.
August 1983	The military government approves the *Ley de Pacificación Nacional*, which grants amnesty to members of the police and armed forces guilty of human rights violations.
30 October 1983	**Raúl Alfonsín** is elected president.

December 1983	President Alfonsín revamps the military, repeals the *Ley de Pacificación Nacional*, and establishes the **Comisión Nacional sobre la Desaparición de Personas** (CONADEP, National Commission on the Disappearance of Persons).
April 1985	Former junta members are put on trial.
December 1985	Five former junta members are sentenced to prison—including General Videla and Admiral **Eduardo Massera**, who are sentenced to life imprisonment.
December 1986	The government proposes, and Congress approves, the *Punto Final* (Full Stop) Law, which sets 22 February 1987 as the deadline for bringing new cases of human rights violations before civil and military courts.
May 1987	In the face of an army rebellion by a group of junior officers (the *carapintadas*), the government announces the *Obediencia Debida* (Due Obedience) Law, which declares an amnesty for all members of the police and armed forces except senior officers.
1988	The government suppresses two more *carapintada* army rebellions—one in January led by Lieutenant Colonel Aldo Rico and another in December led by Colonel Mohammed Alí Seineldín. The demands are higher pay, a larger military budget, and an amnesty for officers accused of **human rights** violations.
23 January 1989	The **Movimiento Todos por la Patria** (MTP, Everyone for the Motherland), a grassroots human rights organization, attacks and occupies the army garrison at La Tablada. The military is called in to crush the rebellion.

8 July 1989	**Carlos Saúl Menem**, a Peronist, takes office as president.
September 1989	A massive human rights demonstration takes place in Buenos Aires following reports of an amnesty agreement between the Menem government and the military.
October 1989	The government pardons senior military officers, NCOs, and soldiers accused of participating in the "dirty war." Eight remain in prison, including Videla and Massera.
3 December 1990	Another *carapintada* rebellion, the last, is put down by loyalists in the military.
December 1990	Menem pardons those remaining in prison, including Videla and Massera and the Montonero leader Mario Firmenich.
June 1998	Videla is arrested in connection with the illegal adoption of children—a crime not covered by the pardon. Ten more officers are arrested by April 2000.
2001	In separate rulings, two federal judges declare *Punto Final* and *Obediencia Debida* to be unconstitutional.
July 2002	A federal judge orders the arrest of more than 30 former military officers on charges of human rights violations.

Chile

1964	President **Eduardo Frei Montalva** of the **Partido Demócrata Cristiano** (PDC, Christian Democratic Party) takes office and begins a reformist government.

4 September 1970	Dr. **Salvador Allende Gossens**, leading the left-wing coalition **Unidad Popular** (UP, Popular Unity), wins a plurality of votes in the presidential election. The lack of a majority places the outcome of the election in the hands of Congress.
22 October 1970	Elements in the **military**, hoping to prevent the confirmation of Allende Gossens, attempt to kidnap General René Schneider, a constitutional loyalist. Schneider is fatally wounded in the attempt.
24 October 1970	The Chilean Congress declares Allende Gossens the winner of the presidential election.
3 November 1970	Allende Gossens is inaugurated, becoming the first democratically elected Marxist president in the world.
April 1971	A strong economy helps the UP garner more than 50 percent of the vote in municipal elections.
June 1971	The PDC leader Edmundo Pérez Zújovic is assassinated by left-wing **guerrillas**.
1971–1973	Economic decline leads to labor strikes, and growing resistance to Allende Gossens' socialist agenda. Inflation rises from 22 to 600 percent. Food and other consumer goods become scarce.
October 1972	Truck owners stage a strike.
November 1972	Allende Gossens appoints several members of the military to his cabinet.
1973	Bus owners and copper miners strike.

1907 and 1911–1915), Batlle y Ordóñez transforms the country into a welfare state.

1907	Legislation passes that introduces the "double simultaneous" ballot, which allows factions in each party to field their own candidates for office.
1919	A new constitution goes into effect, creating a bicephalous executive: Now serving alongside the president is a council composed of elected members from both the majority and minority parties.
1929	Batlle y Ordóñez dies. The Great Depression begins.
31 March 1933	President Gabriel Terra initiates a 10-year period of moderate dictatorship known as the *dictablanda*.
1938	Elections are allowed, presaging the end of the *dictablanda*, in 1942.
1952	A new constitution eliminates the office of president; all executive functions now reside in a nine-member Colegiado, composed of elected members from both parties.
1958	Economic crisis helps the Blancos win a national election, becoming the majority party for the first time in 93 years.
1963	The **Tupamaro** urban **guerrilla** movement is formed.
1966	The elections, won by the Colorados, include a plebiscite that abolishes the Colegiado and returns the country to a presidential system.

1966–1970

Oscar Gestido, the new president, dies in his first year in office. His vice president and successor, Jorge Pacheco Areco, faces a poor economy, labor unrest, and increasing gurerrilla violence. Pacheco uses strong measures to repress opposition.

1970

The Tupamaros execute Daniel Mitrione, a police advisor provided through the **United States** Agency for International Development.

January 1971

Sir Geoffrey Jackson, the British ambassador to Uruguay, is abducted by the Tupamaros.

9 September 1971

More than a hundred Tupamaros escape from prison; Pacheco calls upon the **military** to help thwart guerilla violence.

September 1971

The Tupamaros release Sir Geoffrey Jackson.

November 1971

Juan María Bordaberry, a Colorado, is elected president.

1 March 1972

Bordaberry takes office and continues the previous administration's campaign against the Tupamaros.

14 April 1972

The Tupamaros assassinate several government officials in Montevideo. In response, Bordaberry declares a "state of internal war," putting the military in charge of combating subversion. By midyear the Tupamaros are crushed.

June 1972

The government extends the state of internal war indefinitely; The **Catholic Church** calls for peace.

12 February 1973

Military officers insist on having a stronger role in government. Bordaberry creates the Consejo de Seguridad Nacional (COSENA, National Security Council), which is dominated by the military.

27 June 1973   Bordaberry, with the support of the military, dissolves Congress, an act that sets off two weeks of demonstrations. The military suppresses opposition and consolidates its rule.

June 1976   The military deposes Bordaberry and suspends national elections, removing any pretense of civilian rule.

July 1976   Dr. Aparicio Méndez Manfredini is appointed president for a five-year term.

August 1977   The government announces a plebiscite, scheduled for November 1980, on a constitution drafted by the military.

30 November 1980   In a plebiscite, voters reject the constitution proposed by the military.

September 1981   General Gregorio Alvarez Armellino becomes president and announces a timetable for national elections and a return to civilian government.

November 1984   In national elections, **Julio María Sanguinetti** becomes president.

1 March 1985   Sanguinetti is inaugurated. By the end of the month, all political prisoners are released under an amnesty law passed by Congress.

August 1986   The government proposes legislation that would grant an amnesty to all military and police personnel accused of **human rights** abuses.

December 1986   Legislation is passed (the *Ley de Caducidad*, or the Law of Caducity) that puts an end to investigations of human rights abuses. The law is widely opposed.

22 February 1987   A campaign is begun to collect enough signatures to force a referendum on human rights.

April 1989   In a referendum, voters uphold the *Ley de Caducidad.*

August 2000   President Jorge Batlle Ibáñez creates the Comisión para la Paz (Peace Commission) to investigate the fate of the missing (***desaparecidos***).

October 2002   The Peace Commission issues a preliminary report showing evidence that the military government in Uruguay was responsible for the deaths of 26 Uruguayans.

Introduction

In the 1970s the countries of the Southern Cone fell under military dictatorship. Under the authoritarian rule of a succession of juntas in Argentina (1976–1983) and of Augusto Pinochet in Chile (1973–1990), thousands were abducted, illegally detained, tortured, exiled, and murdered. Many became *desaparecidos*, vanishing without a trace. The regime in Uruguay (1973–1985), though far less deadly, transformed the country into what Eduardo Galeano described as "a vast torture chamber."[1] In a region noted for political repression, Uruguay had more political prisoners than any Latin American country, and 300,000 people (20 percent of its population) went into exile.[2]

Attempts to explain how the Southern Cone came to such a pass place the events of the period in the context of social aspirations and right-wing reaction. The 1970 election of Salvador Allende Gossens in Chile (the first democratically elected Marxist president in the world) and the activities of leftist guerrilla movements in Argentina and Uruguay are seen as provoking a deadly response from the armed forces. By way of explaining the mindset of the Latin American military, many scholars invoke the National Security Doctrine, which emerged during the Cold War period. Inculcated into Latin American military personnel at the United States Army's School of the Americas and in training courses, the doctrine equated movements for social justice with the spread of international, Soviet-led communism. Other scholars, while not denying the dominant role of the United States in the region, question the emphasis placed on the National Security Doctrine to account for the actions of the military. Carina Perelli, for example, in her case study of Argentina and Uruguay, argues that the armed forces there were not simply doing the bidding of the United States. They were reacting to social and political unrest in their own countries, having been asked to intervene by the dominant sectors of society.[3]

Military ideology in Latin America—whether imported from the United States or developed locally—shifted focus away from an external, geographical enemy to an internal, ideological one. The armed forces perceived a threat, not from an invading enemy across a battlefield, but from "subversives" within their own borders. "Subversive" was broadly defined.

1

The category included armed guerrillas and their supporters, certainly, but also came to include anyone or anything perceived as challenging the status quo. To the military mind, what was at stake was nothing less than "Western, Christian civilization."

A change in enemy, the armed forces argued, necessitated a change in strategy. After all, an ideological enemy is not out in the open as in conventional warfare. Instead, it is hidden and pernicious and needs to be rooted out. Hence a different kind of warfare—a "dirty war" (*guerra sucia*). Suspected subversives were kidnapped (sometimes under cover of night, sometimes in broad daylight), taken to secret prisons, subjected to intense physical and psychological abuse, and often killed or exiled. Torture was routine, and information obtained during sessions led to another wave of arrests. A by-product of this process was fear, which paralyzed society and stifled protest.

Fear breeds complicity and collaboration, and it was easy for many to say that the military knew what it was doing and that those who were disappearing must have been guilty of something. Yet groups and individuals, at great risk to themselves, spoke out. Local human rights groups emerged, collaborating with regional organizations like the Organization of American States and international organizations like the United Nations. The Madres (Mothers) de Plaza de Mayo and their offshoot, the Abuelas (Grandmothers) de Plaza de Mayo, in Argentina; the Vicaría de la Solidaridad in Chile; and Servicio Paz y Justicia-Uruguay, were just a few of the groups that gave witness to the disappearances and offered support (material, social, psychological, and spiritual) to those affected by the violence. Many individuals refused to be silenced. Among them were the lawyer Jaime Castillo Velascas and the journalists Jacobo Timerman, Patricia Verdugo, and Rodolfo Walsh.

Even protesting from outside the country became dangerous as the countries of the region fell, one by one, under military rule. Argentina, Chile, and Uruguay were part of Operation Condor, a secret network that allowed the military regimes of the region to share information and work together in silencing dissent. In 1975, when Condor was formed, Brazil and Paraguay had already been under dictatorship for 10 years. As the other countries followed suit, political refugees seeking sanctuary in neighboring countries were tracked downed, seized, and killed.[4]

Despite the similarities among the three countries, there are differences as well. Chile and Uruguay, unlike Argentina, had strong democratic traditions before succumbing to dictatorship. Democratic rule in Chile ended abruptly in a bloody coup on 11 September 1973, whereas the coup in Uruguay, also in 1973, played out over several months. The coup in Argentina on 24 March 1976, sudden but bloodless, was expected by many and considered at first to be just another in a long line of military interventions. Each country had its own manner of operating. Chile, under Pinochet, was brazen about leaving the bodies of some of its victims out in the open as an example to others. The juntas in Argentina, learning from Chile and hoping to avoid the international condemnation incurred by its methods, adopted the strategy of vanishing people into thin air. Uruguay, as already mentioned, killed fewer, though allegations of torture numbered in the thousands.

Equally diverse were the transitions from military to civilian rule and the attempts to achieve some semblance of national reconciliation. The military in Argentina, unable to control the economy and humiliated by its performance in the Falkland Islands/Islas Malvinas conflict of 1982, turned over the reins of government a year later. Chile's transition was as protracted and tedious as its military coup had been sudden and dramatic. Pinochet allowed national elections to take place in 1989, having first rewritten the constitution and arranged to retain control of the army and assume the position of senator for life. In Uruguay both the coup and the return to democracy were drawn-out affairs. After civility was restored, Argentina and Chile established truth commissions. In Argentina President Raúl Alfonsín created the Comisión Nacional sobre la Desaparición de Personas (CONADEP, National Commission on the Disappearance of Persons); in Chile President Patricio Aylwin Azócar created the Comisión Nacional de Verdad y Reconciliación (National Commission on Truth and Reconciliation). Although both commissions issued reports, the two countries differed in what they did or failed to do with the testimony. Argentina took the unprecedented step of putting its former junta commanders on trial, even sentencing several of them to terms of varying lengths, including life. (The convicted later received a pardon from President Carlos Saúl Menem.) In Chile, Pinochet has to date evaded all attempts to bring him to justice; his advanced age and declining health make it unlikely he will ever face trial. In Argentina and Uruguay, the incoming governments invoked the theory "of the two demons," taking the position that both the guerrillas and the armed forces shared responsibility for the violence. In Argentina, the guerrilla leader Mario Firmenich, for example, was imprisoned by Alfonsín and later released under Menem's blanket pardon. In Uruguay, President Julio María Sanguinetti freed all political prisoners and then proposed a blanket amnesty for the military. In the interest of national reconciliation, the argument went, everyone should forget what happened and move on. After much debate, the people of Uruguay agreed, voting in a referendum not to dredge up the past.

Despite efforts to leave the past behind, the events of the "dirty wars" are not easily forgotten. Calls persist for some kind of closure, for those responsible to be punished. Some emanate from such places as Italy and Sweden, France and Spain, in behalf of citizens from those countries who perished in the violence. Others emanate from sources at home. The Madres de Plaza de Mayo (Mothers of the Plaza de Mayo), for example, an organization that first appeared in 1977 at the height of the dictatorship in Argentina, is still active, keeping up protests and also—through its publications and courses (it operates its own university)—seeking to transform society. Meanwhile, some groups and individuals have meted out a small measure of punishment on their own. Outraged that the perpetrators of the "dirty wars" still walk the streets, the Argentine organization Hijos por la Identidad y la Justicia contra el Olvido y el Silencio (HIJOS, Children for Identity and Justice against Oblivion and Silence) has adopted a practice used in Chile, Uruguay, and other countries: members post signs on the houses of former torturers, letting the neighbors know who is living in their midst. Random street justice occurs, too. Jorge Videla, former army commander and president of Argentina during the first junta, has been jeered and spit upon when recognized in public. And Alfredo Astiz, a cashiered officer in the Argentine navy and a notorious dirty warrior easily recognized for his boyish good looks, has been kicked and pummeled.

Both the advocates of collective amnesia and the advocates of justice often defend their position by pointing to the need for national reconciliation. Although both sides of the argument have merit—truth can stir resentment as easily as it can heal—there is a growing awareness that truth in itself is beneficial, even if it does not always lead to reconciliation.[5] What victims find most important—more important than retribution or reconciliation—is that their sufferings be recorded for future generations.[6] The events of the "dirty wars" are duly recorded, not only in the reports of truth commissions and of national and international organizations, but also in the outpouring of nonfiction, testimonial, and creative works. More books have been written on Chile since 1970 (the year of Salvador Allende Gossens's election) than in the previous 150 years.[7] There is a sense in which, for much of the world (especially the United States and Europe), Chile first came to people's attention in the 1970s in spite of its long history.[8] The same could be said for Argentina. Uruguay has continued to remain overshadowed by its neighbors, and has not attracted as much attention. Yet Uruguay has more than held its own in producing works of literature with "dirty war" themes.[9] The testimonial and creative output from the region (including the exile communities) during and after the dictatorships is extensive, and survivors of the period seem to have directed much of their anguish into testimonials, novels, poems, and films.

The sheer number of books and films inspired by the "dirty wars" raises the question whether this period in the region's history was thoroughly unlike anything in recent memory—a period so extreme that it might fall into the category of radical evil. According to one definition, radical evil is that which compels representation or conceptualization but at the same time resists it. The Holocaust, for example, continues to inspire writers and artists to use their talent in an attempt to do justice to the period. Yet how would they begin to convey—through a novel or painting or sculpture—the reality of six million victims? Nevertheless, writers and artists accept the challenge. Not to do so would consign the victims to the fate of suffering twice.[10] Similarly, one could argue that the "dirty wars" make good candidates for the term *radical evil*. Even for Argentina, which had had a long tradition of political violence and where police use of torture had had a long history, one could argue that its "dirty war" was not only *quantitatively* different (more arrests, more torture) from what preceded it but also *qualitatively* so. One scholar, writing about testimonial literature and collective memory in Argentina, argued that to explain the repression of the recent dictatorship in purely historical terms is essentially to explain it away. It is something more than an item in a chronology—instead, it is "an exceptional moment in the history of Argentina."[11] If so, readers will have to make up their own minds whether Lawrence Thornton's novel *Imagining Argentina*—or any other work of fiction or nonfiction on the "dirty wars"—can, in fact, capture the repression. What the authors were trying to capture may be beyond representation, beyond imagination.[12]

Nunca más (Never Again) is the title of the report of the Argentine truth commission, expressing a fervent hope that atrocities like those documented never be repeated. The words "never again" also appear in the title of a similar report on Uruguay (*Uruguay nunca más*), written by two of the country's human rights groups. Although many are rightly skeptical about humanity's ability to learn from the past, there is still reason for optimism about the region's future. Although the military in Latin America remains a force to be reckoned with, and although the region has a long history of authoritarianism, yet alongside this authoritarianism exists a long tradition of respect for human rights. In the aftermath of World War II, Latin Americans—especially from Chile, Panama, and Cuba—played a leading role in the drafting of the United Nations Universal Declaration of Human Rights.[13] Steeped in Latin American socialism, delegates like Santa Cruz from Chile were especially adamant about the inclusion of social, economic, and cultural rights—the "social security rights" (work and education, food and health care, leisure and the arts)—arguing that these were the best defense against the return of fascism.[14] Resistance to the recent military dictatorships—from lawyers and journalists, writers and artists, religious and family members of the missing—is grounded in a tradition that could be termed counterauthoritarianism. Today, many of the human rights groups that emerged during the repression are still active, having reinvented themselves to work on general issues in the public interest such as civil rights, community development, the environment, women and violence, and the rights of children.

The lessons of the "dirty wars" extend well beyond the Southern Cone. The term "dirty war" is applied in a wide range of contexts both past and present—the French in Algeria during the 1950s and early 1960s, the Mexican government's response to leftists in the 1970s and 1980s, the Russian war in Chechnya, the dictatorship in Morocco, the tactics of the Los Angeles Police Department in combating gangs, and the current "war on terrorism" conducted by the United States and its allies, to list only a few examples.[15] Concerning the war on terrorism, Horacio Verbitsky, a journalist who is known as "el perro" (the dog) for his aggressive journalism style and who is well acquainted with terror in his native Argentina, offered advice to his North American colleagues. Speaking at a Press Freedom Awards Dinner after the "appalling Sept. 11 terrorist attacks" in the United States, he shared what Argentineans had learned: "that sacrificing civil liberties and human rights standards in the name of security has devastating effects."[16]

NOTES

1. Quoted in John King, Introduction to *El infierno*, by Carlos Martínez Moreno (London: Readers International, 1988), ii.

2. John King, Introduction to *El infierno*, by Carlos Martínez Moreno (London: Readers International, 1988), ii; James Polk, "No Middle Ground," review of *El infierno*, by Carlos Martínez Moreno, *New York Times Book Review*, 30 October 1988, 22.

3. Carina Perelli, "From Counterrevolutionary Warfare to Political Awakening: The Uruguayan and Argentine Armed Forces in the 1970s," *Armed Forces and Society* 20, no. 1 (1993): 25–49.

4. J. Patrice McSherry, "Operation Condor: Clandestine Inter-American System," *Social Justice* 26, no. 4 (1969): 144.

5. Serge Schmemann, "Transitional Justice: How to Face the Past, Then Close the Door," *New York Times*, 8 April 2001, national edition.

6. Ibid; "Art and the Moral Imagination," a course taught by David H. Fisher, North Central College, Naperville, Ill., 1998.

7. Mark Falcoff, *Modern Chile, 1970–1989* (New Brunswick, N.J.: Transaction, 1991).

8. Ibid.

9. Ruffinelli, Jorge, "Uruguay: Dictadura y re-democratización: Un informe sobre la literatura, 1973–1989," *Nuevo texto crítico* 3, no. 5 (1990): 37–66.

10. "Art and the Moral Imagination."

11. Liria Evangelista, *Voices of the Survivors: Testimony, Mourning, and Memory in Post-Dictatorship Argentina (1983–1995)*, translated by Renzo Llorente, Garland Reference Library of the Humanities, Latin American Studies, vol. 13 (New York: Garland, 1998), 116.

12. The definition of "radical evil," that which demands and resists representation, comes from "Art and the Moral Imagination," a course taught by David H. Fisher, North Central College, Naperville, Ill., 1998.

13. Johannes Morsink, *The Universal Declaration of Human Rights: Origins, Drafting, and Intent* (Philadelphia: University of Pennsylvania Press, 1999), 130–134; Paolo Carozza, "Of Conquest, Constitutions and Catholics: Retrieving a Latin American Tradition of the Idea of Human Rights," *On Catholic Christianity and Western Civilization,* lecture presented in the Yves R. Simon Memorial Lecture Series, The Lumen Christi Institute, the University of Chicago, April 2002.

14. Morsink, *The Universal Declaration of Human Rights*, 89–90, 132.

15. Eric Stener Carlson, "The Influence of French 'Revolutionary War' Ideology on the Use of Torture in Argentina's 'Dirty War,'" *Human Rights Review* 1, no. 4 (2000): 71–84; "Mexican Human Rights Commission Releases Report on 1970s 'Dirty War,'" *NACLA Report on the Americas* 35, no. 4 (January/February 2002): 2, 46–47; Anna Politkovskaya, "Chechnya's Dirty War," *Maclean's*, 14 January 2002, 16; Eric Goldstein, "Morocco's Dirty War," *Nation*, 21 January 2002, 7–8; Andrew Murr and Ana Figueroa, "L.A.'s Dirty War on Gangs," *Newsweek*, 11 October 1999, 72; Peter Maass, "Dirty War: How America's Friends Really Fight Terrorism," *New Republic*, 11 November 2002, 18–21.

16. Clarence Page, "Friendly Warning from a Lover of Liberty," *Chicago Tribune*, 25 November 2001, final edition.

The Dictionary

–A–

ABRAMS, ELLIOTT (1948–). United States assistant secretary of state for inter-American affairs under the administration of President **Ronald Reagan**, replacing **Langhorne A. ("Tony") Motley,** who resigned in 1985. Abrams was a neoconservative lawyer who had been the assistant secretary of state for **human rights,** also under Reagan, since 1981. By mid-1985, Abrams and other officials in the Reagan administration adopted a consistently critical stance toward the regime of **Augusto Pinochet Ugarte** in **Chile.** Abrams feared that the regime's continuing repression jeopardized a peaceful return to democracy. In addition, the Reagan administration opposed the leftist Sandinista regime in Nicaragua, and failing to pressure the rightist regime in Chile would lead to charges of inconsistency. Abram's efforts against the Sandinistas resulted in his indictment in the Iran-Contra Scandal and a temporary departure from government service.

ABUELAS DE PLAZA DE MAYO / GRANDMOTHERS OF THE PLAZA DE MAYO. A human rights nongovernmental organization in **Argentina.** An offshoot of the **Madres de Plaza de Mayo** (Mothers of the Plaza de Mayo), the group was formed in 1977 by 12 women in search of their grandchildren, who had been abducted along with their parents or born in captivity. The children had become spoils in the government's "dirty war" against suspected subversives, illegally adopted and raised by **military** families or by other families considered "decent" and "patriotic." The Abuelas compiled and distributed lists of missing children, petitioned government officials, and marched with the Madres in the **Plaza de Mayo.** Finding that their status as grandmothers offered no protection from harassment by the military and police, they adopted undercover methods to carry on their work, devising a secret code and meeting in public places while pretending to be engaged in traditional family activities.

9

Once the children were found, a serious obstacle to reuniting them with their families of origin was the lack of proof of a biological connection. Parenthood testing was of no use—more often than not, the parents were dead. What was needed was a test to establish grandparenthood. In 1981 the Abuelas began traveling to hospitals and research centers throughout the world in search of such a test. Their hopes were realized in 1984 when they were introduced to Mary Claire King, a geneticist at the University of California. She traveled to Argentina and helped develop a grandparenthood test that can establish—with up to 99.95 percent certainty—a genetic relationship between a child and a particular family. The Abuelas then persuaded President **Raúl Alfonsín** to create a National Genetic Data Bank, which has helped the Abuelas recover the past of 71 of the estimated 200 to 500 kidnapped children. Many of the recovered children have been united with their families of origin. Others have chosen to remain with their adoptive families. Many more children remain unaware of who their biological parents are.

The Abuelas have also sought help from the **United States**, asking the administration of President William Clinton to declassify **Central Intelligence Agency** (CIA) files that can help them trace kidnapped children. They would also like the CIA to shed light on **Operation Condor**, a plan whereby several South American dictatorships shared security information and arrested one another's political enemies. *See also* CHILDREN FOR IDENTITY AND JUSTICE AGAINST OBLIVION AND SILENCE; *DESAPARECIDOS.*

ACOSTA, JORGE EDUARDO. Also known as "El tigre" (the Tiger). **Argentine** navy captain and head of GT-3/32, a navy task group based at the **Escuela Mecánica de la Armada** (ESMA, Navy Mechanics School). Along with colleagues like Rear Admiral **Rubén Jacinto Chamorro**, Acosta was responsible for the kidnapping, detention, and murder of at least 5,000 political prisoners, many of them thrown alive into the Atlantic Ocean from navy aircraft. He was also responsible for ordering the deaths of Dagmar Hagelin, a 17-year-old Swedish girl; Léonie Renée Duquet and Alice Domon, French nuns; and Azucena Villaflor de Vicenti, founder of the **Madres de Plaza de Mayo**. He escaped trial and punishment, however, benefiting from the controversial law *Obediencia Debida* (Due Obedience), which exonerated junior officers (those below the rank of brigadier general). *See also* ASTIZ, ALFREDO.

AGOSTI, ORLANDO RAMÓN (1924–1997). Brigadier general, commander of the air force, and member of the first junta (1976–1981) during the **"dirty war"** in **Argentina**. In 1985, at the trial of the nine junta commanders following the return to civilian rule, Agosti was sentenced to four and a half years in prison for his role in the repression. (The air force was found to have been less active in the repression than the army and navy.) A year later the Argentine Supreme Court upheld the conviction, but reduced the sentence to three years and nine months. Agosti was the only member of the **military** to serve a full sentence for participating in the repression. He was released from prison in 1989. The two other members of the first junta, **Jorge Rafael Videla** and **Emilio Massera,** who had received life sentences, were released from prison following a pardon in 1990 by President **Carlos Saúl Menem.**

AGRUPACIÓN DE FAMILIARES DE DETENIDOS-DESAPARECIDOS (AFDD) / ASSOCIATION OF RELATIVES OF THE DETAINED-MISSING. A human rights nongovernmental organization in **Chile.** The AFDD was founded in 1975 under the name Agrupación de Familiares por la Vida (Association of Relatives for Life). Like many other human rights organizations that were formed in response to the repressive campaign of General **Augusto Pinochet Ugarte** following the 1973 coup, the AFDD was under the auspices of the **Catholic Church.** The AFDD's immediate goal was to assist the thousands of Chileans searching for the status of family members detained by the **military** and security forces. Like the **Vicaría de la Solidaridad** (Vicariate of Solidarity), the AFDD focused on documenting cases of abduction and disappearance, but its demands for truth and justice gave rise to a protest movement that gained international attention.

The inspiration behind this movement was Sola Sierra Henríquez, who joined in 1976 after her husband, Waldo Ulises Pizarro Molina, was abducted and disappeared. Henríquez organized public marches of women like herself who were searching for their loved ones. Parades of women marching through Santiago holding pictures of their missing relatives were a regular annoyance to Pinochet Ugarte and the armed forces. Other methods used by the AFDD to call international attention to its cause were unique. The AFDD sponsored workshops for the making and selling of *arpilleras*, cloth pictorials that relatives of the missing embroidered to illustrate their stories. Another method was chaining, in which large groups of people used link chains to attach their bodies to highly visible public structures such as guardrails or government buildings, while several protesters made speeches explaining the significance of the spectacle.

When democracy returned to Chile in 1990 under President **Patricio Aylwin Azócar**, the AFDD provided documentation and testimony for the human rights investigation conducted by the **Comisión Nacional de Verdad y Reconciliación** (National Commission on Truth and Reconciliation). The commission issued its report, but the Chilean people have been divided over how to proceed. Some want to pursue justice; others prefer not to delve into the past. And there are many others who are too young to remember the Pinochet Ugarte era. For this last group, in June 1999, Henríquez staged a rock concert and commemorative program at the Estadio Nacional (National Stadium), the Estadio having served as a detention and torture center during the repression. The program was both a reminder of the truth and a call for justice. One of the songs on the program, "They Dance Alone," was written by the British rock star Sting in honor of the AFDD. *See also DESAPARECIDOS.*

AGRUPACIÓN DE FAMILIARES DE EJECUTADOS POLÍTICOS (AFEP) / ASSOCIATION OF RELATIVES OF THE POLITICALLY EXECUTED. A human rights nongovernmental organization in Chile. Its members were originally part of the Agrupación de Familiares de Detenidos-Desaparecidos (AFDD, Association of Relatives of the Detained-Missing in Chile) when it was founded in 1975 to denounce the systematic disappearance of individuals perceived to be enemies of the junta. Early AFDD activities focused on documenting abduction cases and staging mass protests demanding information about abducted relatives. By 1978, as the AFDD shifted its focus from documenting cases to seeking justice for the missing, members whose relatives were known to have been victims of execution decided that their cause was specific enough to establish a separate group. Founded in November 1978, the AFEP has sought to obtain official acknowledgment of the deaths—for example, through death certificates, expressions of regret, and reparations. *See also DESAPARECIDOS.*

AGRUPACIÓN DE FAMILIARES POR LA VIDA. *See* AGRUPACIÓN DE FAMILIARES DE DETENIDOS-DESAPARECIDOS.

ALFONSÍN, RAÚL (1927–). President of **Argentina** (1983–1989). He was born in Chascomús, a small farming town 70 miles southeast of Buenos Aires. His father, Serafín Alfonsín, the owner of a general store, was a Spanish immigrant who supported the republican cause in the Spanish Civil War and opposed the dictator Francisco Franco. Serafín also supported the **Unión Cívica Radical** (UCR, Radical Civic Union or Radicals), a middle-class party founded in 1890, under whose banner his son would be elected president. Raúl attended the Liceo Militar General San Martín, a **military** secondary school with a reputation for being the best school in the area. He graduated at 18 with the rank of second lieutenant in the army reserve, but in lieu of a military career, he attended the National University of La Plata, where he studied liberal arts and law and became active in the Radicals.

After graduating in 1950 with a law degree, Alfonsín entered politics and won a seat on the local council of Chascomús. An outspoken legislator, he endured verbal attacks, death threats, and a brief internment at the hands of the **Peronists**. He advanced steadily in his political career, winning a seat on the provincial legislature of Buenos Aires in 1958 (reelected in 1960) and then a seat on the Congreso Nacional (National Congress) in 1963. He made a presidential bid in the primary elections of 1972, hoping to wrest control of the party from its veteran wing, whom he accused of collaborating with the military. He lost by a wide margin to Ricardo Balbín.

Although some observers thought his political career was over, Alfonsín proceeded to build a large following. He won the support of many young people by forming the Movimiento de Renovación y Cambio (Movement of Renovation and Change), a Radical faction committed to social issues. Following the military coup of 1976, he spoke out openly against the disappearances and demanded that the government account for the missing. He cofounded the **Asamblea Permanente por los Derechos Humanos** (APDH, Permanent Assembly for **Human Rights**), and used his legal background to defend political detainees. He sought international support for human rights, finding allies in Europe and the United States. (He praised the policies of President **Jimmy Carter**, but criticized those of his successor, **Ronald Reagan**.) During Argentina's invasion of the **Falkland Islands/Islas Malvinas** in 1982, he was one of the few to speak out against the action, though he did support his country's claim to the islands.

In 1983, as the leader of the Radical party, he was elected president on 30 October, winning 52 percent of the vote and defeating the Peronist candidate Italo Argento Luder. Alfonsín had built his campaign around the issue of human rights, promising to investigate the thousands of disappearances that took place under military rule and to bring those responsible to justice. Meanwhile, Luder had come out on record as supporting the *Ley de Pacificación Nacional* (Law of National Pacification), an amnesty that the military granted itself before handing power back to civilians. Shortly after taking office on 10 December, Alfonsín repealed the military's amnesty and ordered the prosecution of the nine former junta leaders as well as such well-known **"dirty war"** participants as General **Ramón Juan Alberto Camps** and General **Suárez Mason**. And working from the idea that the **guerrillas** shared responsibility with the military for plunging the country into violence—an idea that became known as the "doctrine of the two demons"—he ordered the prosecution of former guerrilla leaders, among them Mario Firmenich, Fernando Vaca Narvaja, and Enrique Gorriarán Merlo.

To prosecute, he needed evidence. In December 1983 Alfonsín appointed a truth commission, the **Comisión Nacional de Investigación de Desaparición de Personas** (CONADEP), or National Commission on the Disappearance of Persons. On the strength of the facts collected by the commission, the civilian trial in 1985 of the former dictators—the first of its kind in the history of Latin America—resulted in the conviction of five, including life sentences for **Jorge Rafael Videla** and **Emilio Massera**. A second trial, in December 1986—in which a corporal and a police doctor were convicted along with three generals—was noteworthy for assigning responsibility for human rights violations to lower-ranking officers.

A public outpouring of testimonials from victims made it likely that many more convictions would follow. But the junior-officer corps, threatened with prosecution and angered by military reforms that included forced retirements and budget cuts, fought back. A series of encounters with the military forced the Alfonsín government to pass two laws that significantly limited the scope of prosecution. The *Ley de Punto Final* (Full-Stop Law) set a 60-day limit for the filing of human rights suits, and the *Ley de Obediencia Debida* (Due Obedience Law) reduced the number of indicted (about 400) to 39, exonerating junior officers on the grounds that they were following orders. His successor, **Carlos Saúl Menem**, took the additional step of pardoning the 39 as well as Videla, Massera, the other junta leaders, and the former **Montonero** leader Mario Firmenich.

ALIANZA ANTICOMUNISTA ARGENTINA (AAA or TRIPLE A) / ARGENTINE ANTICOMMUNIST ALLIANCE. A collection of right-wing **death squads** formed in 1973 in **Argentina** and active until the coup of 24 March 1976, when its functions were absorbed by the

serve twice as its secretary-general. He began his government career in 1937, when he was elected to the Chamber of Deputies as a Socialist. In 1945 he was elected to the first of three consecutive eight-year terms in the Senate, serving as Senate vice president for five years and then as Senate president (1965–1969).

After losing three consecutive bids for the presidency (in 1952, 1958, and 1964), Allende Gossens participated in the presidential election of 4 September 1970 as the candidate of **Unidad Popular** (UP, Popular Unity), a coalition including the **Partido Comunista de Chile** (PC, Communist Party of Chile), the PS, and breakaway members of the **Partido Demócrata Cristiano** (PDC, Christian Democratic Party). The three-way race was close. Allende Gossens won 36.2 percent of the vote; Jorge Alessandri, an ex-president representing the right, 34.9 percent; and Radomiro Tomic, a left-leaning candidate of the PDC, 27.8 percent. Because Allende Gossens obtained a plurality, not a majority, of the vote, the Chilean Congress was to decide the winner in a run-off election. Ordinarily, Congress would favor the front-runner, but a Marxist candidate was a different matter. Many Chileans feared a left-wing dictatorship. Of the 200 votes available in Congress (150 members of the Council of Deputies and 50 senators), 80 were in the hands of the UP. To win, Allende Gossens would have to find support from other parties, most likely the PDC, which controlled 75 votes. In October he reached an understanding with the PDC. In return for their support in the runoff, he agreed to sign a Statute of Guarantees, affirming such principles as the freedom of political parties, **trade unions**, and private education. On 24 October 1970 Congress confirmed Allende Gossens over Alessandri by a vote of 153 to 35.

Succeeding **Eduardo Frei Montalva**, a Christian Democrat who was president from 1964 to 1970, Allende Gossens was inaugurated on 3 November 1970, becoming the first freely elected Marxist president in the world. Though lacking a majority of support in both the electorate and Congress, he embarked on a wide-ranging program of socialist reforms. His government nationalized industry (including copper and banking), took over factories and farms, and raised the standard of living. For his UP followers—peasants, factory workers, students—the reforms held the promise of an end to capitalism and the creation of a more just society. Among many in the working, middle, and upper classes, however, the program caused anger and resentment. Economic policies like boosting salaries while freezing prices led to bankruptcies and high inflation. The wealthy lost property and social standing. And shortages of basic goods—exacerbated by truckers' strikes—led to food lines and rationing. At the same time, right-wing groups engaged in acts of economic sabotage, and in the **United States** the administration of Richard Nixon worked to destabilize the Chilean economy and support the opposition.

By 1973 Congress was at an impasse. In that year's mid-term elections, the UP had failed to win a majority that would allow it to continue its program of reforms through legislation. On the other side, the opponents of Allende Gossens lacked enough seats to force him from office. While Allende Gossens sought compromise, some of his radical supporters called for violent confrontation. On 11 September 1973 the socialist experiment ended in a bloody **military** coup. Allende Gossens died during the ground assault on the presidential palace, La Moneda. For many years, his followers and widow claimed that he was killed; evidence would later indicate, however, that the president committed suicide rather than surrender. Allende Gossens was buried in an unmarked grave in Viña del Mar, and later reinterred in a state funeral when democratic government returned to Chile in 1990.

ALMEYDA MEDINA, CLODOMIRO (c. 1923–1997). A leader of the **Partido Socialista** of **Chile** (PS, Socialist Party), a Marxist scholar, and a high official in the **Unidad Popular** (UP, Popular Unity) government of **Salvador Allende Gossens**—all of which made him a target of the junta that ousted Allende Gossens on 11 September 1973. Like Allende Gossens, Almeyda Medina joined the PS as a student, and spent his life a committed Marxist. He held a variety of positions within the UP, including foreign minister, defense minister, and vice president. Although a voice of moderation in government, he would adopt a more hardline stance after the coup.

On 11 September the army captured Almeyda Medina along with the other UP officers as they exited what was left of the heavily bombed La Moneda (the presidential palace). He was immediately sent to **Dawson Island** prison camp and then transferred to Santiago prior to his ejection from the country in 1975. During his **exile** (1975–1987), most of it spent in East Germany, he became an advocate for exiles forcibly expelled from the country and unable to return because of the junta's ban on political dissidents. In 1987, however, defying the ban, he returned to Chile, where he was seized by the security forces of **Augusto Pinochet Ugarte**. The **military** government referred to him as an "apologist for violence" and sentenced him to internal exile, or *relegación*. However, an international campaign for his freedom led the **Supreme Court** to commute his sentence after he had served 300 days.

As a member of the PS central committee, Almeyda Medina became active in the Movimiento Democrático Popular (MDP, Popular Democratic Movement), a leftist coalition formed in 1983 by the **Partido Comunista** (PC, Communist Party of Chile). In 1990 he reentered government service as ambassador to the Soviet Union under President **Patricio Aylwin Azócar**. He resigned his post under controversy, having sheltered his friend Erich Honecker, the former leader of Communist East Germany, in Moscow in 1991. Germany, now reunited, wanted Honecker extradited to face charges in connection with the East German government's policy of shooting people trying to escape communist rule. (Honecker was granted asylum in Chile, where he died in 1992.) Before his death in 1997, Almeyda Medina returned to writing and teaching at the Universidad de Chile in addition to his work on behalf of the PS. He was buried with a state funeral and military honors.

AMNESTY INTERNATIONAL (AI). An international **human rights** nongovernmental organization. Created in 1961 by Peter Benenson, an English lawyer, AI works to free "prisoners of conscience"—those detained not only for political reasons but also for race, ethnicity, religion, or language. It is especially concerned with victims of **torture**. It tries to be as apolitical as possible, careful not to take up the case of anyone—a member of an armed **guerrilla** movement, for example—who advocates violence. Its mode of operation is simple. AI members are encouraged to write courteous letters on behalf of prisoners to authority figures in the prisoners' countries—a government official or bishop, for example. The chain of letters, combined with reports sent to the media, shines a spotlight on the offending government, which, embarrassed, is often pressured into freeing the prisoner. AI also funnels reports to intergovernmental organizations like the **United Nations**. In the 1970s, the **military** regimes of **Argentina**, **Chile**, and **Uruguay** attracted considerable attention from AI. The organization made site visits to Argentina (6–15 November 1976) and to Chile (1973).

ANAYA, JORGE I. Admiral and the commander of the navy in the third junta (December 1981 to June 1982) during the **"dirty war"** in **Argentina**. He was the principal planner of the ill-fated **Falkland Islands/Islas Malvinas** invasion. Like his fellow members of the third junta, **Leopoldo Fortunato Galtieri** and **Basilio Lami Dozo**, he was acquitted in the 1985 trial of the junta commanders, in which it was found that the worst of the repression had ended by the time they took office.

ANTI-SEMITISM. A disproportionate number of the victims of the **"dirty war"** in **Argentina** were Jewish. In the mid-1970s the country's Jewish population was estimated at 400,000—the largest in Latin America. Although this number was only about 2 percent of the total population of 23 million, Jews made up between 12 percent and 19 percent of the missing (*desaparecidos*). Efforts have been made to explain the variance by noting that Jews were drawn to the professions and thus more likely to be recruited into opposition groups through the universities. Nevertheless, evidence suggests that anti-Semitism was a dominant factor. Bookstores and kiosks were well stocked with Nazi and neo-Nazi literature, Jewish neighborhoods were machine-gunned, and bombs were placed in Jewish-owned establishments. "Dirty war" survivors attest to the especially cruel and degrading punishments inflicted on Jewish prisoners.

Jews began immigrating to Argentina in large numbers during the 19th century. Although ostracized by the **military** and the wealthy landowners, they were not widely persecuted until the early 1940s, when the government openly sympathized with the Axis powers. After World War II, President **Juan Perón** opened the doors to Nazis and Jews alike. Anti-Semitism has remained an issue ever since, becoming overt in times of political crisis. Repression against Jews increased dramatically after the coup of 1976. Unlike Nazi Germany, the junta never made anti-Semitism official policy. Yet it did nothing to discourage the attitude either.

ARGENTINA (1976–1983). On 24 March 1976 the **military** seized control of a deeply divided nation and instituted its **Proceso de Reorganización Nacional**, commonly known as the "Proceso." As part of its plan to restore order and eradicate leftist subversion, the junta launched its **"dirty war,"** institutionalizing a practice that continued for the next four years. People were kidnapped by members of military "task forces" and illegally held in any of about 340 Centros Clandestinos de Detención (Secret Detention Centers) across the country. There they were kept in squalor and regularly subjected to humiliation, rape, and **torture**. Victims were commonly forced to witness the torture of their children or spouses, and children born in captivity were taken from their mothers and given to military families. Most of the victims were eventually murdered, vanishing without a trace. Many were buried in common graves. Some victims were used as *relleno* ("stuffing")—made to look as if they were **guerrillas** killed in shootouts. Others were drugged, weighted, and thrown alive into the ocean out of navy aircraft.

Inquiries made at police stations or military headquarters by worried relatives were met with official silence.

After the return to democracy in 1983, President **Raúl Alfonsín** created the **Comisión Nacional sobre la Desaparición de Personas** (CONADEP, National Commission on the Disappearance of Persons) to investigate the fate of the missing. In 1984 CONADEP issued its report, *Nunca más* (*Never Again*), finding evidence for the torture and murder of at least 8,960 persons (though **human rights** groups place the actual figure at 20,000 or even 30,000). Although the fight against leftist insurgents was one of the military regime's rationales for taking power and waging its "dirty war," CONADEP reported that very few of the missing had had any ties to guerrilla organizations. Most of the victims were unarmed but were perceived to be threats to the regime. They included intellectuals; union and student activists; teachers and performers; priests and nuns; journalists writing about the missing; lawyers working on cases of habeas corpus; and family members, friends, and acquaintances.

Background to the "Dirty War"

Unlike its neighbors **Chile** and **Uruguay**, both stable democracies until succumbing to dictatorship in 1973, Argentina has had a long history of political violence and civil unrest. When General José Uriburu ousted President Hipólito Yrigoyen in 1930, the country's Supreme Court ruled that the armed forces may legally overthrow an elected government. The military succeeded in removing five more elected governments during the century, the last in 1976. From 1928 onward, no *civilian* president succeeded another until **Carlos Saúl Menem** took office in 1989. It was in this tradition that the military overthrew President Ramón S. Castillo on 4 June 1943 and installed General Edelmiro Farrell as head of government. The dominant force in the administration, however, was Colonel (later General) **Juan Perón**, who had helped engineer the coup. The energetic and eloquent Perón quickly accumulated the titles of secretary of labor and social welfare, minister of war, and vice president. He allied himself politically with urban workers, the *descamisados* (shirtless ones), demanding higher wages and the enforcement of labor laws. But his social reforms and growing popularity angered many, and on 9 October 1945, the military, encouraged by the ruling classes, arrested him and removed him from government. His *descamisados* came to his rescue. On 17 October, thousands of workers demonstrated in the **Plaza de Mayo** next to the presidential palace and forced his release, an event that carried him into the presidency the following year.

Perón's policies were characterized by nationalism and social reform. His first administration (1946–1952) was an economic success, regarded by some as Argentina's golden age. Prosperity was based on capital reserves accumulated during World War II. Investment in national industry increased real wages and expanded the domestic market. Workers benefited from minimum-wage laws, 40-hour workweeks, paid holidays and vacations, and pensions. **Eva ("Evita") Perón**, the president's glamorous wife and political partner, increased his popularity with the working class as founder and director of the Social Aid Foundation. But his rule was also characterized by dictatorship, as the president placed his stamp on every aspect of Argentine life, taking control of universities, newspapers, and organized labor. Opponents of his regime were often jailed and tortured. His second administration (1952–1955) faced a series of problems. Worldwide recession and the depletion of wartime reserves forced him to scale back his economic reforms, and the death of Evita in 1952 decreased his popularity. He also ran afoul of the **Catholic Church** by such acts as replacing religious instruction in the schools with **Peronist** instruction and legalizing divorce and prostitution. On 16 September 1955 General Eduardo Lonardi, a pro-Catholic nationalist, initiated a coup that succeeded three days later when Admiral Isaac Rojas threatened to bombard Buenos Aires. Perón went into **exile**, eventually settling in Spain, from where he plotted his return.

The administration of President Lonardi was short-lived. Although he had helped overthrow Perón, he failed to crack down on the Peronist movement itself and was, in turn, overthrown. The palace coup on 13 November 1955, the so-called Liberating Revolution, brought to power General Pedro Aramburu, who set out to eliminate any trace of Peronism. The **Confederación General del Trabajo** (CGT, General Labor Federation)—the major trade organization and mainstay of the Peronist movement—was placed under military control. The Peronist, or Justicialist, party was banned. The mere mention of Perón's name was prohibited, and the body of Evita (whom many regarded as a saint) was stolen by the military and secretly reburied in Italy.

Far from removing Perón from popular memory, the harshness of Aramburu's regime awakened Perón's followers. On 9 June 1956 two Peronist generals, Juan José Valle and Raúl Tanco, led an unsuccessful rebellion against the government. The repression that followed—in which Valle and his supporters were shot by firing squad—earned

Aramburu the enmity of Peronists and later cost him his life. Peronists also had a hand in deciding the 1958 presidential election, even though they were not allowed to field candidates. The winner, Arturo Frondizi, had secured Perón's endorsement by promising to legalize Peronism. The promise was Frondizi's undoing. Peronist candidates won so many votes in the March 1962 national elections—even capturing the governorship of Buenos Aires—that the outraged military annulled the results and forced him from office.

Following the interim government of José María Guido, Dr. Arturo Illia became president in 1963—again in an election in which Peronists were not allowed to participate. The new administration was widely viewed as illegitimate (Illia had won only 23 percent of the vote) and was vigorously opposed by Peronists, especially the CGT. Like Frondizi, he tried to pacify the opposition by allowing Peronist candidates to run in legislative elections. As in 1962, Peronist victories in 1965 paved the way for a military takeover. Illia further angered the military by refusing to send troops to the Dominican Republic in May to assist the **United States** in fighting **communism**.

The military toppled Illia on 28 June 1966, installing General Juan Carlos Onganía, the army commander in chief, as president. Unlike previous military regimes, his administration made no promise to return civilians to power any time soon. The recipient of U.S. counterinsurgency training, Onganía no longer saw the defense of physical borders as the military's primary focus. Instead, fighting internal, ideological enemies—rooting out subversion—became its main concern. Battle lines were formed. The military—long divided into nationalists and liberals, colorados (reds) and azules (blues)—began to close ranks. In contrast, organized labor split into factions. The CGT, controlled by orthodox Peronists in league with the government, gave birth to a left-wing splinter group, CGT de los Argentinos (CGTA, CGT of the Argentines), which protested the regime's pro-business policies. The Catholic Church was divided, too: the traditional hierarchy supported the military; more progressive Catholics turned to **liberation theology** and aligned themselves with the poor. The government took control of the universities, and as early as 29 July 1966 (the Night of the Long Sticks), police were dispatched to break up assemblies at the University of Buenos Aires. Newspapers, movies, and other media were added to the regime's list of enemies. Opposition to Onganía came to a head on 29 May 1969 when the CGTA organized a labor demonstration in the city of Córdoba. Students, incensed over cuts in higher education, joined the workers in protest, and the result was the *cordobazo*—two days of mayhem that quickly spread to other cities. The army joined the police in quelling the unrest, and two weeks of fighting left more than 100 persons dead or injured.

The *cordobazo* was followed by an increase in armed guerrilla activity. Guerrilla groups had begun to form in rural Argentina in the late 1950s and early 1960s, inspired by the Cuban Revolution. Early formations, however, like the **Uturuncos** and the **Ejército Guerrillero del Pueblo** (EGP, People's Guerrilla Army), were unsuccessful. By the early 1970s, the death of Che Guevara in Bolivia (1967), the *cordobazo* uprising (1969), and the recognition that Argentina was primarily an urban society gave rise to effective guerrilla organizations based in cities. The two principal urban groups—the **Montoneros** and the **Ejército Revolucionario del Pueblo** (ERP, People's Revolutionary Army)— quickly established themselves as thorns in the side of the government, carrying out kidnappings, bank robberies, bombings, and attacks on military installations.

Civil unrest, or even its threat, played an important role in deciding who remained in power and who was deposed—the incumbent being judged on the ability to maintain order. The *cordobazo* eventually brought down Onganía. On 8 June 1970 he was replaced by General Roberto Levingston, who, following a second uprising in Córdoba in March 1971, was himself replaced by General Alejandro Lanusse. The task of the new administration was to return Argentina to civilian rule, even if that meant bringing back Perón. The military scheduled a presidential election for March 1973, but disqualified the exiled Perón from being a candidate, citing a residency law. During a brief visit to Argentina in November 1972, however, Perón endorsed the left-leaning **Héctor José Cámpora** to run in his place. Cámpora's victory cleared the way for the return of Perón.

Perón was indeed popular, but his millions of devoted followers were politically divided. The Peronist Movement accommodated both a right wing and a left wing. The right saw Perón as the country's only hope in combating communism; the left saw him as a revolutionary. During his years in exile he managed to maintain both sides of his image. On the one hand, he ignored the entreaties of his representative John William Cooke to forsake the Spain of Francisco Franco for the Cuba of Fidel Castro. On the other hand, he encouraged his "special formations"—the Montoneros and other armed Peronist guerrillas—in their attacks on Peronist traitors and government targets. The movement held together until Perón's return, when each side feared that the other would try to take control. On 20 June 1973, when millions gathered at Ezeiza International Airport to welcome Perón back from exile, rightists opened fire on columns of left-wing marchers. The Ezeiza Massacre portended Perón's drift to the right. In July a right-wing palace coup forced Cámpora to resign, clearing the way for a special presidential election in September, which Perón won with 62 percent of the vote.

Millions had coalesced around the Perón ticket, hoping his victory would heal political division and reverse economic decline. But the rift between the factions only widened, and guerrilla activity continued. Although many guerrillas had laid down their weapons forever after Perón returned, or at least called a cautious truce, others—especially the non-Peronist and traditionally leftist ERP—persisted in armed struggle. The ERP was outlawed in September 1973 after carrying out an attack on an army installation in Buenos Aires. In October the Montoneros were blamed for the killing of CGT head José Rucci, for which they claimed responsibility the following year. Whether the Montoneros were, in fact, Rucci's killer is a subject of dispute (some attribute the act to right-wing Peronists); but belief in their guilt made Perón determined to eliminate the special formations. In January he reformed the penal code so that arms possession could carry a stiffer penalty than murder. Out of the Ezeiza Massacre rose a right-wing **death squad** called the **Alianza Anticomunista Argentina** (AAA), or Argentine Anticommunist Aliance, formed by José López Rega (*"El brujo,"* "the sorcerer") and operated—with implicit state sanction—out of his Ministry of Social Welfare. Although some of its victims were armed insurgents, most were "soft targets"—leftist politicians and other progressives. Perón made his official break with the leftist Peronists in a May Day speech in 1974.

Despite the seeming finality of that pronouncement, many on the Peronist left remained loyal to the general. Some attributed his position to "error" and hoped he would reverse direction; others attributed his public statements to political maneuvering. All hope for negotiation, however, was lost when Perón died on 1 July 1974. **Isabel ("Isabelita") Perón,** his vice president and third wife, assumed the presidency, inheriting a government facing serious economic decline and increasing political violence. Unlike his second wife, Evita, who was known for her advocacy of the working class, Isabel was associated with the Peronist right. Along with López Rega—her personal secretary, social welfare minister, and longtime spiritual advisor—she unleashed a wave of repression against the media, universities, and **trade unions**. Guerrilla organizations (primarily the Montoneros and ERP) quickened the tempo of violence in turn, carrying out more operations, some of them spectacular assaults on military targets. In November 1974 Isabel Perón, who made no secret of her enmity toward guerrillas, declared a state of siege, suspending constitutional guarantees. The following year, she placed the armed forces in charge of counterinsurgency, giving them a free hand. They took the opportunity to test "dirty war" tactics that they would put into full production a year later. Meanwhile, the economy continued its downward trend. Inflation, running at a rate of 600 percent in 1975, was expected to reach 1,000 percent by the end of 1976. The peso plummeted, dropping from 36 to the dollar in 1975 to 320 in early 1976. Her administration was also noted for being corrupt. It was in this context of economic and political crisis that the military intervened.

Argentina under the Juntas

The coup of 24 March 1976 placed Isabel under house arrest (she was later exiled) and imposed a junta consisting of General **Jorge Rafael Videla**, Admiral **Emilio Massera**, and Brigadier **Orlando Ramón Agosti**—the commanding officers of the army, navy, and air force, respectively. Led by General Videla, the junta dissolved Congress, provincial legislatures, and municipal councils; appointed a cabinet composed of military officers; replaced all members of the Supreme Court and other judges; suspended all political activity and political parties at the national, provincial, and municipal levels; took control of universities and trade unions; and censored the media. It also maintained the state of siege called by the preceding administration and waged its "dirty war," or "holy war," against subversion. The junta argued that armed guerrilla organizations posed a serious threat to national security and that the state was justified in using any means necessary to defend itself. Subversion, however, was broadly defined. In addition to armed insurgents, the term included dissenters of all types. According to General Videla, terrorists were not necessarily those with guns and bombs; they were also those who spread ideas that fell outside the scope of "Western, Christian civilization." Thought itself became subversive.

Given this wide definition, the war against subversion took both conventional and unconventional forms. Alongside the traditional encounters with armed insurgents was a clandestine campaign of terror waged against the civilian population. Tens of thousands of innocent people were "sucked off" the streets and disappeared. The two levels of warfare continued in tandem. Most of the disappearances occurred in

1976 and 1977, at the height of the military's antiguerrilla campaign. The number of disappearances decreased sharply in 1978—the ERP and Montoneros having been largely defeated the year before—then tapered off until 1982. The junta, meanwhile, categorically denied any violation of human rights, attributing any disappearances to the work of groups acting independently of the government. The death squads that had operated during the previous Peronist administrations, however, had been absorbed by the new regime and brought under military control.

Despite official denial, the facts became known. A few torture victims survived and related their experiences, and families untouched by violence most likely knew others that lost children or friends. Most people, however, were too intimidated to protest or accepted the explanation that extraordinary methods were needed—that those who had been taken must have been involved in something subversive. Nevertheless, individuals and groups managed to break the silence and attract international attention. In 1977 a group of women who later formally organized as the **Madres de Plaza de Mayo** (Mothers of the Plaza de Mayo) began demonstrating every Thursday outside the Casa Rosada (the Pink House, or presidential palace), calling on the government to account for their missing children or grandchildren. Besides the *Madres*, several other major Argentine human rights organizations appeared by the end of dictatorship. The media largely failed to speak out, but there were exceptions. The editors of the *Buenos Aires Herald* (an English-language newspaper) and **Jacobo Timerman**, editor of *La Opinión*, both insisted on publishing the names of the missing (*desaparecidos*), though at great personal risk. (Timerman was abducted and tortured.) Voices outside the country joined in protest of the regime. **Amnesty International** and the **Organization of American States** both reported on the human rights situation, and President **Jimmy Carter**, at least early in his administration, made human rights integral to U.S. foreign policy.

In March 1981 the junta led by Videla was replaced by a second junta, again composed of the commanding officers of the army, navy, and air force: General Roberto Viola, Admiral **Armando Lambruschini**, and Brigadier **Omar Graffigna**. Viola's junta was itself replaced in December by another set of commanding officers: General **Leopoldo Fortunato Galtieri**, Admiral **Jorge Anaya**, and Brigadier **Basilio Lami Dozo**. By 1982 a faltering economy and growing labor unrest threatened military rule. The third junta, composed of Galtieri, Anaya, and Lami Dozo, employed a common diversionary tactic: it started a war. On 2 April 1982 it invaded the **Falkland Islands/Islas Malvinas**, a group of sparsely populated islands off the coast of southern Argentina. Long claimed by Argentina, the islands were ruled by Great Britain, which sent troops to recover them. Argentina suffered a swift and humiliating defeat, surrendering on 18 June. General Galtieri, held responsible for the debacle, resigned in disgrace, and representatives from the navy and air force were removed from the junta. On 1 July 1982 General **Reynaldo Benito Bignone** became president and eased the country back to civilian rule. Before leaving office, the military government approved the *Ley de Pacificación Nacional* (Law of National Pacification), which granted amnesty to members of the police and armed forces involved in the "dirty war." In the election of 30 October 1983, Raúl Alfonsín, representing the **Unión Cívica Radical** (UCR, Radical Civic Union) party became president.

The Aftermath of the "Dirty War"

Alfonsín set out to fulfill his promises to investigate the disappearances and to bring those responsible to justice. He repealed the *Ley de Pacificación Nacional* and charged CONADEP, led by **Ernesto Sábato**, with conducting the investigation. The pursuit of justice, however, required caution. Unlike the Nuremberg trials, in which the victors prosecuted the vanquished, criminal prosecutions in Argentina risked the intervention of the ever-present military. Especially troublesome were issues regarding whom to prosecute and where. One of Alfonsín's first acts had been to arrest the nine members of the three juntas and order them to stand trial; but the question remained of how to proceed against those lower in the hierarchy—whether to prosecute the junior officers in charge of abductions and torture and the soldiers ordered to participate in such illegal activities. There was also the question of jurisdiction—whether to prosecute members of the military in military or civilian courts.

Law 23.049, drafted by one of Alfonsín's advisors and passed by the Argentine Congress, assigned original jurisdiction to the military (though with automatic appeal by a civilian court) and absolved junior officers of criminal responsibility unless they participated in atrocities. Human rights advocates attacked the law, highly skeptical of the military's ability to judge itself. But after months of deliberation, the Supreme Council declared in October 1984 that it could not reach a verdict against the junta members, and as a result, the cases were transferred to a civilian court. On 22 April 1985 the trial of the nine junta commanders began in the Federal Criminal Court of Appeals in Buenos Aires. It lasted five months, during which a panel of six judges heard testimony from several hundred witnesses. Verdicts were handed down on 9 December. The court made it clear that the commanders were being held responsible not for any acts of their own but for the acts of others. And while acknowledging that the army, navy, and air force may have operated independently of one another in conducting the repression, it held each commander responsible for what happened within his own service. Four defendants were acquitted: Leopoldo Galtieri and Jorge Anaya, commanders of the army and navy, respectively, after the repression largely ceased, and Omar Graffigna and Basilio Lami Dozo, commanders of the air force after Ramón Agosti. (The air force was thought to be far less active in repression than the other two services.) Life sentences were handed to Jorge Videla and Emilio Massera, commanders of the army and navy during the height of the "dirty war" (1976–1979). Agosti, who commanded the air force during the first junta, was sentenced to four and a half years in prison. Roberto Viola was sentenced to 17 years, and Armando Lambruschini to eight, having commanded the army and navy when state violence had begun to wane. In December 1986 the Supreme Court upheld the convictions, affirming the life sentences given to Videla and Massera and the eight-year sentence for Lambruschini. It made two minor reductions, cutting Viola's 17-year sentence by six months and reducing Agosti's four-and-a-half year sentence to three years and nine months.

The search for justice did not stop with the junta commanders. A second level of trials spread responsibility for the repression even further. On 2 December 1986 the former chief of police of Buenos Aires province and four other former police officials were convicted on charges of torture. Two of the defendants, **Ramón Juan Alberto Camps** and Ovidio Pablo Riccheri, held the rank of general. Camps, the torturer of the journalist **Jacobo Timerman**, was sentenced to 25 years in prison; Riccheri, Camps's successor as chief of police, was sentenced to 14. It was noteworthy, however, that the trial led to the conviction of those further down the chain of command. **Miguel Etchecolatz**, Camps's aide, received 23 years; Dr. Jorge Berges, a former police physician accused of assessing the degree to which prisoners could withstand pain, received six; and Norberto Cozzani, a corporal, received four.

By extending criminal responsibility, the second level of trials threatened more than a thousand other junior officers with prosecution. Human rights organizations advocated a wholesale purging of the military, arguing that it was impossible to decide who had committed which atrocities. After all, many of the victims had been killed, most survivors had been blindfolded, and the dirty warriors had concealed their identities. Yet the government feared that a general prosecution of the military would provoke a military rebellion. Unlike the former junta commanders, who were retired or tainted by the Falklands Islands/Islas Malvinas debacle, junior officers were still in the field. The government sought a way to limit prosecution. In late 1986 it proposed legislation that would allow new cases of human rights violations to be brought before civilian and military courts—but only within a 60-day period. The *Ley de Punto Final* (Full-Stop Law), passed on 24 December 1986, set 22 February 1987 as the cutoff date for new cases. Despite the time limitation, about 400 officers were indicted. On 15 April 1987 the approaching judicial proceedings, combined with increasing pressure from human rights groups, set off a military rebellion known as *Operación Dignidad* (Operation Dignity), led by Lieutenant Colonel Aldo Rico, one of a group of military officers known as the *carapintadas* (literally, "painted faces"). Alfonsín met with the rebels and announced on Easter Sunday that they had agreed to surrender.

One month later the government proposed the **Obediencia Debida** (Due Obedience) Law, which granted an amnesty for all officers below the rank of brigadier general. The new law, passed on 4 June, caused widespread public concern, reducing the number of officers due to stand trial from about 400 to 39. In the September gubernatorial and legislative elections, the **Partido Justicialista** (PJ, Justicialist [Peronist] Party) made significant gains against the UCR. Peronist success was attributed partly to political fallout from *Obediencia Debida*, and partly to the government's austere economic program unveiled in July. In 1988 the government suppressed two more *carapintada* rebellions—one in January led by Rico, and another in December led by Colonel Mohammed Alí Seineldín. The demands were higher pay for soldiers, a larger military budget, and an amnesty for officers due to be prosecuted for their involvement in the "dirty war." On 23 January 1989 still another rebellion took place, this one led by a leftist organization called the **Movimiento Todos por la Patria** (MTP, Everyone for the Motherland). The group, fearing that the military would escape prosecution altogether, took the infantry garrison at La Tablada. Alfonsín called in the army to suppress the uprising, and in the end 39 lay dead, most of them rebels.

The elections of May 1989 returned the Peronists to power, and **Carlos Saúl Menem** assumed the presidency on 8 July. In September, reports of an amnesty deal between the new government and the military prompted a massive human rights rally in Buenos Aires. The reports were confirmed the following month. On 8 October the government pardoned 277 officers, including 39 generals due to stand trial for human rights abuses, the three junta members in power during the Falkland Islands/Islas Malvinas war (who had received prison terms for negligence), and participants in the recent military uprisings. Also included in the pardons were 64 Montoneros, who were either exempted from prosecution or set free. Excluded from the pardons were Jorge Videla, Emilio Massera, Orlando Agosti, Roberto Viola, Armando Lambruschini, Ramón Camps, **Carlos Suárez Masón**, and Eduardo Firmenich. The public was told to expect another wave of pardons by the end of 1990, the expectation raising fears that the military would escape punishment altogether. Another *carapintada* uprising in December, the last, was followed later in the month by the announcement of the pardon and release from prison of the former junta leaders (including Videla, Viola, and Massera) and the Montonero leader Mario Firmenich. (They were released on 2 January.) The news prompted a demonstration of more than 40,000 in Buenos Aires, and critics rejected Menem's explanation that the pardon was necessary for national reconciliation.

In 1995 the chiefs of the army, navy, and air force made a public expression of regret for crimes committed by the military during the "dirty war." Human rights issues, however, remained in the political forefront. In January 1998 protesters forced President Menem to halt his plans to demolish the **Escuela Mecánica de la Armada** (ESMA, Navy Mechanics School)—the most notorious torture center operating during the repression—and to erect a monument to national reconciliation in its place; they insisted that the site would better serve as a museum to remind people of the atrocities committed there. Also in January President Menem asked the navy to punish **Alfredo Astiz**, a retired naval captain and notorious participant in the "dirty war," for comments published in a magazine; Astiz had defended the military's role in the repression and threatened journalists and politicians who insisted on dredging up the past. (He was dishonorably discharged.) In February came the discovery of Swiss bank accounts owned by Astiz and other military officers and believed to contain money stolen from the detained and missing. In March Congress passed legislation repealing *Punto Final* and *Obediencia Debida*, but since the new law could not be applied retrospectively, those already pardoned would not be subject to prosecution.

Although by now the issue of impunity seemed to be settled, the quest for justice continued on a different front. Among the victims of the "dirty war" were at least 200 children (perhaps as many as 500). Some of them were abducted with their parents, but many of them were born in captivity—their mothers kept alive until giving birth. Children often disappeared by way of a "baby trade," having been illegally adopted and raised by people connected with the military. In June 1998 Videla was arrested and charged with ordering the abduction and illegal adoption of children—crimes not covered by the pardon. By April 2000 10 more former officers were arrested in connection with the kidnapping of children, including Massera, Bignone, Lieutenant General Cristino Nicolaides, and Vice Admiral Rubén Oscar Franco. A seminal but controversial ruling by a federal court in September 1999 strengthened the case against these officers and provided a potential breakthrough in bringing other "dirty war" participants to justice. The court argued that in cases of disappearance, whether of children or of political prisoners, the criminal acts remain in progress until the children or the bodies are identified. As a result, the 11 arrested former officers remain in detention. (Those, like Videla, who are over 70 years old are allowed by Argentine law the benefit of house arrest.) Meanwhile, since its founding in 1980, the human rights group **Abuelas de Plaza de Mayo** (Grandmothers of Plaza de Mayo) has identified the biological parents of 71 children.

Another front opened as well. **Baltasar Garzón**, the Spanish judge who in 1998 prevailed on Great Britain to arrest General **Augusto Pinochet Ugarte** of Chile, turned his attention to Argentina. On 2 November 1999 he indicted 98 military officers on charges of torture, terrorism, and genocide, and requested their extradition to Spain. Among those named in the indictment were Videla, Massera, and Galtieri. Although the claim had a legal basis (an estimated 600 victims of the "dirty war" were Spanish citizens or of Spanish descent), President Menem refused to cooperate, arguing that Spain (Argentina's former colonial master) was interfering in his country's domestic affairs.

There the matter of justice stood until 2001, when two federal judges, Gabriel Cavallo and Claudio Bonadio, each declared *Punto Final* and *Obediencia Debida* unconstitutional. Their rulings meant that military officers could again face prosecution. In October Bonadio ordered the arrest of Massera and five other former navy officers on charges of stealing property from people kidnapped during the "dirty war." (Massera was already under house arrest for his role in the trafficking of children.) In July 2002 Bonadio ordered the arrest of more than 30 former military officers on charges of human rights violations. Among them were Galtieri, Suárez Masón, and Nicolaides.

ARGENTINE FORENSIC ANTHROPOLOGY TEAM. *See* EQUIPO ARGENTINO DE ANTROPOLOGÍA FORENSE (EAAF).

ARGENTINE LEAGUE FOR THE RIGHTS OF MAN. *See* LIGA ARGENTINA POR LOS DERECHOS DEL HOMBRE.

ASAMBLEA PERMANENTE POR LOS DERECHOS HUMANOS (APDH) / PERMANENT ASSEMBLY FOR HUMAN RIGHTS. A **human rights** nongovernmental organization in **Argentina**. The Asamblea was founded in 1975 in response to the right-wing violence and repression that characterized the regime of **Isabel Perón**. During the dictatorship, the Asamblea documented thousands of disappearances—evidence that was forwarded to international human rights groups like the **Organization of American States** and, once civility was restored, to the government of **Raúl Alfonsín**.

ASOCIACIÓN DE EX-DETENIDOS-DESAPARECIDOS / ASSOCIATION OF FORMER DETAINEES-MISSING. A **human rights** nongovernmental organization in **Argentina**. The Asociación was founded in 1985 by some of the few survivors of the **"dirty war."** Members see it as their mission to testify to the sufferings they endured under detention. Although the group was formed after the 1985 trial of the junta commanders, survivors had helped the **Comisión Nacional sobre la Desaparición de Personas** (CONADEP), or National Commission on the Disappearance of Persons, document cases of disappearance. *See also DESAPARECIDOS.*

ASOCIACIÓN DE LAS MADRES DE PLAZA DE MAYO. *See* MADRES DE PLAZA DE MAYO.

ASSOCIATION OF FORMER DETAINEES-MISSING. *See* ASOCIACIÓN DE EX-DETENIDOS-DESAPARECIDOS.

ASSOCIATION OF RELATIVES OF POLITICALLY EXECUTED PERSONS. *See* AGRUPACIÓN DE FAMILIARES DE EJECUTADOS POLÍTICOS (AFEP).

ASSOCIATION OF RELATIVES OF THE DETAINED-MISSING. *See* AGRUPACIÓN DE FAMILIARES DE DETENIDOS-DESAPARECIDOS (AFDD).

ASTIZ, ALFREDO (c. 1951–). A navy lieutenant and the leader of a kidnapping squad (a unit of the navy task group GT-3/32) that brought suspected subversives to the **Escuela Mecánica de la Armada** (ESMA), or Navy Mechanics School, an infamous **torture** and detention center active during the **"dirty war"** in **Argentina.** He had several aliases—*"Angel," "El rubio,"* "Blondie," "Crow," "Eduardo Escudero," and "Gustavo Niño." He used his boyish good looks to infiltrate the **Madres de Plaza de Mayo** (Mothers of the Plaza de Mayo), a **human rights** group formed by women in search of their missing children and grandchildren. Joining in 1977 under the name Gustavo Niño and pretending to be in search of a real missing person, he betrayed about a dozen members and supporters, who were kidnapped by his squad and never seen again. Among them were two French nuns, Sister Alice Domon and Sister Leonie Duquet, whose bodies were discovered two months later. On 26 April 1982, during the **Falkland Islands/Islas Malvinas** war, Astiz surrendered South Georgia Island to the British within 24 hours.

After the return to civilian government, he was accused of the murder of the two nuns as well as that of Dagmar Hagelin, a 17-year-old Swedish girl. (His boss, **Jorge Eduardo Acosta**, ordered the killing.) None of these victims was associated with any terrorist activity. He escaped trial and punishment, however, benefiting from the controversial law *Obediencia Debida* (Due Obedience), which exonerated junior officers. But because several of his victims were international citizens, other countries have taken an interest in prosecuting him. In 1990 a French court sentenced him, in absentia, to life in prison for the murder of Sisters Domon and Duquet. In 2001 Italy sought his extradition, charging him with the abduction, torture, and disappearance of three Italian citizens. Argentina refused to extradite him.

Astiz was cashiered from the navy in 1998 for remarks he made in an interview published in the magazine *Tres Puntos.* (An English translation of the interview appeared in *Harper's.*) Astiz told the journalist, Gabriela Cerruti, that torture was not in his job description but that he would have tortured if the navy had asked him to do so. He also claimed to be the best-trained man in Argentina to kill a politician or journalist who provoked the **military.** The comments outraged President **Carlos Saúl Menem,** who asked the navy to punish Astiz.

AYLWIN AZÓCAR, PATRICIO (1918–). President of **Chile** (1990–1994). On 14 December 1989 Aylwin Azócar, representing the **Partido Demócrata Cristiano** (PDC, Christian Democratic Party), was elected to the presidency with the help of some 16 left and center parties. When he took office in March 1990, he was charged with managing the country's return to democracy. He faced opposition from the armed forces, the Chilean court system, and legislators appointed during the regime of **Augusto Pinochet Ugarte**. Despite these challenges, Aylwin Azócar was able to exert his authority on an issue that concerned the majority of voters—the investigation of **human rights** abuses committed by the state under Pinochet Ugarte. Aylwin Azócar appointed the **Comisión Nacional de Verdad y Reconciliación** (National Commission on Truth and Reconciliation), an apolitical group of investigators with legal and human rights expertise, and charged it with uncovering the truth. Although the Commission, under the direction of Raúl Rettig, compiled extensive documentation of human rights abuses, including evidence presented in a lengthy report, it was cut short in its attempts to assign culpability or to seek justice for the victims of state violence. Aylwin Azócar was also unsuccessful in reconciling the issues surrounding the rights and responsibilities of the state. He was successful, however, in laying a foundation for debate.

–B–

BAÑADOS, ADOLFO. Supreme Court justice in **Chile**. Appointed by President **Patricio Aylwin Azócar** after the return to civilian rule, Bañados was one of the first appointees to a high court dominated by judges from the **military** regime of **Augusto Pinochet Ugarte**. In 1993 Bañados presided over the **Orlando Letelier del Solar** assassination case, the first case excluded from Pinochet Ugarte's 1978 Amnesty Law. Bañados sentenced two former military officers from the **Dirección de Inteligencia Nacional** (DINA, Directorate of National Intelligence), Chile's secret police. General **Manuel Contreras Sepúlveda** received a seven-year term, and Brigadier General **Pedro Espinoza Bravo** received a six-year term, for planning the 1976 murders of Letelier del Solar and his assistant, Ronni Moffit, with a car bomb in Washington, D.C.

BARNES, HARRY ("DIRTY HARRY"). Ambassador from the **United States** to **Chile**, replacing **James Theberge** in 1986. Theberge's pro-junta stance ran counter to that of the second administration of **Ronald Reagan**, which supported the opposition movement's demands for a return to constitutional government. The appointment of Barnes, a **human rights** advocate, riled General **Augusto Pinochet Ugarte**, who dubbed Barnes "Dirty Harry," after the movie character played by Clint Eastwood.

BENEDETTI, MARIO (1920–). Uruguayan poet, novelist, playwright, lyricist, essayist, and journalist. Born in Paso de los Toros, in the Tacuarembó province in **Uruguay**. He attended the Colegio Alemán de Montevideo—from which he was withdrawn by his father in the 1930s after the school made the Nazi salute official—and the Liceo Miranda. In 1945, after a three-year residence in Buenos Aires, **Argentina**, he began his journalistic career in the influential weekly *Marcha*, with which he would collaborate until its closing in 1974. Also in 1945 he published his first volume of poetry. He is grouped among the writers known as "generación crítica" by the influential critic Ángel Rama.

During the next decade, Benedetti would direct the literary journal *Marginalia* and collaborate with *Número*, one of the most prestigious literary journals of its day. In 1954 he became the literary editor of *Marcha*; his first novel had been published the year before. Two years earlier, in 1952, Benedetti had taken part in protests against the **military** treaty between Uruguay and the **United States**—an action that marked the beginning of his political activism. In the late 1950s he made his first trip to Europe, as correspondent for *Marcha* and *El Diario*, and later visited the United States for several months. During the 1960s he continued his literary trajectory and became a prominent participant in cultural events in Latin America. He was chosen as a judge of the Casa de las Américas award in Havana, Cuba, in 1966; two years later, he founded and directed the Center for Literary Investigations for the Casa de las Américas editorial board.

In 1971 Benedetti became one of the founders of the Movimiento de Independientes 26 de Marzo, which would later merge with the leftist coalition Frente Amplio. That same year he was appointed director of the Department of Latin American Literature at the University of Montevideo. The next year, he participated in the Frente Amplio campaign. Following the military coup of 1973, he resigned his university post and went into **exile** in Buenos Aires. After receiving several death threats from the **Alianza Anticomunista Argentina** (AAA, Argentine Anticommunist Alliance), Benedetti went into exile in Peru and Cuba. In 1980 he settled in Spain. In 1985, with the restoration of democracy in Uruguay, he returned to his native country, although from that point he would divide his residence between Montevideo and Madrid. That year he became a member of the editorial council of the new journal *Brecha*, a continuation of the editorial project of the weekly *Marcha*, closed by the military in 1974.

A prolific writer—his complete works, first edited in 1994, would eventually comprise 36 volumes—Benedetti is perhaps best known as the lyrical author of nearly 20 books of poetry and song lyrics. Equally prolific as a novelist and short-story writer, his novel *Tregua* (1960) has gone through over 75 editions. Several of his works have been adapted for the stage and screen, notably *Tregua*, directed in 1975 by Sergio Renán and the first Latin American movie nominated for an Oscar. Some Benedetti works associated with the period of the **"dirty wars"** are the play *Pedro y el capitán* (1979), an exploration of the psychology of torturers and victims; *Primavera con una esquina rota* (1982), an examination of two sectors of a nation—Uruguayans under the military dictatorship and Uruguayans in exile—united by a thread of hope; and *Recuerdos olvidados* (1988), which examines the theme of exile and the eventual reconciliation of a divided nation. He is also the author of *El desexilio y otras conjeturas* (1985), in which he proposes the term *desexilio* to denote the experience of those unable or unwilling to go into exile and forced to live under military dictatorship.

During a literary career spanning over 50 years, Benedetti has been distinguished by several governments and organizations. In 1982 and 1989, respectively, he received the Order Félix Varela and the Haydeé Santamaría medal awarded by the Cuban government. In 1986 he received the Jristo Botev award from the Bulgarian government. In 1987, in Brussels, he received the Golden Flame award from **Amnesty International** for his novel *Primavera con una esquina rota*. He was invested Doctor Honoris Causa by the University of Valladolid (Spain) and the University of Alicante (Spain) in 1997. Two years later, the University of Alicante created the Mario Benedetti Center for Latin American Studies. In 1999 he also received the VIII Premio Reina Sofía de Poesía Iberoamericana, awarded by the Spanish government.

BIGNONE, REYNALDO BENITO. An army general and the fourth and last president (1982–1983) of the **military** government in **Argentina** during the **"dirty war."** Two weeks after General **Leopoldo Fortunato Galtieri**, the previous president, resigned in disgrace following Argentina's defeat in the **Falkland Islands/Islas Malvinas** conflict, General Bignone became president, taking office on 1 July 1982. By then the military government had lost all credibility owing to the country's economic disarray, the Falklands debacle, and increasing public unrest over disappearances. Bignone saw his role as twofold—to cover up the military's involvement in **human rights** violations and to return the country to civilian rule. He gave orders to destroy records related to the detained and missing (*desaparecidos*) and then organized elections—not before adopting the *Ley de Pacificación Nacional* (Law of National Pacification), which granted immunity from prosecution to members of the military and police for acts committed in combating "subversion." (The law was repealed by President **Raúl Alfonsín** after he took office in October 1983.)

BONAFINI, HEBÉ. *See* MADRES DE PLAZA DE MAYO.

BORDABERRY, JUAN MARÍA (1928–). President of **Uruguay** (1972–1976). Bordaberry was born into a family of wealthy landowners, and served as the minister of agriculture under President Jorge Pacheco Areco in the late 1960s. In November 1971 he was elected president, representing the Colorado (Red) party. His victory over the Blancos (Whites) and the leftist Frente Amplio (Broad Front) coalition was narrow and widely attributed to electoral fraud. Taking office in March 1972, Bordaberry continued his predecessor's policy of curtailing civil liberties, and gave the **military** a freer hand in combating the **Tupamaros**, an urban **guerrilla** organization. By mid-1972 the guerrillas were crushed, and the military, successful in its counterinsurgency campaign, demanded a greater role in government. In February 1973 the service commanders forced Bordaberry to sign the Boisso Lanza agreement, one of the terms of which required him to create the Consejo de Seguridad Nacional (COSENA, National Security Council), which gave the military veto power over his government. The agreement was the first step in a lengthy coup that culminated on 27 June 1973, when Bordaberry closed Congress and established a dictatorship. The events of that day are often described as an *autogolpe*, or "self-coup," since he essentially overthrew himself. The military was now firmly in control, with Bordaberry a mere figurehead. On 12 June 1976 Bordaberry was forced out of office for being too far to the right—he balked at the idea of an eventual return to civilian rule. The military replaced him with another civilian, Dr. Aparicio Méndez Manfredini.

BORGES, JORGE LUIS (1899–1986). Argentine poet and narrator. Possibly the most important writer in 20th-century **Argentina**. He was born in Buenos Aires into an aristocratic family of Anglo-Spanish heritage, having distinguished connections to the nation's *criollo* past. In his childhood, the Borges family settled in Palermo, a suburb in the northern section of Buenos Aires. Palermo's colorful legacy of violence, tango, and politics would find its way into the early prose of the young writer. In 1914 the family moved to Switzerland, where Borges attended a *lycée* and learned French, German, and Latin. Upon his graduation, his family had an extended stay in Spain, where the young writer soon became a familiar figure among the avant-garde *ultraísta* movement. On his return to Buenos Aires in 1921, Borges immersed himself into the vibrant intellectual life of the Argentine capital and founded an avant-garde journal, *Prisma*. In 1923 he published his first book of poetry, *Fervor de Buenos Aires*. After a year-long stay in Spain, he returned to Buenos Aires and embarked on a decade of productive literary work. He became associated with the most influential journals of the day, most notably *Martín Fierro*, *Proa*, and, later, *Sur*, edited by Victoria Ocampo. In 1927 he underwent an operation for cataracts, the first of what would be a long series of attempts to save his vision. None would succeed; by the end of his life he would be totally blind. In 1928 Borges campaigned for the reelection of former president Hipólito Yrigoyen. Two years later, Yrigoyen was deposed by a **military** junta, the first of several repressive governments in 20th-century Argentina.

In 1937 Borges accepted a position as First Assistant in the Miguel Cané Branch of the Buenos Aires Municipal Library. It was a job he would hold for nine years and one that he would later describe as a "menial and dismal existence." The last years of the 1930s would also bring a series of setbacks to the writer. Earlier, in 1935, his English-born grandmother, Frances Haslam de Borges—a key figure in introducing the young Borges to English literature—died, a death followed in 1938 by that of his father, Jorge Guillermo Borges. Soon after, the writer suffered a head wound—an incident he later retold in his short story "El Sur"—and spent several weeks in the hospital near death from septicemia. He soon began working on his most important stories, collected in *El jardín de senderos que se bifurcan* (1941), which would later be incorporated into another collection and retitled *Ficciones* (1944).

In 1946 **Juan Perón** was elected president of Argentina. Owing to his association with the Yrigoyen campaign and his presidency of the Sociedad Argentina de Escritores (Argentine Writers' Society), a professional group with anti-Peronist overtones, Borges was demoted to

"Inspector of Poultry and Rabbits in the Public Market." He resigned and soon accepted a number of teaching and lecturing jobs across Argentina and **Uruguay**. In 1951 the first foreign translation of his work—a French edition of *Ficciones*—was published. After the fall of Perón in 1955, Borges was appointed director of the National Library, and soon after, the University of Buenos Aires named him Professor of English and American Literature, a post he would hold for 12 years. In 1956 he won the National Prize for Literature. Worldwide recognition of his work—which had eluded him until then—followed in 1961, when Borges and Samuel Beckett shared the International Publishers Prize (the Formentor Prize), awarded by a group of European and American publishers. That year, he visited the **United States** for the first time as a visiting professor at the University of Texas in Austin, a period followed by travels and lecture across the United States, Europe, and several Latin American countries. In 1967 and 1968 he held the Charles Eliot Norton Chair of Poetry at Harvard University and lectured extensively throughout the United States. As with the earlier visit to the United States, this period was followed by travels in Europe—where he received numerous official honors and was invested a Doctor Honoris Causa by Oxford University—and by visits and lectures in Israel.

In 1973 Borges resigned his post at the National Library following Perón's return from **exile** and his reelection to the presidency of Argentina. That same year he received major awards from Mexico and Spain. A one-volume edition of his *Obras completas* was published in 1974, though he would continue to publish new works for a few more years. In 1975, his mother and longtime traveling companion, Leonor Acevedo Suárez de Borges, died at the age of 99. An invitation by the Japanese Ministry of Education to visit Japan in 1976 preceded by a few months the right-wing military coup that overthrew the government of **Isabel Perón**, Juan Perón's widow and successor. Given Borges's stature as perhaps Argentina's most internationally known writer in 1976, the Argentine intellectual community was dismayed at his initial lack of condemnation of the military coup. Although Borges would later denounce what he termed the "absurd war" over the **Falkland Islands/Islas Malvinas**, his reputation would suffer a severe blow owing to his apparent endorsement of the regime of General **Jorge Videla** and its tactics. Borges died on 14 June 1986 in Geneva, Switzerland.

–C–

CÁMPORA, HÉCTOR JOSÉ (1909–1980). **Peronist** politician and president of **Argentina** from May to July 1973, when he was forced out of office by a right-wing Peronist faction to make room for **Juan Perón** himself, who had recently returned from **exile**. As Perón's handpicked representative in Argentina, Cámpora had been designated to run in his place in the March 1973 presidential election. Perón was barred from being a candidate owing to a residency requirement. Cámpora won easily under the slogan "Cámpora in government, Perón in power." Taking office in May, Cámpora, who had ties to the **Montoneros**, an urban **guerrilla** organization, freed all political prisoners, many of them guerrillas, and reopened diplomatic relations with Cuba. The drift toward the left angered Perón, who returned to Argentina in June, engineered Cámpora's resignation, and ran for president himself. After the **military** coup of 24 March 1976, Cámpora took refuge in the Mexican embassy in Buenos Aires with the intention of fleeing to Mexico. The junta, however, refused to let him leave, and he spent most of his remaining years as a refugee in the embassy.

CAMPS, RAMÓN JUAN ALBERTO (c. 1927–1994). Argentine Army General who was chief of the Buenos Aires provincial police until his retirement in 1981. Of the 9,000 to 30,000 people who disappeared in **Argentina** during the 1976–1983 **"dirty war,"** Camps claimed responsibility for the disappearance of 5,000. His most famous prisoner was **Jacobo Timerman**, who wrote about his imprisonment and **torture** under Camps in his best-selling book *Preso sin nombre, celda sin número* (published in English as *Prisoner without a Name, Cell without a Number*). In 1986, Camps was sentenced to 25 years in prison for **human rights** crimes, but was freed in 1990 under a general amnesty for "dirty war" participants granted by President **Carlos Saúl Menem**. He died on 22 August 1994.

CARABINEROS. Members of the Chilean national police force. The primary responsibilities of the carabineros are to maintain public order, investigate crimes, and patrol the country's borders. After the **military** coup of 11 September 1973, the department carried out a systematic campaign of **human rights** abuse against Chilean citizens. Under the direction of General **César Mendoza Durán** (until 1985) and then General Rodolfo Stange Oelckers—both of whom served in the ruling junta—the carabineros took part in abduction, illegal detention, **tor-**

ture, summary execution, murder, and disappearance. During the first two years of military rule, their principal victims were demonstrators, workers, opposition-party members, and poor urban dwellers. The poor who resided in shantytowns suffered *allanamientos*, or surprise raids, in which people were rounded up while their homes were destroyed. The carabineros would later extend their campaign of state-sponsored terror to include members of local and international human rights organizations active in recording and denouncing the department's repression. In the 1980s, when popular protests were directed against the government, the carabineros renewed their violent assaults against demonstrators. After the transition to democracy, attempts to charge carabineros of human rights violations were frustrated by the amnesty law of 1978.

CARAPINTADAS. A group of junior army officers, who, from 1987 to 1990, staged a series of revolts against the democratic governments of **Raúl Alfonsín** and **Carlos Saúl Menem**. They were called *carapintadas* (literally the "painted faces") in reference to their practice of wearing comando fatigues and smearing their faces with black camouflage. The *carapintadas* were angered by civilian attempts to persecute the **military** for waging what they saw as a justified war against subversion.

In April 1987 and January 1988, Lieutenant Colonel Aldo Rico, a veteran of the **"dirty war"** and the **Falkland Islands/Islas Malvinas** conflict, led uprisings against Alfonsín. The first uprising, *Operación Dignidad* (Operation Dignity), began on 15 April 1987, the Thursday of Holy Week. (The uprising is also known as the revolt of *Semana Santa*, Easter Holy Week.) An army major accused of **human rights** violations had fled prosecution and taken refuge in a military compound in Córdoba. The rebels took over the compound and demanded a general amnesty for all officers facing trial for participating in the "dirty war." Alfonsín met with the rebels and announced, on Easter Sunday, that they had agreed to surrender. Although he claimed that the rebels had given in without conditions, two months later the government passed *Obediencia Debida* (Due Obedience law), which exempted all but the most senior officers from prosecution.

Although the *carapintadas* escaped the possibility of standing trial for any involvement in the "dirty war," they did not escape the army's efforts to discipline them for their part in the rebellion. In January 1988, Rico, who had been imprisoned since the revolt, resisted the army's call for his resignation, fled confinement, and led a second uprising, the *Rebelión de Monte Caseros* (Rebellion of Monte Caseros), which was put down by army loyalists. Rico and his followers were sentenced by a military court and imprisoned in Magdalena military prison. In December 1988 a third uprising against Alfonsín took place. This one, at the Villa Martelli military base, was led by Colonel Mohammed Alí Seineldín, a charismatic right-wing figure. Like Rico, Seineldín surrendered and received a prison term. Both were freed on 8 October 1989 in a blanket presidential pardon issued by **Carlos Saúl Menem**. They were still subject to military discipline, however. Rico was discharged from the army later that month. Seineldín, however, fought any attempt to remove him, and on 3 December 1990 launched another *carapintada* rebellion—the last and most violent. It was crushed by loyalist forces the same day. The rebels were sentenced in a military court to long prison terms, including life sentences for Seineldín and other leading officers.

CARAVAN OF DEATH. Also known as the "Mission of Death" or "Death Tour." A covert **military** operation ordered by General **Augusto Pinochet Ugarte** in **Chile**. Less than a month after the junta takeover on 11 September 1973, Pinochet Ugarte authorized a traveling war tribunal to supervise the trial and execution of political prisoners. Led by General Sergio Arellano Stark, the contingent included Lieutenant Colonel Sergio Arredondo González, Majors **Pedro Espinoza Bravo** and Marcelo Moren Brito, and Lieutenant Armando Fernández Larios. The group began its mission on 4 October 1973 at the military camp in Cauquenes. From there the group traveled northward by helicopter from one military camp to another—to La Serena, Copiapó, Antofagasta, and, finally, on 19 October, Calama. Along the way it revised sentences (usually making them more severe) and ordered summary executions. The tour resulted in the deaths of 75 prisoners, all believed to have been associated with leftist political organizations. Three of the officers involved in the caravan of death—Espinoza Bravo, Fernández Larios, and Moren Brito—were later promoted to positions in the **Dirección de Inteligencia Nacional** (DINA, Directorate of National Intelligence), the secret police.

CARTER, JAMES EARL, JR. ("JIMMY") (1924–). President of the **United States** (1977–1981). Unlike **Henry Kissinger**, secretary of state under the administrations of presidents Richard Nixon (1969–1974) and Gerald Ford (1974–1977), President Jimmy Carter made the promotion of **human rights** one of the goals of his foreign policy.

Whereas Kissinger regarded human rights concerns as being in potential conflict with the practice of foreign policy, Carter argued that the United States was legally bound—by virtue of its membership in the **United Nations**—to speak out against abuses. The U.S. commitment to human rights, he thought, was especially strong in the Americas—the United States being a member of the **Organization of American States** (OAS) and signatory to the OAS's American Declaration of the Rights and Duties of Man. He argued further that the pursuit of human rights could coexist with political, **military**, and economic goals in foreign policy; that it could expand democracy abroad, creating a world friendly to the United States; and that it could distance the United States from repression.

One of Carter's first acts as president was to activate the Bureau of Human Rights and Humanitarian Affairs, which had been created in 1976 during the final months of the Ford administration. Citing a lack of concern for human rights in U.S. foreign policy, Congress had passed the International Security and Arms Export Control Act, section 301 of which established the bureau and placed it within the State Department. Whereas Ford and Kissinger had disregarded the new agency, Carter appointed **Patricia Derian**, a 1960s civil-rights activist, as its coordinator and empowered her to speak out strongly on human rights issues. As early as August 1977, Derian's position was upgraded from coordinator to Assistant Secretary for Human Rights.

The Southern Cone quickly became the main focus of Carter's human rights policy. In the context of the region, human rights abuse was defined as the violation of a person's physical integrity. Abuses of this type were severe and had been well documented by the UN, the OAS, and private human rights groups. The administration used a wide range of methods to try to halt abuses. It practiced "quiet diplomacy" through private channels; issued public statements; compiled "Country Reports" on the status of human rights in the region and around the world; imposed military and economic sanctions; and supported the efforts of the UN, the OAS, and other international organizations to make site visits and publish their findings.

Carter's policy has been criticized on a number of grounds. First, its legal basis: Some ask whether UN declarations on human rights are legally binding or merely voluntary. Second, its definition of human rights abuse: Should the emphasis be on violations of personal integrity, or on economic, social, civil, and political rights? Third, its lack of consistency: The policy was applied to "soft" targets like **Argentina**, **Chile**, and **Uruguay** rather than to nations perceived to be of more strategic importance to the United States at the time. And although human rights tended to improve during the Carter years, it is unclear whether improvements were due to policy or to the destruction of the perceived leftist threat in the region. Nevertheless, there are indications that the policy was successful: the region's military governments celebrated Carter's defeat to **Ronald Reagan** in the 1980 election, and President **Raúl Alfonsín** of Argentina asserted that Carter's policy saved many lives during the repression.

CASTILLO VELASCO, JAIME. A Chilean jurist, Castillo Velasco had served as minister of justice under President **Eduardo Frei Montalva** (1964–1970) and as a representative to the Human Rights Commission of the **United Nations**. During the dictatorship, he posed a challenge to the Chilean legal community. He was one of five prominent Chilean lawyers who sent an "open letter" to the **Organization of American States** (OAS) when it met in Santiago in June 1976. The letter deplored the **human rights** abuses of the junta and the unwillingness of the courts to intervene. Two months later, Castillo Velasco and a second letter writer, Eugenio Velasco Letelier, were abducted by agents of the **Dirección de Inteligencia Nacional** (Directorate of National Intelligence, DINA) and forced into **exile**. A copy of the letter was included in the second supplement to *Final Report of Mission to Chile: Arrests and Detentions and Freedom of Information in Chile*, published by the **International Commission of Jurists** in September 1976.

CATHOLIC CHURCH. Since their independence from Spain and Portugal, the countries of Latin America have been dominated by a triumvirate consisting of the **military**, the landed elite, and the Catholic Church. In the 1960s, **liberation theology** challenged the Latin American Church to abandon its traditional alliances and side instead with the region's poor. A decade later, during the height of the repression brought on by the **"dirty wars,"** the Church was further challenged to shift its allegiance from those defending the status quo to those suffering **torture**, disappearance, and **exile**.

In **Argentina**, the Church was largely conservative, and many priests and bishops not only supported the coup of 24 March 1976 but also justified the repression. Yet the Argentine Church was by no means homogeneous. Many Catholics opposed the military regime and suffered the consequences. Monsignor Enrique Angelelli, the bishop of La Rioja, for example, was assassinated by the air force on 4 August 1976, shortly after the assassination of two of his diocesan priests. Two

French nuns disappeared on 13 December 1977 because of their involvement with the **Madres de Plaza de Mayo** (Mothers of the Plaza de Mayo). And **Adolfo Pérez Esquivel**, a lay Catholic and leader of **Servicio Paz y Justicia** (SERPAJ, Peace and Justice Service), was imprisoned for his nonviolent efforts in behalf of the missing (*desaparecidos*).

Although some members of the Catholic hierarchy in **Chile** supported the coup of 11 September 1973, the Church emerged as the only institution in the country capable of applying consistent pressure on the military regime of **Augusto Pinochet Ugarte**. Shortly after the coup, the bishops condemned socialism, but stopped short of publicly embracing the new regime. Cardinal Raúl Silva Henríquez, though uncommitted at first, created the **Comité de la Paz** (COPACHI, Committee for Peace) in October to aid victims of the repression. After COPACHI was dissolved by the government two years later, its work was continued by the **Vicaría de la Solidaridad** (Vicariate of Solidarity), established under Church protection. In 1984, Archbishop Juan F. Fresno Larraín urged the regime to return the country to democratic rule.

In **Uruguay**, bishops opposed the dissolution of Congress on 27 June 1973, which capped a four-month-long coup. Although the bishops often spoke of the need for reconciliation, they openly opposed the military government in a document issued on 30 April 1975. On 1 April 1984, in anticipation of the return to democracy, Monsignor Carlos Partelli delivered a sermon on "the good news of the dignity of man." Partelli had spent many years defending the Uruguayan branch of SERPAJ against the military government.

CENTER FOR LEGAL AND SOCIAL STUDIES. *See* CENTRO DE ESTUDIOS LEGALES Y SOCIALES (CELS).

CENTRAL INTELLIGENCE AGENCY (CIA). A clandestine agency of the **United States** government, responsible for foreign intelligence and counterintelligence. Established by the National Security Act of 1947, the CIA has been used by presidents as a tool of analysis and covert activity. During the Cold War, combating **communism** was the agency's primary mission. In 1954, during the administration of President Dwight D. Eisenhower, the CIA staged the overthrow of Jacobo Arbenz, the left-wing president of Guatemala. In 1961, during the administration of President John F. Kennedy, the CIA attempted to oust Fidel Castro of Cuba by directing the Bay of Pigs invasion. Among the agency's Cold War activities were experiments on mind control and (unsuccessful) attempts on the lives of foreign leaders—Castro, in particular.

In 1975 the CIA's covert operations came under the investigation of the Select Committee to Study Governmental Operations with Respect to Intelligence Activities. Chaired by Frank Church, the Committee looked into possible CIA involvement in the 1973 coup that deposed the Marxist president **Salvador Allende Gossens** of **Chile**. The CIA had tried for many years to prevent Allende Gossens from gaining the presidency. Once he took office in 1970, the United States reduced aid, curtailed trade, and cut off supplies. The CIA was instructed to sabotage the Chilean economy, following the orders of President Richard Nixon to "make the economy scream." The CIA also carried out Track II—a top-secret plan to instigate a **military** coup. From 1970 to 1973 the CIA spent $8 million to undermine the Allende Gossens government, supporting the opposition in business, labor, media, and politics. Although the Church Committee found no evidence that the CIA took a direct part in overthrowing Allende Gossens, the agency knew about the plan for the coup and encouraged those who put it into action.

CENTRO DE ESTUDIOS LEGALES Y SOCIALES (CELS) / CENTER FOR LEGAL AND SOCIAL STUDIES. A **human rights** nongovernmental organization in **Argentina**. CELS was founded in 1978 by a group of lawyers that included the lawyer-educator Emilio F. Mignone, whose daughter Monica had disappeared in May 1976. During the dictatorship, CELS offered legal defense and documented human rights abuses. It has since become a civil rights organization, promoting the rule of law and human rights.

CENTRO NACIONAL DE INFORMACIÓN (CNI). *See* DEATH SQUADS; DIRECCIÓN DE INTELIGENCIA NACIONAL (DINA).

CHAMORRO, RUBÉN JACINTO (d. 1986). Nicknamed "Dolphin" or "Máximo." An **Argentine** navy captain (later rear admiral) who commanded the most notorious of the Centros Clandestinos de Detención (Secret Detention Centers). While he was chief of the **Escuela Mecánica de la Armada** (ESMA, Navy Mechanics School) from 1976 to 1979, at least 5,000 suspected subversives were detained, tortured, and murdered, many of them thrown alive into the Atlantic Ocean from navy aircraft. *See also DESAPARECIDOS.*

CHICAGO BOYS. The name for a large, diverse group of neoliberal economists, some of whom studied at the University of Chicago. Among them were many Chileans who had received fellowships in the 1960s to study under such Chicago monetarist theorists as Milton Friedman and Arnold Harberger. After the military coup in **Chile** in 1973, the generals wanted to transform the economy but did not know where to begin. Admiral José Toribio Merino Castro, the junta member in charge of economic policy, sought the advice of Chile's Chicago Boys, who had produced a massive plan for instituting free-market reforms. The junta was not easily convinced, but after much spirited debate and a visit to Chile by Milton Friedman in 1975 (the first of a series of consultations), the Chicago Boys took control of the economy. Their recommended "shock treatment" called for drastically reducing the supply of money, expanding free trade, and encouraging private investment.

The treatment was painful, especially for the working class. Chilean industry, accustomed to producing for domestic consumption, felt the pressure of foreign competition, and some companies went bankrupt. Industries that did adapt to competition became leaner, wages plummeted, unemployment and self-employment rose, and thousands entered government make-work programs. **Trade unions** lost much of their traditional bargaining power. By the end of the 1970s, however, the Chicago policies resulted in what many described as the "Chilean miracle." Between 1973 and 1980, inflation dropped from 600 to 31 percent, growth was significant, and a fiscal deficit was transformed into a surplus. There was an increase in demand for consumer goods, mostly imports. The economic boom improved the lot of many Chileans. At the same time, its benefits failed to reach the large percentage of people living in poverty, particularly dwellers in Santiago's *poblaciones* (shantytowns).

The boom ended in 1982, a victim of worldwide recession, and the Chicago Boys fell out of favor. The government continued to embrace the free-market model, but from then on economic policy became less doctrinaire and more pragmatic.

CHILDREN FOR IDENTITY AND JUSTICE, AGAINST OBLIVION AND SILENCE. *See* HIJOS POR LA IDENTIDAD Y LA JUSTICIA, CONTRA EL OLVIDO Y EL SILENCIO (HIJOS).

CHILE (1973–1990). On 11 September 1973 the Chilean **military** overthrew **Salvador Allende Gossens**, a democratically elected Marxist president. Led by General **Augusto Pinochet Ugarte**, the military coup unleashed a reign of terror over the civilian population. The victims included Allende Gossens himself, who died (an apparent suicide, later confirmed) during the air and ground assault on the presidential palace, La Moneda. Pinochet Ugarte began a series of campaigns against leftists and other perceived subversives. **War tribunals** appeared—military courts that detained and executed prisoners without benefit of a trial. The two main sports arenas in the capital city of Santiago—Chile Stadium and National Stadium—became holding centers for detainees. Thousands of political prisoners were arrested and subjected to **torture**; many were killed.

Immediately after the coup, a junta was formed consisting of General Pinochet Ugarte, commander in chief of the army; Admiral José Toribio Merino Castro, commander in chief of the navy; General Gustavo Leigh Guzmán, commander in chief of the air force; and General César Mendoza Durán, Director General of the **Carabineros** (the national police force). The junta was led by Pinochet Ugarte, who declared Chile to be in a state of civil disorder and economic chaos caused by the proliferation of Marxist ideas. The junta had two main objectives: the first was to extirpate Marxism from Chilean society and ensure the return of civilian government; the second was to rescue the government from the economic chaos caused by Allende Gossen's socialist reforms.

To fulfill the first objective, the junta declared a state of siege and implemented a plan of organized repression. During the first few weeks after the coup, thousands of Chilean citizens, refugees from other countries of Latin America, and foreign nationals became the victims of raids, attacks, searches and seizures, arrests and detentions, torture and executions, forced disappearances, and **exile**. The junta assured the country that once all leftist elements had been eliminated, the military would return the country to civilian rule. Members of the once-powerful **Partido Demócrata Cristiano** (PDC, Christian Democratic Party), many of whom tacitly supported the coup, entertained hopes of leading a new government. Their expectations were cut short by what resulted—the one-man totalitarian regime of Pinochet Ugarte, who would rule for 17 years.

To fulfill the second objective, that of stabilizing the economy, the junta sought the help of a group of economists called the **Chicago Boys**. Drawing upon the monetarist ideas of University of Chicago economics professor Milton Friedman, the Chicago Boys believed that the chief impediment to economic growth in Chile was the welfare state. They envisioned replacing it with a model of unrestrained free-market capitalism.

Background to the "Dirty War"

After brief military interventions in 1924 and 1931, Chile settled into one of the longest-running, most representative democracies in Latin America. From 1932 to 1973, political representation from the center, left, and right parties achieved a fairly even balance, and elections resulted in multiparty alliances.

The government of **Eduardo Frei Montalva**, president from 1964 to 1970, represented an era of social and political advancement for many Chileans. His PDC, traditionally centrist, had aligned itself with the Chilean right in the previous election in order to defeat Salvador Allende Gossens, the candidate representing an alliance of leftist groups. Frei Montalva's social reforms (in education, labor, and agriculture) expanded opportunities for the middle and working classes. His land-reform program, however, angered the wealthy, who saw their estates converted into farm cooperatives. In the presidential election of 4 September 1970, the right turned against the PDC, allowing Allende Gossens to win a narrow plurality over the two other candidates, the conservative former president Jorge Alessandri and the left-leaning PDC candidate Radomiro Tomic. Allende Gossens promised a peaceful transition to socialism and headed a coalition of leftists and moderates called **Unidad Popular** (UP, Popular Unity). Since Allende Gossens failed to win a majority, Congress was called on to decide between the two front-runners. In past elections, congressional confirmation had been a formality. This time, however, the leading candidate was a socialist, and conservative members of the PDC tried to block the confirmation.

By early October the two sides had reached a compromise. In return for PDC votes necessary for confirmation, Allende Gossens agreed to sign a Statute of Guarantees, promising to respect democratic principles. Not all of Allende Gossens's opponents, however, were willing to accept his impending confirmation. Two groups within the military were already planning to disrupt the process. On 22 October one of the groups attempted to kidnap General René Schneider, the commander in chief of the army and a strict defender of the constitution. The plan went awry, and Schneider was fatally wounded. Constitutionalists in the military were now in a stronger position to let the process continue. On 24 October Congress declared Allende Gossens president.

Inaugurated on 3 November 1970, Allende Gossens became the first democratically elected Marxist president in the world. He continued implementing his predecessor's reforms while introducing many of his own. He appropriated and redistributed land, purchased banks, and nationalized major industries. He completed the nationalization, begun under Frei Montalva, of Chile's most important industry, copper mining.

Although Allende Gossens enjoyed wide popular support, Congress and members of the right and center parties thought he was going too far with his socialist reforms. Many of his younger supporters, meanwhile, thought he was not going far enough. Some encouraged peasants to seize land illegally; others called for armed struggle. The urban **guerrilla** group **Movimiento de la Izquierda Revolucionaria** (MIR, Movement of the Revolutionary Left) and a wing of the **Partido Socialista** (PS, Socialist Party) both advocated revolution as opposed to reform. Allende Gossens tolerated their militant stance in the hope of preserving the UP coalition, though he did denounce the June 1971 murder of the PDC leader Edmundo Pérez Zújovic by the Vanguardia Organizada del Pueblo (VOP, People's Organized Vanguard), a splinter group of the MIR.

Left-wing extremism met with right-wing extremism, especially from the vigilante group Patria y Libertad (PL, Fatherland and Liberty). While leftists sought to create the conditions for revolution, PL sought to provoke a military coup. The right found an ally in the **United States**. The administration of President Richard Nixon was openly antagonistic toward Allende Gossens, and the **Central Intelligence Agency** (CIA) worked covertly in an attempt to sabotage the Chilean economy and destabilize the government.

During Allende Gossens's first year in office, the economy grew, and both unemployment and inflation declined. Wage increases, coupled with a freeze on prices, stimulated consumer demand. In the municipal elections of April 1971, the UP was rewarded with more than 50 percent of the vote. But the UP's economic policies also had a downside, leading to decreased production, government deficits, capital flight, and (following another wage increase) high inflation. Between 1971 and 1973, inflation would rise from 22 to 600 percent. By 1972 food and other consumer goods were in short supply. Shortages became more acute in October 1972, when the *gremio* (trade association) representing independent truck owners staged a strike to protest an attempt at bringing the transport industry under state control. The strike ended when Allende Gossens asked the military for support, inviting three commanders into his cabinet.

More strikes—by bus owners and copper miners—took place in 1973. In the May 1973 congressional elections, the PDC and the conservative National party won 55.7 percent of the vote; the UP, 43.9 percent. The results left Congress deadlocked. On the one hand, the UP lacked the majority necessary to legislate additional reforms; on the other hand, the opposition lacked the two-thirds majority necessary to remove Allende Gossens from office.

The country moved close to civil war. In June young military officers mounted an armored tank rebellion, or *tancazo*. This attempt at a coup, quickly put down by General **Carlos Prats González**, the commander in chief of the army, revealed a growing public support for military intervention as a possible solution to the economic crisis. More rebellion followed in July, when truck owners, merchants, and white-collar workers organized strikes. Cardinal Raúl Silva Henríquez, the Archbishop of Santiago, tried to help Allende Gossens and the PDC reach an agreement, but negotiations broke off in August. In the opinion of high-ranking members of the military, such civil disorder warranted military intervention.

The "Dirty War": The Junta of Augusto Pinochet Ugarte

Within the first few days of the 11 September coup, international **human rights** groups such as **Amnesty International** and the Red Cross began to arrive. As the violence became more systematic (for example, abductions and disappearances under the cover of a dusk-to-dawn curfew), local human rights organizations were formed not only to provide assistance but also to document and denounce the repression. One was the **Comité de la Paz** (Committee for Peace), which later became the **Vicaría de la Solidaridad** (Vicariate of Solidarity). Both provided medical, legal, and social services despite protest and harassment from the government. Foreign embassies, with the exception of the embassy of the United States, provided refuge and assistance to foreign nationals and Chileans who wanted to leave the country. Although at first Pinochet Ugarte refused attempts by the **United Nations** (UN) to investigate reports of state terror, the UN would eventually observe and document human rights abuses in Chile.

In the months following the coup, the junta consolidated its power. The courts, including the **Supreme Court of Justice**, generally stood behind the junta and allowed the rulings of military tribunals to take precedence. The junta issued a series of decree laws aimed at bringing the government under military control, and replaced officials who had been appointed by Allende Gossens. It authorized the infamous **caravan of death**, a cross-country helicopter tour led by General Arellano Stark, which led to the deaths of 75 political prisoners. The junta closed Congress and burned the official election registries. It suspended political activity and outlawed leftist parties. The military and police then instituted a plan intended to eliminate all members of leftist opposition groups through the detention, interrogation, and execution of political prisoners. In 1974 a secret-police organization appeared, the **Dirección de Inteligencia Nacional** (DINA, Directorate of National Intelligence), followed in 1975 by the Comando Conjunto (CC, Joint Command), a rival **death squad** created by the air force. Both recruited from the right-wing vigilante group Patria y Libertad. Their initial targets were members of the MIR, the Partido Socialista, and the **Partido Comunista de Chile** (PC, Communist Party of Chile).

In December 1977 the UN condemned Chile for human rights violations. Furious, Pinochet Ugarte called a referendum seeking national support for his policies in the "defense of the dignity of Chile." In January 1978, 75 percent voted their approval, though the referendum was conducted without electoral safeguards. Pinochet Ugarte interpreted the results as a mandate, and reduced the state of siege (in effect since 1973) to a state of emergency. He also pressured the junta into signing an amnesty law. Promulgated on 19 April 1978, Decree Law 2191 had the effect of absolving the military and police of human rights abuses committed after 11 September 1973, the day of the coup. In September 1980 voters were called to the polls again, this time to endorse a new constitution written by Pinochet Ugarte and scheduled to take effect in March 1981. Approved by 67 percent of the vote in a plebiscite widely considered fraudulent, the **constitution of 1981** provided for President Pinochet Ugarte to remain in office until 1989.

In addition to extirpating Marxism, the junta had a second objective: to transform the economy. The subject stirred much debate. The Chicago Boys argued passionately for a free-market model; in contrast, the junta's early economic ministers were influenced by PDC members and business interests who wanted the economy to remain under state management. In the end, the Chicago Boys prevailed, and in 1975 took charge of policy. The "shock treatment" they administered caused immediate hardship. Those who escaped unemployment saw their wages drastically reduced. By the end of the decade, however, the treatment began to show positive results—significantly lower inflation and substantial growth. Hailed by many as a "miracle," the economic boom brought many Chileans into the middle class. It also made those who were well off even wealthier. According to theory, this wealth would eventually "trickle down" to the poor. Nevertheless, in 1982 world recession ended the boom, and by the mid-1980s, anywhere from 14 percent (the government's figure) to 45 percent of the population remained in poverty.

By 1983 economic recession was taking its toll in bankruptcies and unemployment. Antigovernment sentiment began to build, taking the form of organized demonstrations and protest marches. Political parties revived, and in June 1983 the PDC formed a coalition of moderate parties, the Alianza Democrática (AD, Democratic Alliance), which called for the resignation of Pinochet Ugarte and a return to democratic rule. Excluded from the AD were the PC and the militant wing of the PS, owing to their refusal to rule out armed struggle as a means of ending the dictatorship. The PC responded by creating a left-wing coalition called the Movimiento Democrático Popular (MDP, Popular Democratic Movement).

Pinochet Ugarte refused to step down, and protests continued into 1984 and 1985, many of them violent confrontations with security forces. By then a new guerrilla organization had formed, the **Frente Patriótico Manuel Rodríguez** (FPMR, Manuel Rodríguez Patriotic Front), which carried out thousands of operations, including a failed attempt to assassinate Pinochet Ugarte in September 1986. The incident provoked another state of siege and renewed death-squad activity, especially from the Centro Nacional de Información (CNI, National Information Center), an intelligence agency that had replaced DINA in 1977.

The government announced in mid-1987 that Pinochet Ugarte would be the candidate in a plebiscite scheduled for 1988. A "yes" vote would give him eight more years as president. A "no" vote would mean a general election with a choice of candidates. By mid-1988 the opposition had begun to rally around the Comando por el No (Command for the No), an alliance of some 16 political parties established in February to campaign against Pinochet Ugarte and guard against electoral fraud. That the country was moving toward democracy was evident in the **plebiscite of 1988**, which took place on 5 October. A majority of voters (54.7 percent) rejected another term in office for Pinochet Ugarte and opened the way for national elections the following year. On 14 December 1989 **Patricio Aylwin Azócar**, representing a center-left coalition, was elected president with 55.2 percent of the vote. Hernán Büchi, the government candidate and a former minister of finance under Pinochet Ugarte, came in second with 29.4 percent.

Aftermath of the "Dirty War"

On 24 April 1990, one month after taking office, President Aylwin Azócar established the **Comisión Nacional de Verdad y Reconciliación** (National Commission on Truth and Reconciliation) to investigate and document human rights abuses committed during the dictatorship. Chaired by the judge Raúl Rettig and given nine months to complete its work, the commission issued its report in 1991, having documented more than 2,000 cases of human rights abuse involving death. The commission's charge, however, did not extend to naming those responsible, nor was the commission allowed enough time to identify the victims and find their bodies. Some remains had already been recovered through the efforts of the Vicariate of Solidarity: 15 were found in 1978 in an abandoned lime kiln in Lonquén; 126 were found in 1991 in a Santiago cemetery—many in graves marked NN (*ningún nombre*, no name) and some two to a coffin. The task of locating the remaining missing (*desaparecidos*) and politically executed fell to the commission's successor, the Corporación Nacional por la Reconciliación y la Reparación (National Corporation for Reconciliation and Reparation). Established in January 1992, it was originally given two years to complete its work, though Congress would grant it an additional year. By the time it was dissolved in December 1994, however, the corporation had made little progress in determining the whereabouts of the more than 1,500 missing Chileans.

An important reason for this lack of progress was the military's refusal to cooperate. Members of the armed forces and carabineros saw no advantage to getting involved, having been granted amnesty in 1978. Moreover, the administration was careful not to threaten the military for fear of provoking a coup—Pinochet Ugarte remaining a force to be reckoned with. After stepping down as president in 1990, he continued to lead the army, and after his retirement in 1998, he took office as senator for life, a position provided for him by the constitution of 1981. It seemed as if he were well situated to thwart any attempt at assigning responsibility for the "dirty war" to specific members of the military, including himself. Yet his immunity from prosecution would be challenged when he went abroad.

On 16 October 1998, while in London for back surgery, Pinochet Ugarte was placed under house arrest by British authorities at the request of the Spanish judge **Baltasar Garzón**, who sought his extradition to Spain to face charges of gross human rights violations. On 28 October the British High Court rejected the request, ruling that Pinochet Ugarte was immune from prosecution for crimes committed while he was head of state. A committee of the House of Lords, however, reversed that ruling in November, rejecting the claim of immunity. Extradition proceedings began the following month, but were discontinued when it became known that one of the law lords who had ruled against Pinochet Ugarte had failed to disclose a possible conflict of interest—a link to the human rights group Amnesty International. A new House of Lords committee was formed in January 1999 to appeal the initial High Court ruling. Its decision, announced on 24 March, agreed with the November ruling that rejected the claim of immunity. Extradition proceedings resumed in September, and a court ruled on 8 October that the extradition of Pinochet Ugarte to Spain could proceed. Pinochet Ugarte, however, would be spared a second time. Independent doctors reported that he was medically unfit to stand trial, and in March 2000 he was allowed to return to Chile.

Pinochet Ugarte's detention in Britain had divided Chilean society, prompting demonstrations for and against a trial. Yet even some of his opponents argued that he should be tried not in Spain but in Chile. The likelihood of bringing him to trial increased as a new generation of judges appeared, replacing the old guard as it retired from the bench. In August 2000 the Supreme Court divested Pinochet Ugarte of his immunity, and Judge Juan Guzmán Tapia, known for his independence, pursued the case against him. On 1 December Pinochet Ugarte was placed under house arrest, indicted on charges of kidnapping and murder in connection with the caravan of death. An appeals court overturned the case on a technicality. The Supreme Court upheld that decision, but ordered Guzmán Tapia to question Pinochet Ugarte. First, however, Pinochet Ugarte was required to undergo a medical examination—required by Chilean law for citizens over 70 years old—to see if he was mentally competent. An appeals court ruled on 9 July 2001 that he was mentally unfit to stand trial, and the effort to bring him to justice came to an end.

CHILEAN HUMAN RIGHTS COMMISSION. *See* COMISIÓN CHILENA POR LOS DERECHOS HUMANOS.

CHRISTIAN DEMOCRATIC PARTY. *See* PARTIDO DEMÓCRATA CRISTIANO (PDC).

COMANDO CONJUNTO. *See* DEATH SQUADS.

COMISIÓN CHILENA POR LOS DERECHOS HUMANOS / CHILEAN HUMAN RIGHTS COMMISSION. A **human rights** nongovernmental organization in **Chile.** Founded in 1978 by lawyers, the Comisión documented and reported human rights abuses. The group also established a network of neighborhood human rights defense committees. Like many other human rights organizations during the dictatorship, the group was the target of repression. Its president, **Jaime Castillo Velasco**, was **exiled** in 1981, and other high-ranking members were detained and tortured by government security forces.

COMISIÓN NACIONAL DE VERDAD Y RECONCILIACIÓN / NATIONAL COMMISSION ON TRUTH AND RECONCILIATION. Also known as the Rettig commission. A truth commission established in 1990 by President **Patricio Aylwin Azócar** of **Chile**. It was charged with investigating and documenting **human rights** violations committed in Chile between 11 September 1973 and 11 March 1990. Judge Raúl Rettig headed the commission, which was composed of six lawyers, an historian, and a civil rights worker, all representing different political affiliations. The commission reviewed more than 3,000 cases of human rights violations that resulted in death. The Commission's charge stopped short of allocating responsibility to the members of the armed forces, including **Augusto Pinochet Ugarte** and other high-ranking officials. The Supreme Court and the **military** publicly vilified the commission and its report. In spite of the rancor, President Aylwin Azócar established the Corporación Nacional por la Reconciliación y la Reparación (National Corporation for Reconciliation and Reparation) to finish the work of the commission.

COMISIÓN NACIONAL SOBRE LA DESAPARICIÓN DE PERSONAS (CONADEP) / NATIONAL COMMISSION ON THE MISSING. Also known as the Sábato Commission. A blue-ribbon panel charged with investigating the fate of those who disappeared in **Argentina** during the **"dirty war."** Formed in 1983 after the return to democracy, CONADEP was asked to hear evidence and to report its findings. Its charge was limited to documenting cases and making recommendations. The task of assigning responsibility for what happened would fall to the courts. Of the 13 CONADEP members, President **Raúl Alfonsín** selected 10, including **Ernesto Sábato**, who headed the commission. These 10 individuals represented a cross section of Argentine society and politics. What they had in common was national and international respect and a commitment to **human rights**. The remaining three members were representatives of the Chamber of Deputies. (Both chambers of Congress had been asked to elect representatives, but only the Chamber of Deputies chose to do so.) Aided by staff and human rights organizations, CONADEP collected thousands of depositions and testimonies. Its report, summarizing 50,000 pages of information, was published in Spanish in 1984 under the title *Nunca más* (Never Again). In 1986 an English translation appeared under the title *Nunca Más (Never Again). See also DESAPARECIDOS.*

COMITÉ DE DEFENSA DE LOS DERECHOS DEL PUEBLO (CODEPU) / COMMITTEE FOR THE DEFENSE OF THE RIGHTS OF THE PEOPLE. A **human rights** nongovernmental organization in **Chile**. CODEPU was founded in 1980 to defend those accused of terrorism, and expanded to provide legal and psychological assistance to **torture** victims and their families.

COMITÉ DE LA PAZ (COPACHI) / COMMITTEE FOR PEACE. Also known as the Committee of Cooperation for Peace. A **human rights** nongovernmental organization in Chile. COPACHI, established in October 1973 under the leadership of the Chilean **Catholic Church**, is an example of the strong role that the Church played in opposition to the **military** government of **Augusto Pinochet Ugarte**. Although some members of the Church hierarchy supported military intervention as a solution to restoring governmental order before and during the coup, the Church denounced the severe repression and human rights abuses that followed, organizing support for the victims. As a humanitarian organization, COPACHI started with basic programs involving food distribution and medical services, but later expanded its scope to include legal services for detainees and sanctuary to those being persecuted as part of the military's campaign against subversives. In 1975 COPACHI's practice of providing sanctuary brought the organization under the scrutiny of the **Dirección de Inteligencia Nacional** (DINA, Directorate of National Intelligence), a newly formed state intelligence agency. After the forced **exile** of some of COPACHI's strongest activists, the organization finally acceded to Pinochet Ugarte's constant demands for formal dissolution. Work on behalf of victims of the state was continued by a new religious organization created by one of COPACHI's founders, Cardinal Raúl Silva Henríquez. The **Vicaría de la**

Solidaridad (Vicariate of Solidarity) opened its offices in 1976 under the protection of the Catholic Church.

COMMITTEE FOR PEACE. *See* COMITÉ DE LA PAZ (COPACHI).

COMMITTEE OF COOPERATION FOR PEACE IN CHILE. *See* COMITÉ DE LA PAZ (COPACHI).

COMMUNISM. Although the **"dirty wars"** were a Cold War phenomenon, communism—as well as anarchism, socialism, and other variants of the left—has had a long tradition in the Southern Cone, closely connected with the rise of **trade unions**. The traditional left in **Chile**, dominated by the Marxist **Partido Comunista** (PC, Communist Party) and **Partido Socialista** (PS, Socialist Party), was more successful politically than in **Argentina** and **Uruguay**. In 1970 the PC and PS, as part of the **Unidad Popular** (UP, Popular Unity) coalition, helped elect **Salvador Allende Gossens** to the presidency. In Uruguay leftist parties long dominated union elections but regularly lost to the mainstream Colorados (Reds) and Blancos (Whites) in national elections. Not until 1971, with the rise of the Marxist-led coalition **Frente Amplio** (FA, Broad Front), did leftists gain a significant percentage of the national vote. In Argentina **Juan Perón** wrested control of the trade unions from leftists in the 1940s, and since then national politics became a contest between **Peronists** and anti-Peronists.

After 1959 the left in Latin America was strongly influenced by the Cuban Revolution, which gave rise to rural and urban **guerrilla warfare** across the region. Although sometimes dismissed by senior party members as amateurism or adventurism, guerrilla movements attracted young people who rejected party bureaucracy for the chance to effect radical change. When "dirty war" regimes came to power, guerrillas became prime targets for repression, along with radical trade unionists and Marxist parties like the Frente, the PC, and PS. In Argentina the Communist and Socialist parties, aging and conservative, were spared.

COMMUNIST PARTY OF CHILE. *See* PARTIDO COMUNISTA DE CHILE (PC).

CONCERTACIÓN NACIONAL PROGRAMÁTICA (CONAPRO) / NATIONAL PROGRAMMATIC AGREEMENT. A multiparty agreement made in **Uruguay** in 1984, calling for truth and justice. President **Julio María Sanguinetti**, however, who took office in 1985 after the return to civilian rule, never signed the agreement, allowing it to fade into oblivion.

CONDOR. *See* OPERATION CONDOR.

CONFEDERACIÓN GENERAL DEL TRABAJO (CGT) / GENERAL LABOR CONFEDERATION. The principal labor confederation in **Argentina**. Founded in 1930, the CGT was originally under the control of leftists, but was absorbed into the **Peronist** movement during the administration of **Juan Perón** (1946–1955). The succeeding **military** government, as part of its anti-Peronist efforts, took control of the CGT (*intervención*). Nevertheless, in 1957 the CGT split into two factions. Sixty-two unions declared loyalty to Perón; 32 would be led by leftists or independents. Although the exact number would vary, the Peronist faction became known as the "62 organizations." In 1968 the CGT split again, this time into two separate organizations. A radical group broke away to form the CGT de los Argentinos (CGTA, CGT of the Argentines). The CGTA opposed the efforts of Augusto Vandor to reach an agreement with the military government of Juan Carlos Onganía. Vandor, who had hoped to establish "Peronism without Perón," was assassinated the following year. The CGTA was banned, and its leaders jailed. In 1970 the two organizations reunited, but the CGT, like the Peronist movement itself, remained deeply divided.

CONFEDERACIÓN GENERAL DEL TRABAJO DE LOS ARGENTINOS (CGTA). *See* CONFEDERACIÓN GENERAL DEL TRABAJO (CGT).

CONSTITUTION OF 1981 (CHILE). Drafted under the guidance of the junta leader General **Augusto Pinochet Ugarte**, this constitution was approved by a referendum in September 1980, replacing the constitution of 1925. The new constitution established as law the repressive policies of the **military** government while promising an eventual return to civilian rule. It placed the armed forces in a position of considerable power. After a referendum in 1988 rejected Pinochet Ugarte's bid for another presidential term, the military government moved to consolidate its power even further by issuing a series of constitutional amendments. One amendment restricted the president's authority to dismiss high-ranking army officials. Another amendment ensured a disproportional representation in the legislature of members aligned to the rightist military regime, including several appointed institutional senators with extended terms. After the return to civilian rule, these adjustments to the constitution hindered the attempts of President **Patricio Aylwin Azócar** and his successor **Eduardo Frei Ruiz-Tagle** to investigate **human rights** abuses committed during the military regime.

CONTI, HAROLDO (1925–1976?). Argentine teacher, journalist, actor, playwright, and screenwriter. Born in Chacabuco, a province of Buenos Aires, Conti won early acclaim in the theater with his play *Examinados* (1955). Several later works of fiction were published to critical acclaim. His novel *Mascaró el cazador americano* received the prestigious Casa de las Américas award in 1975. This work, which incorporates realist elements and fantasy, has been described as "a study of freedom." Earlier Conti was the recipient of several literary awards in Latin America and Spain. His novel *Alrededor de la jaula* was filmed in 1977 under the title *Crecer de golpe*. Conti was abducted by members of the Argentine secret police on 5 May 1976 and remains among the *desaparecidos*.

CONTRERAS SEPÚLVEDA, MANUEL. A colonel (later general) in the armed forces and the director of the **Dirección de Inteligencia Nacional** (DINA, Directorate of National Intelligence), the secret police in **Chile**. Attempts to charge Contreras Sepúlveda with **human rights** violations were blocked by an amnesty law announced by the junta in 1978. In 1993, however, after the return to civilian government, a Chilean court convicted General Contreras Sepúlveda and his former deputy, Brigadier General **Pedro Espinoza Bravo**, of complicity in the 1976 car-bomb assassination of **Orlando Letelier del Solar** and Ronni Moffitt in Washington, D.C. Since the crime had been committed outside the country, the 1978 amnesty did not apply. He was sentenced to seven years and served time in a special **military** prison.

CORDOBAZO. *See* ARGENTINA.

CORPORATION FOR THE PROMOTION AND DEFENSE OF THE RIGHTS OF THE PEOPLE. *See* COMITÉ DE DEFENSA DE LOS DERECHOS DEL PUEBLO (CODEPU).

COSTA-GAVRAS (1933–). French director, writer, actor, and producer. Born in Athens, Greece, as Konstantinos Gavras. A graduate of the Institut de Hautes Études Cinématographiques in Paris, Costa-Gavras captured the attention of the U.S. movie-going public with the first of a trilogy of political thrillers starring Yves Montand. *Z* (1969), a critique of the Greek junta, then in power, was awarded an Oscar for Best Foreign Language Film and earned Costa-Gavras nominations for directing the film and co-writing the screenplay. *Z* was followed by *The Confession* (1970) and *State of Siege* (1973), a critique of U.S. intervention in South America set against the backdrop of **Uruguay**. Costa-Gavras would revisit the politics of South America in his film *Missing* (1982), the first of a string of successful films made in Hollywood. *Missing* examines the issue of the ***desaparecidos*** following the overthrow of **Salvador Allende Gossens** in **Chile**. It won Costa-Gavras an Oscar for co-writing the screenplay and a Palme d'or at the Cannes Film Festival. Later films include *Betrayed* (1988), *Music Box* (1990), which won the Golden Bear at the Berlin Film Festival, and *The Little Apocalypse* (1993). Costa-Gavras directed the Cinémathèque française between 1982 and 1987.

CULTURAL RESISTANCE. Acts of cultural resistance are expressions of solidarity and nonviolent protest. During the **"dirty wars"** of the Southern Cone, protest literature and films were dominant examples of cultural resistance. Media bans and censorship, however—including book burnings and the destruction of both merchant's inventories and personal libraries—moved the production of literature and film underground. To survive, works either had to be allegorical enough to escape the censors or else produced in **exile**. A notable exception was the film *La batalla de Chile: la lucha de un pueblo sin armas. 2. El golpe del estado* (*The Battle of Chile: The Struggle of an Unarmed People. 2. The Coup*), which was made in **Chile** in the direct aftermath of the **military** coup of 11 September 1973. But Patricio Guzmán, who was the producer and director, and the other four members of the film crew paid a heavy price for their efforts. All were detained by security forces, and one member, the cameraman Jorge Muller-Silva, disappeared.

Yet there were other forms of expression not as easy to control—for example, music, clothing, murals, graffiti, and improvised street theater. In **Argentina**, where many of the victims were young people, *rock nacional*, or national rock, developed into a social movement with a mass following. Rock concerts were something more than musical events. They were a means of challenging the values of the dictatorship. In place of violence, authoritarianism, and silence, rock offered peace, freedom, and participation. Within the pages of the thousands of fan magazines spawned by the movement (many of them underground), young people could communicate with one another by way of letters. Many commented on how secure they felt at concerts, confident that no harm could come to them in such large crowds. In Chile, the funeral of prize-winning poet **Pablo Neruda** became a symbol of formalized protest. Another was the performance of songs by traditional folk artists such as **Violeta Parra**, whose work was embodied in the new song cultural movement (*nueva canción chilena*) of the 1960s and 1970s, later reaffirmed in demonstrations against the regime of **Augusto Pinochet Ugarte**. In 1984, a few days before the anniversary of the coup of 11 September 1973, many paused at noon to sing Parra's "Thanks to Life" in a declaration of remembrance.

–D–

DAWSON ISLAND. A remote and desolate place in the Strait of Magellan, where prisoners of the **military** government in **Chile**—especially those sentenced to *relegación*, or internal **exile**—were taken. Because of its poor climate, the island itself was a **torture** center where prisoners suffered and died from pneumonia and other conditions associated with exposure to the elements. After the military coup in 1973, **Clodomiro Almeyda Medina**, vice-president in the government of **Salvador Allende Gossens** and a leader in the **Partido Socialista**, or Socialist Party, was sentenced to *relegación* there along with other **Unidad Popular** officials. He was later exiled.

DEATH SQUADS. As the left in the 1960s and early 1970s made political gains or turned to **guerrilla warfare**, the right formed vigilante groups aimed at political opponents. Prominent among them were Patria y Libertad (PL, Fatherland and Liberty) in **Chile** and the **Alianza Anticomunista Argentina** (AAA, Argentine Anticommunist Alliance). During the socialist government of **Salvador Allende Gossens** in Chile (1970–1973), PL engaged in acts of economic sabotage—vandalizing factories and blowing up electrical towers—in the hope of gaining mainstream support for a **military** coup. From 1973 to 1976 the AAA targeted left-wing **Peronists**, assassinating them or forcing them into **exile**. In **Uruguay** in the late 1960s, the administration of Jorge Pacheco Areco enlisted civilian and police organizations in the fight against the **Tupamaro** guerrillas.

When these countries fell to dictatorship, extremist groups like PL and AAA either disbanded or became subordinate to the military. Various service branches, especially their intelligence operations, took the lead in the fight against subversion. In Argentina groups called *patotas* (gangs), ranging in size from six to two dozen and often traveling in Ford Falcons, made the arrests. *Patotas* were part of larger groups called *grupos de tareas* (GT, task forces). GT 1 was controlled by the federal police; GT 2, the army; GT 3, the navy; and GT 4, the air force.

In Chile the secret police, the **Dirección de Inteligencia Nacional** (DINA, Directorate of National Intelligence), had both a national and an international component. The national component was responsible for attacking the military regime's internal enemies like the **Movimiento de la Izquierda Revolucionaria** (MIR, Movement of the Revolutionary Left), the **Partido Socialista** (PS, Socialist Party), and the **Partido Comunista de Chile** (PC, Communist Party of Chile). DINA's international component, which eliminated the regime's enemies abroad, earned worldwide notoriety and led to DINA's dissolution. DINA's successor, the Centro Nacional de Información (CNI, National Information Center), was more low key but became active in the civil unrest of the mid-1980s. Competing with the DINA was the Comando Conjunto (CC, Joint Command), under the control of the air force. As late as December 2002 the CC was still in existence.

In Uruguay arrests were made by teams ranging in number from three or four to more than 15, depending on the amount of resistance expected. The army, the other service branches, and the police all took part in making arrests.

***DEGOLLADOS* CASE.** The term refers to the murders in **Chile** of three members of the **Partido Comunista de Chile** (PC, Communist Party of Chile) by **carabineros** working out of the Dirección de Inteligencia y Comunicaciones de Carabineros (DICOMCAR, Directorate of Carabinero Intelligence and Communication), a separate investigative unit of the national police. In late March 1985, José Manuel Parada, an archivist for the **Vicaría de la Solidaridad** (Vicariate of Solidarity), and Santiago Nattino and Manuel Guerrero, both suspected intelligence agents of the PC, were abducted by DICOMCAR agents and later found in a ditch with their throats slashed. Commonly referred to as the *degollados* (from the verb *degollar*, meaning "to cut the throat of," "to slaughter"), the crime was reminiscent of the leftist-targeted disappearances and murders following the 1973 **military** coup, and contributed to a growing antigovernment movement. The *degollados* case was one of the few military crimes investigated by the courts. Judge José Cánovas Robles identified the 14 men responsible for the slayings as DI-

COMCAR agents. Ironically, the identifications were made with the assistance of the Centro Nacional de Información (National Information Center), the military secret service agency formed in 1977 to replace the infamous **Dirección de Inteligencia Nacional** (DINA, Directorate of National Intelligence). The case led to the resignation of the longtime police agency director General César Mendoza Durán from the junta.

DERIAN, PATRICIA ("PATT"). Assistant secretary of state for **human rights** under President **Jimmy Carter** (1977–1981). Born in New York City, she became a registered nurse and then moved to Jackson, Mississippi. There, in the 1960s, she became a civil-rights activist and was threatened by the Ku Klux Klan. She served as Democratic National Committeewoman in Mississippi in 1968, ran George McGovern's presidential-election campaign in the state in 1972, and served as deputy director of Carter's national election campaign in 1976. When Carter took office in January 1977, pledging to defend human rights throughout the world, he appointed her coordinator of the revived Bureau of Human Rights and Humanitarian Affairs, a State Department position. Within the year, she was promoted from coordinator to assistant secretary.

Derian was an outspoken critic of human rights violators, and her commitment to the issue put her at odds with others within the State Department. The Bureau was often ignored or ridiculed. Her most vocal critics were Richard Holbrooke, Assistant Secretary of State for East Asian and Pacific Affairs, and Terence Todman, Assistant Secretary of State for Inter-American Affairs, both of whom accused her of promoting human rights to the detriment of national security or economic considerations. Meanwhile, finding it difficult to apply a human rights policy across the board, the Carter administration adopted a case-by-case approach, and in some countries—most notably China—made human rights secondary to other foreign-policy objectives.

By January 1978 the policy was largely applied to Latin America alone. Derian made several trips to **Argentina**, vehemently protesting the *desaparecidos* and raising the issue of **torture**. She lobbied for the release of **Jacobo Timerman**, who later credited her with saving many lives. But she was dismayed that, despite her agency's opposition and Congressional legislation, some types of **military** aid (spare parts and support equipment) continued to flow into Argentina, **Chile**, **Uruguay**, and other countries with dismal human rights records. In 1980 the Carter administration considered renewing military aid to Argentina, hoping to win its cooperation in the U.S.-led grain embargo against the Soviet Union. Derian said she would resign if military aid was restored. The administration decided against the aid, and she remained in her position. Her influence, however, continued to diminish.

DESAPARECIDOS. A Spanish term meaning "the missing," it refers to those who vanish while in the custody of the state. The state often refuses to release information about the victims—indeed, often denies ever having had them in custody. The term originated in Guatemala during the 1960s, and then became associated with **Argentina** during the 1970s. It was adopted into the English language in its original Spanish version, though the Anglicized version "disappeared" is also common. Instances of a transitive use of the verb disappear (meaning to cause to disappear) existed in English long before the **"dirty wars,"** but the events of the period have popularized its use, with or without quotation marks (the security force "disappeared" her; he was "disappeared" by the **military**). Disappearances, however, are by no means peculiar to Latin America. They are a common occurrence in national security states throughout the world, and are condemned by the **United Nations** (UN) as a fundamental violation of **human rights**.

In Argentina the **Comisión Nacional sobre la Desaparición de Personas** (CONADEP, National Commission on the Missing)—the government truth commission established after the return to democracy in 1985—documented 8,960 *desaparecidos*. Estimates by human rights groups, however, reach as high as 30,000. One reason for the discrepancy is that the truth commission reported only *documented* cases collected during the short period it was allowed to work—nine months. During that period, it was able to sift less than half the data it received. Even so, the evidence was strong enough to convict the former junta commanders and middle-ranking officers of human rights crimes, though they were later pardoned by President **Carlos Saúl Menem**. (Lower-ranking members of the military were exempt from prosecution because of the *Obediencia Debida*, or Due Obedience, law.) The evidence also refuted the military's allegation that most of the missing were **guerrillas**. The documentation showed that most of the missing had been abducted at home, 150 were under 15 years old, 125 were over 60, and 268 were pregnant. Some of the victims were physically disabled.

As many as 2,000 of the victims in Argentina were disappeared by being drugged and thrown into the Atlantic Ocean from navy aircraft. At least 200 (perhaps as many as 500) of the missing were children abducted with their parents or born in prison. Many of these children were illegally adopted and raised by military families. Among the local human rights organizations that were formed in the 1970s to protest the disappearances were the **Madres de Plaza de Mayo** (Mothers of the Plaza de Mayo), who brought international attention to their cause by marching every Thursday outside the Casa Rosada (Pink House, or presidential palace). An offshoot of the Madres, the **Abuelas de Plaza de Mayo** (Grandmothers), set out to trace missing children and reunite them with their biological families. In 1979 the military government attempted to rid itself of the issue of disappearance by pronouncing the missing dead. The Madres and other human rights groups challenged the attempt and kept the issue in the forefront. Even after the officers convicted of human rights violations were pardoned and the cause of justice seemed lost, the issue refused to go away. In 1999 a federal court ruled that as long as victims remained missing—bodies unrecovered and children unaccounted for—the crimes of disappearance were still being committed. The ruling gave new life to a case against several former high-ranking military officers, including the junta commanders **Jorge Rafael Videla**, **Emilio Massera**, and **Reynaldo Benito Bignone**, who had been charged in connection with the kidnapping and illegal adoption of children—crimes not covered by their pardons.

Fewer people disappeared in **Chile** and **Uruguay**. The **Comisión Nacional de Verdad y Reconciliación** (National Commission on Truth and Reconciliation), the Chilean truth commission, documented 877 *desaparecidos*. The total number of documented deaths, however, is 2,279—2,115 attributed to the military regime, 164 to left-wing violence. Among the regime's victims, 815 died under **torture** or were executed. The number of missing Uruguayans is estimated at 170, many of whom (about 140) disappeared in Argentina, Chile, and Paraguay, presumably victims of **Operation Condor**. Nevertheless, in Chile and Uruguay there were thousands of cases of temporary disappearance—abduction, rape, and torture—also considered by the UN to be gross violations of human rights.

DESCAMISADOS. A small **guerrilla** organization in **Argentina**, **Peronist** in sympathy, formed in 1968 by Horacio Mendizábal and Norberto Habegger. The group took its name from Perón's working-class supporters (the "shirtless" ones). Mendizábal and Habegger went on to play important roles as members of the **Montoneros**, by whom the group was absorbed in late 1972. *See also* EJÉRCITO NACIONAL REVOLUCIONARIO.

DIRECCIÓN DE INTELIGENCIA NACIONAL (DINA) / DIREC-TORATE OF NATIONAL INTELLIGENCE. The notorious **Chilean** secret police, established in June 1974 under the dictatorship of General **Augusto Pinochet Ugarte.** The explicit purpose of DINA was to gather information from a variety of sources at the national level; its implicit purpose, however, was to gather information on political opponents and to eliminate the leftist influence on Chilean society. The gathering of information actually began in November 1973, when a commission was established under Colonel (later General) **Manuel Contreras Sepúlveda.** When DINA was created, Contreras Sepúlveda continued as its director and, to the dismay of other junta officers, reported directly to Pinochet Ugarte. He recruited from the intelligence units of the armed services—air force, army, **carabineros** (national police), and navy—as well as from vigilante groups active against the **Unidad Popular** (Popular Unity) government of President **Salvador Allende Gossens,** especially Patria y Libertad (Fatherland and Liberty).

DINA agents worked out of secret detention centers throughout the country, the most notorious of which was **Villa Grimaldi,** a former estate mansion. They abducted their victims under cover of curfew, and, using information obtained from **torture,** murdered or disappeared persons perceived as subversives. To eliminate political opponents living in **exile,** DINA participated in a secret regional military network codenamed **Operation Condor.** Condor has been linked to the assassination of **Orlando Letelier del Solar,** a former Chilean cabinet official, and his assistant Ronni Moffitt in the **United States,** and to an assassination attempt on Bernardo Leighton, one of the founders of the **Partido Demócrata Cristiano** (Christian Democratic Party), in Rome.

In 1977, under international pressure owing to the murder of Letelier del Solar and Moffitt, Pinochet Ugarte dissolved DINA and replaced it with the Centro Nacional de Información (CNI, National Information Center).

Attempts to prosecute DINA members have been blocked by an amnesty law declared in 1978. In 1993, however, after the return to democracy, Contreras Sepúlveda (now a general) and Brigadier General **Pedro Espinoza Bravo,** his former deputy, were convicted by a Chilean court of complicity in the murder of Letelier del Solar and Moffitt. The crime, having been committed outside the country, was not covered by the amnesty. Contreras Sepúlveda was sentenced to seven years, Espinoza Bravo to six. Both served time in a special military prison.

DIRECTORATE OF NATIONAL INTELLIGENCE. *See* DIREC-CIÓN DE INTELIGENCIA NACIONAL (DINA).

"DIRTY WAR" ("GUERRA SUCIA"). Although the term is commonly applied to events in **Argentina** from 1976 to 1983, the concept behind it is by no means peculiar to that country or to Latin America. In a "dirty war," the state brings the full weight of its **military** and other resources to bear against individuals, groups, or ideas it considers subversive. The phrase is often enclosed in quotation marks or preceded by *so-called*, suggesting that a "dirty war" is not a war in the traditional sense. Unlike a conventional war, in which standing armies contest territorial boundaries, a "dirty war" combats ideological boundaries. "Dirty-war" tactics are designed to root out an enemy that the state regards as hidden and elusive. Suspects are kidnapped, taken to clandestine detention centers, tortured and raped, and often "disappeared" or **exiled**. Names of additional suspects extracted during **torture** sessions lead to further arrests. Those who authorize and commit such acts enjoy not only the resources of the state but also the impunity it provides. There is no attempt to account for the missing—bodies are buried in secret graveyards or left out in the open as a warning to others. The ensuing climate of terror silences opposition and breeds collaboration.

The "dirty wars" waged in Argentina, **Chile**, and **Uruguay** in the 1970s and 1980s, coming in the final throes of the Cold War, were aimed primarily at the left and those perceived to be its supporters. Political parties and **guerrilla** movements like the **Montoneros** and **Ejército Revolucionario del Pueblo** in Argentina, the **Partido Socialista** and **Movimiento de Izquierda Revolucionaria** in Chile, and the **Tupamaros** in Uruguay all suffered heavy losses, many of its members killed or forced into exile. Not all of the victims, however, were political party leaders or armed insurgents. Journalists, labor activists, school teachers, university professors, progressive church leaders, high-school students—anyone whose ideas were perceived to be antithetical to government notions of "Western, Christian civilization"—could join the ranks of the missing. *See also DESAPARECIDOS.*

DISAPPEARED. *See DESAPARECIDOS.*

DORFMAN, ARIEL (1942–). **Chilean** playwright, poet, novelist, essayist, cartoonist, memoirist, and professor of Latin American literature. Born in Buenos Aires, Argentina, into a family of European émigrés—themselves survivors of Eastern European pogroms—the young

Dorfman followed his family into **exile** in 1944 to the **United States**. In 1954, during the McCarthy era, the family went once again into exile, this time to Chile, where Dorfman obtained a Licenciatura in Comparative Literature from the Universidad de Chile, Santiago (1965), and became a naturalized citizen (1967). An early supporter of President **Salvador Allende Gossens**, Dorfman was a member of the Popular Front and advisor to the president's chief of staff. After the 1973 coup, Dorfman went into exile in France, the Netherlands, and the United States. He returned briefly to Chile in 1983 following eased restrictions on exiles. Another attempt to return, in 1986, resulted in his detention and expulsion from the country. He has taught at the Universidad de Chile, the Sorbonne (Paris), and the University of Amsterdam. He is currently the Walter Hines Page Research Professor of Literature and Latin American Studies at Duke University, North Carolina.

Dorfman's plays include "Widows," winner of a New American Plays Award from the Kennedy Center, and "Reader," winner of a Roger L. Stevens Award from the Kennedy Center. Several of his works have been filmed, most notably the play "Death and the Maiden," first performed to critical acclaim in England in 1991 and later directed for the screen by Roman Polanski in 1994. In 1997 he was awarded, in collaboration with his son Rodrigo, a Writer's Guild of Great Britain Award for the short film *Prisoners of Time*. His latest film, *Dead Line*, another father-son collaboration, is based on Dorfman's collection of poetry *Last Waltz in Santiago and Other Poems of Exile and Disappearance* (1988).

Dorfman's literary works have been translated into 27 languages. His early works, which offer a critique of U.S. popular culture, include *The Emperor's Old Clothes* (1983, first published in 1980 as *Reader's nuestro que estás en la tierra*) and perhaps his best-known work, *How to Read Donald Duck* (1984, first published in 1971), the best-selling collection of essays in Latin America in the 1970s. In addition to plays and poetry, Dorfman works that offer a perspective on the Chilean repression include *Hard Rain* (1990, first published in 1973 as *Moros en la costa*), *Widows* (1983), *The Last Song of Manuel Sendero* (1986), *Mascara* (1988), and *Konfidenz* (1995). In 1998 Dorfman published *Heading South, Looking North: A Bilingual Journey*, a work the author has described as a double memoir—that of his experiences during the Allende Gossens years and the coup and that of his life in exile.

Haunted by memory and chance survival, Dorfman's work grapples with the themes of justice, overcoming distances, liberation, and resistance.

DUE OBEDIENCE. *See OBEDIENCIA DEBIDA.*

–E–

ECUMENICAL MOVEMENT FOR HUMAN RIGHTS. *See* MOVIMIENTO ECUMÉNICO POR LOS DERECHOS HUMANOS (MEDH).

ECUMENICAL SERVICE FOR HUMAN DIGNITY. *See* SERVICIO ECUMÉNICO DE REINTEGRACIÓN (SER).

ECUMENICAL SERVICE FOR REINTEGRATION. *See* SERVICIO ECUMÉNICO DE REINTEGRACIÓN (SER).

EJÉRCITO GUERRILLERO DEL PUEBLO (EGP) / PEOPLE'S GUERRILLA ARMY. A **guerrilla** organization that appeared in 1963 in Salta, a northern province of **Argentina**. It was led by Jorge Masetti, an Argentine journalist who had spent the previous five years in Fidel Castro's Cuba. From there he slipped into Bolivia with three veterans of the Cuban Revolution and, using an intricate recruiting system, attracted young Argentines from the universities and the **Communist** Party. In September 1963 the group crossed the border into Argentina, hoping to put into practice the ideas of Che Guevara. Its first **military** action was its last. Infiltrated by military agents, the EGP was surrounded by the police and defeated in April 1964. Masetti fled into the jungle and presumably died there.

EJÉRCITO NACIONAL REVOLUCIONARIO (ENR) / NATIONAL REVOLUTIONARY ARMY. An Argentine urban **guerrilla** organization credited with only a few operations, among them the assassinations of labor leaders Augusto Vandor (1969) and José Alonso (1970)—both for alleged crimes against **Peronism**. It was closely allied with the group called the *Descamisados*, for which it may have been a front.

EJÉRCITO REVOLUCIONARIO DEL PUEBLO (ERP) / PEOPLE'S REVOLUTIONARY ARMY. The most active of the **guerrilla** organizations in **Argentina** and one of the two principal ones. Unlike the rival **Montoneros**, who were radical Peronists, the ERP represented the traditional left. Its roots can be traced to the Trotskyist Palabra Obrera

(PO, Workers' Word), which gave rise in 1963 to the Comando Buenos Aires, a fledgling guerrilla group that perished when its apartment, filled with explosives, blew up a year later. The Comando's legacy, however, survived. After the PO merged with the Frente Revolucionario Indoamericano Popular (FRIP, Indo-American Popular Revolutionary Front) in 1965 to become the Partido Revolucionario de los Trabajadores (PRT, Workers' Revolutionary Party), the idea of armed struggle was kept alive by Luis Pujals and **Mario Roberto ("Robi") Santucho**, the leaders of the PRT's *El combatiente* wing. In 1968 the PRT broke with Trotskyism (though it maintained formal relations with the international Trotskyist movement until 1973), choosing to follow the path of Che Guevara, and in 1970 it established the ERP as its militant wing, though armed operations had begun the year before.

The earliest actions of the ERP were designed to establish links with workers and took the form of "hunger commandos" (seizing food and distributing it in poor neighborhoods), factory takeovers, and the kidnapping of executives as a means of intervening in worker-management disputes. By 1972 its warfare reached a new level. On 10 April a kidnapping received international press when its victim—Oberdan Sallustro, the head of Fiat-Argentina—died in a gun battle between police and guerrillas, President Alejandro Lanusse having refused to negotiate. A few hours earlier, in a joint operation with the **Fuerzas Armadas Revolucionarias** (FAR, Revolutionary Armed Forces), the ERP assassinated General Juan Carlos Sánchez, who had a reputation for ruthlessness in dealing with strikers and insurgents. The government responded to the escalation with the massacre at Trelew on 22 August 1972, executing 16 political prisoners recaptured after their escape from Rawson prison. The ERP, in turn, sought revenge. In a joint operation with the FAR and Montoneros (who also lost comrades at Trelew), it carried out a number of kidnappings and assassinations of **military** officers thought responsible for the massacre.

The presidential election of March 1973 was divisive for the ERP. Part of the group supported the bid of **Héctor José Cámpora** and broke off to form the ERP-22 de agosto faction (ERP-22 August, named after the date of the Trelew incident); this faction joined the Montoneros a year later. The mainline ERP, however, took a position of critical neutrality toward **Peronism**, which hardened into opposition after the massacre at Ezeiza airport in June. The group continued to engage in armed struggle. It built a war chest of $30 million from robberies and kidnappings in 1973, and on 19 January 1974 launched an attack on an army garrison in the city of Azul. But having failed to build a political base among urban workers (millions had remained loyal to Peronism in the March and September elections), the ERP removed its struggle to the countryside. In 1974 it opened a rural front in the mountainous, sugar-producing province of Tucumán, where it tried to replicate the Cuban Revolution. The ERP's rural company was successful at first, fighting only the police. In February 1975, however, the government of **Isabel Perón** sent in the army. Given a free hand, General Acdel Vilas carried out "Operation Independence," a **"dirty war"** against the local population whose methods were expanded the following year to the entire country. Surrounded by unfriendly countries (Bolivia, **Chile**, and **Uruguay** were all under dictatorships) and deprived of any support in the province, the ERP was easily defeated by the military.

Turning again to urban struggle, the ERP made a desperate attempt to reverse its losses. In December 1975, it attacked the Batallón de Arsenales 601 in Monte Chingolo, Buenos Aires Province. The army was prepared, having been warned by a traitor or infiltrator. About a hundred ERP members were killed in the operation, from which the organization never recovered. The coup de grace came in July 1976, when Mario Santucho and other ERP leaders were killed by the army.

ELTIT, DIAMELA (1949–). Chilean novelist, literary theorist, essayist, and video and performance artist. Born in Santiago, **Chile**, she holds degrees from the Universidad de Chile and the Pontificia Universidad Católica (Chile). Eltit is grouped among the members of the Post-Coup Generation of 1980, those Chilean writers whose works were first published during the years of the dictatorship of **Augusto Pinoche Ugarte**. In the late 1970s, in collaboration with other Chilean artists such as the poet Raúl Zurita and the visual artist Lotty Rosenfeld, Eltit founded the Colectivo de Acciones de Arte, an artistic collective that tested the limits of official censorship through avant-garde and performance-art representations. The group's work has been exhibited in several Latin American countries and Europe. In 1987 Eltit organized the IEI Congreso Internacional de Literatura Femenina Latinoamericana in Santiago. She has promoted literacy campaigns and was a cultural attaché at the Chilean embassy in Mexico City during the presidency of **Patricio Aylwin Azócar**. She was awarded a Guggenheim Fellowship in 1985 and has received several awards and grants in her native Chile. Eltit has lectured on literary theory at Brown University and the Universidad Nacional de Chile and is a frequent speaker in universities in Europe and the **United States**. She is currently a professor at the Universidad Tecnológica Metropolitana in Chile.

Her first novel, *Lumpérica* (1983, translated as *Lumpen* in 1997), sought to dismantle the discourse of authority through the use of extremely experimental and cryptic language. The text makes repeated references to a performance piece, performed at a brothel in the city of Maipu in 1980, where Eltit washed the pavement in front of the brothel, inflicted a series of cuts on her arms, and concluded by reading a portion of the novel. *Lumpérica* received ambivalent reviews from literary critics in Chile, though its use of experimental language is often credited with helping it escape official censorship. Her 1986 novel, *Por la patria* (translated as *For the Fatherland*), offered a critique of the Chilean regime in the form of the protagonist, a woman who has been detained and tortured by the government. Later novels—still rooted in linguistic experimentation but closer to traditional narratives—include *El cuarto mundo* (1988, translated as *The Fourth World* in 1995), *Vaca sagrada* (1991, translated as *Sacred Cow* in 1995), and *Los vigilantes* (1993). She has also collaborated in documentary work such as *El infarto del alma* (1995, with the photographer Paz Errázuriz) and *Los trabajadores de la muerte* (1998).

EQUIPO ARGENTINO DE ANTROPOLOGÍA FORENSE (EAAF) / ARGENTINE FORENSIC ANTHROPOLOGY TEAM. A human rights nongovernmental organization. Founded in 1984 in **Argentina** after the return to civilian rule, the Equipo has concentrated on disinterring and identifying the remains of the missing (*desaparecidos*). The team was trained by Dr. Clyde C. Snow, a leading forensic anthropologist, who first visited Argentina in 1984 as part of a delegation of forensic and genetics specialists sent by the Human Rights and Science Program of the American Association for the Advancement of Science. In addition to carrying out scientific exhumations and collecting evidence for court cases, the EAAF aims at easing the suffering of families by helping them recover the remains of their loved ones. It also works to recover the past in the face of attempts—often by those guilty of human rights crimes—to rewrite history. Since 1986 the EAAF has expanded its mission to many other countries.

ESCUELA MECÁNICA DE LA ARMADA (ESMA) / NAVY MECHANICS SCHOOL. An Argentine naval technical school in the heart of Buenos Aires, the ESMA was transformed during the repression into an infamous detention center. The officers' quarters, one of the school's whitewashed buildings, was put to use in the war against suspected subversives. The cellar contained interrogation rooms, an infirmary, and a photographic laboratory. On the main level, intelligence officers analyzed information extracted from interrogations and planned their operations. On the second and third floors were officers' rooms. The third floor also contained the *Capucha* (hood), an area divided into small cubicles where prisoners lived, and a storeroom, which held furniture, clothes, and other goods taken as spoils of war from prisoners' homes. At the end of 1977, part of the storeroom became the "fishbowl," a series of glass offices where some prisoners were allowed to work. On the top floor was the *Capuchita* (little hood), which held interrogation rooms and more prisoner cubicles.

ESPINOZA BRAVO, PEDRO. A major (later brigadier general) in the armed forces and chief of operations of the **Dirección de Inteligencia Nacional** (DINA, Directorate of National Intelligence), the secret police in **Chile**. He took part in the **caravan of death**, a military helicopter tour across the country in October 1973 that resulted in the deaths of 75 political prisoners. In November 1993 Espinoza Bravo was convicted by a Chilean court of complicity in the September 1976 murders of **Orlando Letelier del Solar** and Ronni Moffit in Washington, D.C. Because the crime had been committed outside the country, the 1978 amnesty law did not apply. He received a sentence of six years, and served time in a special military prison.

ETCHECOLATZ, MIGUEL. Chief inspector for the Buenos Aires Police during the **"dirty war"** in **Argentina**. Reporting to General **Ramón Camps**, Etchecolatz was in charge of 21 secret detention centers throughout Buenos Aires. He is known to have participated in the **"Night of the Pencils,"** an operation in which 10 high-school students were abducted. On 2 December 1986, he was convicted in federal court on charges of **torture** and sentenced to 23 years in prison. He served only a short time, however. He was freed by the law *Obediencia Debida* (Due Obedience), passed in June 1987.

EVERYONE FOR THE HOMELAND. *See* MOVIMIENTO TODOS POR LA PATRIA (MTP).

EXILE. Exile during the **"dirty wars"**—and the years leading up to them—took many forms. Some people, fearing state persecution, sought diplomatic asylum or left the country unofficially. Others were forced to leave—led to the border or put on a plane by security forces, sometimes with nothing but the clothes on their backs. Not all exile, however, was external. In **Chile** some political prisoners were banished to remote parts of the country, suffering a forced internal exile called *relegación*.

It is difficult to know the true number of exiles. One source of statistics is the **United Nations** (UN), but many people never registered with the UN as refugees, having left their own countries unofficially. Still, by some estimates the number for **Argentina** ranges from 500,000 to two million; for Chile, from 40,000 to 200,000, which includes those escaping economic recession from 1982 onward; for **Uruguay**, from 300,000 to 500,000. Exiles took refuge in many parts of the world. Argentines were especially drawn to Italy, Spain, Mexico, and France; many Chileans went to Sweden, France, and Canada; and Uruguayans went to a variety of countries in the Americas, Eastern and Western Europe, and Africa. Countries such as France and Mexico had welcomed past exiles from the Southern Cone—including the right-leaning **Juan Perón** from Argentina and the left-leaning **Pablo Neruda** from Chile—a reminder that the forced exile of political opponents did not originate in the 1970s.

Refuge in another country did not necessarily mean safety from the "dirty wars." **Operation Condor**, a consortium of Latin American **military** regimes, claimed victims not only throughout the region but also farther afield—the **United States**, for example, and Italy.

–F–

FALKLAND ISLANDS / ISLAS MALVINAS. Islands off the coast of **Argentina**, 900 miles southeast of Buenos Aires. Although sparsely populated, cold, and windswept, the Falkland Islands (known as the Islas Malvinas, or Malvinas, in Argentina) have been a subject of dispute between Argentina and Great Britain since 1833. In that year, the British occupied the islands, which Argentina had claimed as an inheritance from Spain. In 1982 General **Leopoldo Fortunato Galtieri**, the leader of the third junta, made the decision to take back the islands—an attempt to divert attention from the country's domestic problems. Diplomatic talks failed, and Argentina turned to force. On 11 March an Argentine construction crew on South Georgia Island (a Falklands dependency) created a diplomatic incident by raising the Argentine flag. Shortly after, events in Argentina persuaded Galtieri to accelerate plans for an invasion. On 18 March the **Madres de Plaza de Mayo** (Mothers of the Plaza de Mayo) staged their largest Thursday vigil yet, and on 30 March the **Confederación General del Trabajo** (CGT, General Confederation of Labor)—revived but illegal—led thousands in a demonstration that was suppressed with violence. On 2 April Argentina invaded the islands.

At first, the move was popular in Argentina. The demonstrations against the junta a few days earlier were replaced with rallies in support of the invasion. Even the labor movement set aside its grievances. The Madres, however, continued their protest, though the Thursday vigils attracted fewer marchers. Outside Argentina, however, the junta found itself virtually isolated. The invasion was condemned by the **United Nations** Security Council and elicited, at most, only lukewarm support from Latin American countries. The **United States** sided with its North Atlantic Treaty Organization ally Great Britain. Domestic support faded, too, when it became clear that Britain intended to recapture the islands. British Prime Minister Margaret Thatcher sent a fleet to the south Atlantic that included eight destroyers, two aircraft carriers, and two nuclear submarines. Because their invasion plan had been hastily drawn up, the Argentines found themselves at a disadvantage. The occupying force, the Third Army Brigade, was made up largely of recent conscripts who lacked training and equipment. It was no match for the experienced British force, and the Argentines surrendered on 14 June.

The next day, when Galtieri reported Argentina's defeat to a crowd assembled in the **Plaza de Mayo**, the crowd hurled insults at him and the other junta members and began rioting in the streets. On 17 June Galtieri was forced to resign. He was replaced by **Reynaldo Benito Bignone**, a retired general, who would return the country to civilian rule the following year.

FAMILIARES / RELATIVES. A small **human rights** nongovernmental organization in **Uruguay**. Founded in 1977, the group was originally called the Madres y Familiares de los Uruguayos Desaparecidos en Argentina, or Mothers and Relatives of Uruguayans Who Disappeared in Argentina. Owing to repression within Uruguay, the group concentrated most of its efforts at first on those who disappeared in **Argentina**, but expanded its efforts to Uruguayan victims a few years later. The group collaborated with **Servicio Paz y Justicia** (SERPAJ), or Peace and Justice Service, and participated in the **Concertación Nacional Programática**.

**FAMILIARES DE DESAPARECIDOS Y DETENIDOS POR RA-
ZONES POLÍTICAS / RELATIVES OF THE MISSING AND
DETAINED FOR POLITICAL REASONS.** A **human rights** nongovernmental organization in **Argentina**. Familiares was founded in
1977. Unlike the **Madres de Plaza de Mayo** (Mothers of the Plaza de
Mayo) and the **Abuelas de Plaza de Mayo** (Grandmothers), two other
human rights groups formed by family members of the missing (*desaparecidos*), Familiares included male relatives and directed more attention to political prisoners in the official prison system, trying to secure
their release and to improve the conditions under which they were held.

FATHERLAND AND LIBERTY. *See* DEATH SQUADS.

FIRMENICH, MARIO EDUARDO. *See* MONTONEROS.

FORD, GERALD. *See* KISSINGER, HENRY; UNITED STATES.

**FOUNDATION FOR THE PROTECTION OF CHILDREN IN-
JURED BY STATES OF EXCEPTION.** *See* FUNDACIÓN PARA
LA PROTECCIÓN DE LA INFANCIA DAÑADA POR LOS ESTA-
DOS DE EMERGENCIA (PIDEE).

FREI MONTALVA, EDUARDO (1911–1982). President of **Chile**
(1964–1970). Representing the **Partido Demócrata Cristiano** (PDC,
Christian Democratic Party), he was elected president in 1964 under the
slogan "Revolution in Liberty." His administration was reformist—he
partially nationalized the copper industry, for example—though his
reputation suffered after he forcibly put down strikes in 1966 and 1968.
Prevented by the constitution from running for president again in 1970,
he was elected to the Senate in 1973, and supported the coup that toppled his successor, **Salvador Allende Gossens**, in September. He
would later turn against the **military** regime, however, and when he
died in 1982, his funeral drew thousands of mourners.

FREI RUIZ-TAGLE, EDUARDO (c. 1941–). President of **Chile** (1994–
2000). On 11 March 1994 Eduardo Frei Ruiz-Tagle, head of the **Partido Demócrata Cristiano** (PDC, Christian Democratic Party), and the
son of former president **Eduardo Frei Montalva**, led Chile into its
second term as a constitutional democracy following **military** rule,
capturing over half of the majority votes in the December 1993 six-way
electoral race. Like his predecessor **Patricio Aylwin Azócar**, Frei

Ruiz-Tagle faced the task of continuing the investigation of **human rights** abuses during the 17 years of military rule under General **Augusto Pinochet Ugarte** and of contending with a powerful and solidly entrenched armed forces. After General Pinochet Ugarte was rejected for another eight-year term in the **plebiscite of 1988**, the General made amendments to the **constitution of 1981** that clearly favored the military.

FRENTE PATRIÓTICO MANUEL RODRÍGUEZ (FPMR) / MANUEL RODRÍGUEZ PATRIOTIC FRONT. An urban **guerrilla** movement in **Chile**. It was formed in 1983 as an offshoot of the **Partido Comunista de Chile** (PC, Communist Party of Chile). Named after an independence hero, the group conducted thousands of bombings and other operations, but is best known for Operation Twentieth Century, its plot to assassinate General **Augusto Pinochet Ugarte**. On 7 September 1986, 25 FPMR commandos directed machine-gun and rocket fire on the General's motorcade. Five bodyguards were killed, but the general escaped—the rocket that hit his car never exploded. The regime retaliated by arresting hundreds of leftists, including nine of the commandos involved in the attack.

FUERZAS ARMADAS PERONISTAS (FAP) / PERONIST ARMED FORCES. An **Argentine** urban **guerrilla** organization, formed in 1968 under the leadership of Envar El Kadri. Inspired by the Cuban Revolution, it began as a rural insurrection, or *foco* (literally "center," "nucleus"). It abandoned the countryside, however, after a defeat in September at Taco Ralo, Tucumán, where police surprised and captured the group's first detachment, the "17th of October" (named in solidarity with the workers who freed **Juan Perón** in 1945). By 1970 the group had moved its operations to the cities. In late 1970, it came to the aid of another Peronist group, the **Montoneros**, sheltering it from government persecution. It changed its militant strategy after Perón's return from **exile** in 1973, when many of its members put down their weapons in favor of political activity above ground, including organizing workers. A splinter group, the Comando Nacional, continued armed struggle, later merging with the Montoneros.

FUERZAS ARMADAS REVOLUCIONARIAS (FAR) / REVOLUTIONARY ARMED FORCES. A militant organization begun in 1966 as the **Argentine** branch of Che Guevara's **guerrillas**. Che's death in 1967 and the popular uprising in Córdoba (the *cordobazo*) led the group, under the leadership of Carlos Enrique Olmedo and Roberto Jorge Quieto, to initiate urban struggle in 1969. The FAR originally described itself as Marxist-Leninist-Peronist, but by 1971 had shifted to **Peronism**. It had a reputation for technical expertise, earned in such operations as the 1969 bombing of a supermarket chain owned by Nelson Rockefeller and the July 1970 capture of the small town of Garín (population 30,000) near Buenos Aires. The group's development was hampered by the capture of several members in 1970 and 1971 and the resulting disclosure of vital information. Protected by the **Fuerzas Armadas Peronistas** (FAP, Peronist Armed Forces), the FAR survived and continued to conduct operations, often with other guerrilla groups, until their merger with the **Montoneros** in October 1973.

FULL STOP. See *PUNTO FINAL*.

FUNDACIÓN DE AYUDA SOCIAL DE LAS IGLESIAS CRISTIANAS (FASIC) / CHRISTIAN CHURCES SOCIAL ASSISTANCE FOUNDATION. A **human rights** nongovernmental organization in **Chile**. Founded in 1975 by protestant churches, especially the Evangelical Lutheran Church, FASIC collected cases of torture, **exile**, political prisoners, and those who returned from exile. It also provided legal assistance and medical-psychiatric treatment to victims.

FUNDACIÓN PARA LA PROTECCIÓN DE LA INFANCIA DAÑADA POR LOS ESTADOS DE EMERGENCIA (PIDEE) / FOUNDATION FOR THE PROTECTION OF CHILDREN INJURED BY STATES OF EMERGENCY. A **human rights** nongovernmental organization in **Chile**. It was founded in 1979 with assistance from the **Fundación de Ayuda Social de las Iglesias Cristianas** (FASIC, Christian Churches Social Assistance Foundation). PIDEE provided assistance—medical, psychological, and educational—to children and teenagers who suffered directly from the repression or whose parents had been disappeared or executed.

–G–

GALEANO, EDUARDO (1940–). Uruguayan journalist, essayist, and historian. Born in Montevideo into a middle-class family of Welsh, German, Spanish, and Italian ancestry as Eduardo Hughes Galeano. In 1954 he began his career in journalism as a political cartoonist for the socialist weekly *El Sol*. He signed his cartoons "Gius," a word play on the difficult pronunciation of his paternal surname, Hughes, in Spanish. In the 1960s he published his first articles, adopting his maternal surname, Galeano, as *nom de plume*. From 1960 to 1964 he was editor-in-chief of the influential weekly *Marcha* and editor of the daily *Época*. From 1965 to 1973 he was editor-in-chief of the University Press in Montevideo. He was jailed in the months leading to the 1973 coup. Upon his release, he went into **exile** in **Argentina**. In Buenos Aires he founded and edited the cultural magazine *Crisis*. After the Argentine **military** coup in 1976, Galeano went into exile in Barcelona, Spain. He returned to Uruguay in 1985 after the restoration of democracy and the election of **Julio María Sanguinetti** as president. He is presently editor-in-chief of the editorial house El Chanchito.

A vigorous critic of capitalist models, Galeano's best-known work is *Las venas abiertas de América Latina* (1971, translated as *Open Veins of Latin America*), an economic analysis of five centuries of exploitation in Latin America. *Las venas* was a best-seller in Latin America and was routinely banned in several countries. Galeano continued his trajectory in the trilogy *Memoria del fuego* (1982–1986, translated as *Memory of Fire* in 1985–1988). Translated into more than 20 languages, *Memoria del fuego* weaves fiction and history, folklore, and memoirs into a narrative that defies easy classification. In 1978 he published *Días y noches de amor y de guerra* (translated as *Days and Nights of Love and War* in 2000), which one critic has described as "a testimony to the power of fear to silence a population . . . a testimony to the courage of those who refuse to be silenced."

The author of more than 30 books, Galeano received the prestigious Casa de las Américas award in 1975 and 1978. In 1993 he was honored by Danish editors with the Aloa award. In 1989 *Memoria del fuego* received awards from the Uruguayan Ministry of Culture and the American Book Award from Washington University. In 1999 the Lannan Foundation of New Mexico awarded its first Cultural Prize for Freedom to Galeano in recognition of his work.

GALTIERI, LEOPOLDO FORTUNATO (1926–2003). General, army commander, and the leader of the third junta (December 1981 to June 1982) during the **"dirty war"** in **Argentina**. To distract public attention from the country's economic and social unrest, he ordered the invasion of the **Falkland Islands/Islas Malvinas**, which were governed by Great Britain. On 17 June 1982, after Argentina's defeat at the hands of the British in the brief Falklands War, Galtieri resigned from the presidency in disgrace, replaced by **Reynaldo Benito Bignone**. In the 1985 trial of the nine former junta commanders, Galtieri was acquitted of **human rights** crimes. He was, however, convicted in 1986 of negligence in his role as army commander during the Falklands War. He was released from prison in October 1989 following a blanket amnesty decreed by President **Carlos Saúl Menem**.

GAMBARO, GRISELDA (1928–). Argentine novelist and playwright. Born in Buenos Aires, Gambaro began her literary trajectory as a novelist, a career she combined with that of a playwright. Although she began to write early, amid a variety of jobs and occupations, her first works were not published until the 1960s. In 1965 her play "El desatino" was first performed in the Sala de Experimentación Audiovisual del Instituto Di Tella in Buenos Aires, under the direction of Jorge Petraglia. Three years later, her play "El campo" debuted in the Teatro Sha in Buenos Aires, under the direction of Augusto Fernández. "El campo," rooted in the tradition of Artaud's "theatre of cruelty," presents a stark vision of life in a concentration camp and is often read as a presage to the Argentine situation under the **military** regime. In 1977 her novel *Ganarse la muerte* was banned by the government of General **Jorge Rafael Videla** as being "against the institution of the family" and "against the social order." The ban, and the increasing political repression, sent Gambaro into **exile** in Barcelona, Spain. After her return to Buenos Aires, her play "La malasangre" (1982) was first staged in the Teatro Olimpia under the direction of Laura Yusem. "La malasangre" offers an oblique commentary on the political situation in **Argentina** during the period of the **"dirty war."**

A prolific playwright and novelist—with nearly 30 plays and novels to her credit—Gambaro has had her plays staged abroad in England, France, Belgium, and Mexico. Some of her works have also been adapted for the radio by the BBC of London, Sverige Radio, and France Culturel. In 1982 she was the recipient of a Guggenheim Fellowship. She has received numerous awards in her native Argentina for both her dramatic and narrative work, notably the Argentores Award on four occasions (1976, 1990, 1992, and 1996) and the Academia Argentina de Letras award of 1997/1999 for her collection of short stories *Lo mejor que se viene.* She has also received several distinctions abroad, most notably in Spain and Mexico, where she has lectured on theater. A frequent lecturer abroad, Gambaro has participated in symposia at Dartmouth College in 1987, Universidad de Valencia (Spain) in 1992,

University of Bordeaux (France) in 1992 and 1994, and the Universidad de Cuenca (Spain) in 1998.

GARZÓN, BALTASAR. Spanish magistrate who initiated the arrest of General **Augusto Pinochet Ugarte** for crimes against humanity. On 16 October 1988 Garzón instructed Interpol to place Pinochet Ugarte under armed guard at the private clinic in London where the general was recuperating from back surgery. Pinochet Ugarte's name appeared often in the jurist's investigation of the **torture** and murder of Spanish nationals in **Chile**. Among the more high-profile victims named in the investigation was Carmelo Soria, a United Nations employee and Spanish citizen. Garzón's case would be further supported with evidence from the files of author and former **Unidad Popular** (Popular Unity) official Juan Garcés, who, like Garzón, had spent several years documenting the Pinochet Ugarte government's abuse of Spanish citizens. Garzón's indictment was welcomed by **human rights** organizations and by victims of the Pinochet Ugarte regime. For more than a year, the British House of Lords debated whether to extradite Pinochet Ugarte to Spain to face formal charges. In the end, however, doctors declared Pinochet Ugarte medically unfit to stand trial and he was returned to Chile on 3 March 2000.

Garzón also exposed the international terror network centered in Chile and operating under the code name **Operation Condor**, as well as the murder and disappearance of hundreds of Spanish citizens during the repression in **Argentina**.

GELMAN, JUAN (1930–). Argentine poet and journalist. Born in Buenos Aires, the child of Ukrainian immigrants—his father participated in the Russian revolution of 1905—Gelman spent his childhood in the historic *porteño* neighborhood of Villa Crespo. An early member of the literary group El Pan Duro, Gelman published his first book of poetry, *Violín y otras cuestiones*, in 1956. In the 1970s Gelman began his career in journalism. He directed the cultural supplement of the newspaper *La Nación*, was editor-in-chief of the newspaper *Noticias*, and was the Spanish-language editor of the journal *Ceres*, published by the Food and Agriculture Organization (FAO) of the **United Nations**.

An early opponent of **Peronism**, Gelman abandoned the Communist Party in favor of the **Fuerzas Armadas Revolucionarias** (FAR, Revolutionary Armed Forces), which in 1973 joined the **Montoneros**. He served as Montonero press secretary for Europe until his break with the organization in 1979. In 1976 the **military** invaded his home with orders to arrest him. Instead, they arrested his son, Marcelo, and his daughter-in-law, Claudia Irueta, then pregnant. The younger Gelman was killed in captivity, and his wife was transported to an Uruguayan prison as part of **Operation Condor**. There, Claudia gave birth to a daughter and was executed. Juan Gelman's granddaughter was located and identified in **Uruguay** in March 2000 following the intervention of Uruguayan president Jorge Batlle Ibáñez.

Exiled in 1976, Gelman spent 12 years in several European and Central American countries. In 1989 he settled in Mexico City, where he still resides. In 1987 he received **Argentina**'s Premio Nacional de la Poesía, and in 2000 received the Premio Juan Rulfo, Latin America's most prestigious award for poetry.

The author of over 20 volumes of poetry translated into 10 languages, Gelman is hailed as one of Argentina's most important contemporary poets. Themes of family and lost friends, Argentina, his beloved tango, his Jewish heritage, exile, **torture,** and disappearances, and an almost obsessive need to remember are all present in his oeuvre. In 1997 a compilation of his poetry, translated into English, was made available in the United States under the title *Unthinkable Tenderness.* He is also the author, with Mara La Madrid, of the collection of essays *Ni el flaco perdón de Dios/Hijos de desaparecidos* (1997).

GRAFFIGNA, OMAR D. Brigadier general, commander of the air force, and member of the second junta (March to December 1981) during the **"dirty war"** in **Argentina**. (The other members of the junta were Roberto Viola and **Armando Lambruschini**.) Graffigna was acquitted in the 1985 trial of the nine former junta commanders.

GRANDMOTHERS OF THE PLAZA DE MAYO. *See* ABUELAS DE PLAZA DE MAYO.

GUERRA SUCIA. See "DIRTY WAR."

GUERRILLA WARFARE. The success of Fidel Castro's Cuban Revolution in 1959 inspired guerrilla movements across Latin America, as did the teachings of such revolutionary theorists as Regis Debray and the **Argentine**-born Ernesto ("Che") Guevara. The movements drew heavily from the urban middle class, and most of the members were young—under 30 and sometimes under 20. Of groups that operated in urban settings, a large percentage of members were women. Young people were attracted to the cause, not only by the romance of being revolutionaries, but by a number of material issues that included bleak employment prospects, sensitivity to a lack of social justice, and the growing abandonment of hope for peaceful social change. Although some groups purported to be Castroist, Trotskyist, **Peronist**, or some combination, ideology seems not to have been an important factor in the decision of which group to join. Indeed, the most successful groups, the **Montoneros** in Argentina and **Tupamaros** in **Uruguay**, were not known for ideological purity.

In Argentina, groups first appeared in the late 1950s and the 1960s, guided at first by Guevara's theory of the rural guerrilla *foco* (focus). Deviating from traditional Marxist thought, the theory held that, instead of waiting for history to produce the objective conditions for revolution, a small group of committed revolutionaries, joined by the masses, could manufacture those conditions. These early groups, following the Cuban example, took their struggle to the countryside. Among them were the **Uturuncos** ("Tigermen"), the **Ejército Guerrillero del Pueblo** (EGP, People's Guerrilla Army), the **Fuerzas Armadas Peronistas** (FAP, Peronist Armed Forces), and the **Fuerzas Armadas Revolucionarias** (FAR, Revolutionary Armed Forces). These rural movements failed, however, as did their counterparts in Bolivia, Brazil, and Ecuador. The reasons were tactical and geographical. As **military** focus shifted from foreign invaders to internal subversives, the training given to Latin American military and police officers in the **United States** and elsewhere turned from conventional warfare to counterinsurgency. The military had also made an effort to reach out to rural populations by building roads and schools and performing other civic functions. The guerrillas, meanwhile, mostly urbanites, stood out in a rural setting, where peasants were more likely to report them to the army or police than to embrace them as liberators. One of the victims of local informants was Guevara himself, who was captured and executed in Bolivia in 1967.

Guevara, like Castro, had been a cult hero of the guerrilla movement. His death, though by no means diminishing his mystique, led many guerrillas to rethink their rural strategy. By 1970 the FAP and FAR had moved their operations to the city. Meanwhile, the Montoneros, the Tupamaros, and the Chilean **Movimiento de la Izquierda Revolucionaria** (MIR, Movement of the Revolutionary Left) had been established as urban organizations. (The Uturuncos and EGP had perished long before.) An exception to this change in strategy was the **Ejército Revolucionario del Pueblo** (ERP, People's Revolutionary Army), which, though it carried out operations in the city after its formation in 1970, remained Guevarist at heart and returned in 1974 to its origins in the countryside. Urban guerrillas, unlike their rural counterparts, could take part in operations (bombings, bank robberies, kidnappings, assassinations) and then blend back into society. Some guerrillas believed that by carrying out violent acts and provoking a violent response, one could reveal the repressive nature of the state and win over the masses to the revolutionary side.

The urban guerrillas built impressive organizations. By 1975 the Peronist Montoneros fielded anywhere from 3,000 to 10,000 combatants. (Their military adversaries estimated their numbers to be higher.) During the same period, their tactical operations increased in frequency, technical expertise, and scale, and were eventually directed at military targets. The Tupamaros took a similar route, making leaps (*saltas*) to increasingly higher levels of warfare. In the end, however, neither group attracted a mass following, and when the military took charge of counterinsurgency, each found itself fighting a lost cause.

GUEVARA, ERNESTO ("CHE"). *See* GUERRILLA WARFARE.

–H–

HIGH COURT OF JUSTICE. *See* SUPREME COURT OF JUSTICE (CHILE).

HIJOS POR LA IDENTIDAD Y LA JUSTICIA, CONTRA EL OLVIDO Y EL SILENCIO (HIJOS) / CHILDREN FOR IDENTITY AND JUSTICE AGAINST OBLIVION AND SILENCE. A **human rights** nongovernmental organization in **Argentina**. It was founded in 1995 by the children of people who were disappeared or **exiled** by the **military** during its **"dirty war."** Although the group seeks justice for all members of the armed forces guilty of human rights violations, its first objective is to find the children (some estimates put the figure at more than 500) who were kidnapped with their parents or born to political prisoners. It was not uncommon for women in captivity to be killed after giving birth and their children illegally adopted by military personnel—sometimes the very people who tortured and killed the parents. The idea behind the practice was to ensure that the children would not be raised by those the military considered subversive. HIJOS conducts investigations—aided by young people who come forward and by telephone leads—and if evidence suggests that someone is the offspring of *desaparecidos,* it will inform that person of its suspicions.

HOLY WEEK REVOLT. *See CARAPINTADAS.*

HORMAN, CHARLES. One of two **United States** citizens killed in **Chile** by the regime of **Augusto Pinochet Ugarte.** Charles Horman, 31, and his friend Frank Teruggi, 24, the second victim, were leftist supporters of the overthrown Marxist president **Salvador Allende Gossens.** Both worked as journalists, contributing to a newsletter that criticized U.S. policy. A few days after the coup of 11 September 1973, security forces abducted Horman from his apartment; he would become one of the missing (*desaparecidos*). About the same time, security forces abducted Teruggi and his roommate, David Hathaway, who were taken to the *Estadio Nacional* (National Stadium), which had been converted into a detention center. Hathaway, also a U.S. citizen, was released; Teruggi's body was discovered in the government morgue. The story of the two men's deaths is told in the book *Missing* (1982), by Thomas Hauser (originally published in 1978 as *The Execution of Charles Horman*), and dramatized in the film *Missing* (1982), directed by **Costa-Gavras.**

Owing to State Department internal reviews conducted in 1976 and the recent declassification of United States documents on Chile, there is wide conjecture about a possible **Central Intelligence Agency** (CIA) involvement in the killing of Horman and Teruggi. The CIA might have supplied information on the two men to the Chilean government that led to their being labeled as subversives or, aware of the danger they were in, failed to prevent their deaths. In his book *Missing,* Hauser suggests that Horman may have been perceived as especially dangerous to Chilean and United States interests. On the day of the coup, Horman was at the coastal resort of Viña del Mar, where he met some United States **military** officers and may have come across evidence that the United States was involved in the overthrow of Allende Gossens. In her book *Soldiers in a Narrow Land: The Pinochet Regime in Chile,* however, Mary Helen Spooner finds it unlikely that the military officers would have leaked such information, speculating that Horman may have been just one of the hundreds of foreigners arrested after the coup, some of whom were tortured and killed.

HUMAN RIGHTS. Human rights are inalienable human freedoms that states are called upon to recognize and defend. According to this definition, states do not grant rights; instead, they guard rights that already exist. The Universal Declaration of Human Rights, adopted by the **United Nations** (UN) in 1948, proclaims a wide range of freedoms—civil and political, economic, social, and cultural. Among them are the right to an adequate standard of living; the right to leave the country, and to return; the right to obtain and deliver information; the right to participate in government; and the right to the integrity of the person, or due process (freedom from extralegal detention, **torture**, and execution). Human rights advocates tend to regard the right to the integrity of the person as fundamental. During the **"dirty wars,"** the **military** regimes violated any number of rights—they banned political parties, censored the press, forced people into **exile**. The most common and serious violation, however, was abducting and torturing people, many of whom were never seen again.

In Latin America the concept of human rights is reinforced by the American Declaration of the Rights and Duties of Man, which is similar to the UN declaration, and was adopted by the **Organization of American States** (OAS) in 1948. The OAS document preceded the UN declaration by several months, and was the first to recognize that rights are inherent in humanity and not granted by states. Neither document is legally binding, but in 1967 the OAS adopted a protocol making the American Declaration the standard for member nations. Both the UN and the OAS helped draw world attention to human rights violations in the Southern Cone. But both organizations, composed of states, were put in the awkward position of investigating crimes committed by some of their own members. Human Rights Nongovernmental Organizations (HRNGOs), in contrast, are independent of government control and thus freer to investigate and report abuses. HRNGOs like **Amnesty International** (AI) and the **International Commission of Jurists** (ICJ) are accredited with the UN, and in the 1970s supplied it with evidence that helped to build cases against **Argentina**, **Chile**, and **Uruguay**. At the regional level, the HRNGO **Servicio Paz y Justicia** (SERPAJ, Peace and Justice Service) lent support to victims of state violence (especially the poor) throughout Latin America. The branches of SERPAJ in Argentina, Chile, and Uruguay were among many local HRNGOs that came into existence during the "dirty wars" to contest authoritarian rule.

In Argentina one of the first HRNGOs to appear after the coup of 1976 was the **Movimiento Ecuménico por los Derechos Humanos** (MEDH, Ecumenical Movement for Human Rights), which was formed by progressive **Catholics** and which concentrated on providing assistance to victims of abuse. Jewish leaders resisted dictatorship early on as well, and later formed the **Movimiento Judío por los Derechos Humanos** (Jewish Movement for Human Rights). Women turned to social activism, directly confronting the regime through the **Madres de Plaza de Mayo** (Mothers of the Plaza de Mayo) and the **Abuelas de Plaza de Mayo** (Grandmothers of the Plaza de Mayo). The **Familiares de Desaparecidos y Detenidos por Razones Políticas** (Relatives of the Missing and Detained for Political Reasons) took up the cause of those charged with political crimes. The **Centro de Estudios Legales y Sociales** (CELS, Center for Legal and Social Studies) specialized in documenting abuses and providing legal defense. Other groups opposing the military regime in Argentina had been formed during earlier periods of repression. The **Liga Argentina por los Derechos del Hombre** (The Argentine League for the Rights of Man) had been in existence since 1937, and the **Asamblea Permanente por los Derechos Humanos** (APDH, Permanent Assemby for Human Rights) was founded in 1975 to oppose the right-wing violence that was a forerunner to the "dirty wars." After the return to civilian rule, the **Equipo Argentino de Antropología Forense** (EAAF, Argentine Forensic Anthropology Team) was founded to recover the remains of the missing (*desaparecidos*).

In Chile, as in Argentina, the first HRNGOs to form after the military takeover were connected to religious organizations. In Argentina, however, the Catholic Church hierarchy tended to be conservative, and it was dissident members of the Church who took the initiative on human rights. In contrast, the Chilean Church, though hesitant at first and by no means homogeneous, assumed a leading role in resisting military rule. In 1973 Cardinal Raúl Silva Henríquez, along with Protestant and Jewish leaders, formed the **Comité de la Paz** (COPACHI, Committee for Peace in Chile), which offered social and legal assistance to victims. After COPACHI was forced to dissolve under pressure from the regime, its functions were absorbed by the **Vicaría de la Solidaridad** (Vicariate of Solidarity), which was placed under the auspices of the Catholic Church. Also connected with the Catholic Church were the **Agrupación de Familiares de Detenidos-Desaparecidos** (AFDD, Association of Relatives of the Detained-Missing) and its offshoot, the **Agrupación de Familiares de Ejecutados Políticos** (AFEP, Association of Relatives of the Politically Executed). Another religious-based organization was the **Fundación de Ayuda Social de las Iglesias Cristianas** (FASIC, Christian Churches Social Assistance Foundation), which helped found the **Fundación para la Protección de la Infancia**

Dañada por los Estados de Emergencia (PIDEE, Foundation for the Protection of Children Injured by States of Emergency). Legal and psychological assistance was provided by the **Comité de Defensa de los Derechos del Pueblo** (CODEPU, Committee for the Defense of the Rights of the People). About a dozen more HRNGOs were active at one time or another during the dictatorship in Chile, including the **Movimiento contra la Tortura Sebastián Acevedo** (Sebastián Acevedo Movement against Torture).

In Uruguay the most important HRNGOs were SERPAJ-Uruguay and the **Instituto de Estudios Legales y Sociales** (IELSUR, Institute for Legal and Social Studies), which was composed of progressive lawyers. After the return to democracy, in the absence of an Uruguayan truth commission, the two groups combined to produce the report *Uruguay Nunca Más: Human Rights Violations, 1972–1985.* Two other HRNGOs were the **Familiares** (Relatives), a small group of family members of the missing, and the **Servicio Ecuménico de Reintegración** (SER, Ecumenical Service for Reintegration), which assisted those released from prison or returning from exile.

–I–

INSTITUTE FOR LEGAL AND SOCIAL STUDIES. *See* INSTITUTO DE ESTUDIOS LEGALES Y SOCIALES (IELSUR).

INSTITUTO DE ESTUDIOS LEGALES Y SOCIALES (IELSUR) / INSTITUTE FOR LEGAL AND SOCIAL STUDIES. A **human rights** nongovernmental organization in **Uruguay.** The Instituto was officially founded in 1984, though its activities began a few years earlier. In response to the lack of human rights activity from the Colegio de Abogados—the country's traditionally conservative lawyers' association—a group of progressive lawyers joined forces with **Servicio Paz y Justicia** to provide legal assistance to victims of human rights abuse. IELSUR still exists and is active in the field of public interest law.

INTER-AMERICAN COMMISSION ON HUMAN RIGHTS. *See* ORGANIZATION OF AMERICAN STATES (OAS).

INTER-AMERICAN DEFENSE COLLEGE (IADC). *See* UNITED STATES.

INTERNAL EXILE. *See RELEGACIÓN.*

INTERNATIONAL COMMISSION OF JURISTS (ICJ). An international **human rights** nongovernmental organization, established in Berlin in 1952 and composed of legal professionals. Six months after the **military** coup of 11 September 1973 in **Chile**, the ICJ sent a three-member team to examine the human rights conditions under the junta led by General **Augusto Pinochet Ugarte.** From 19 April to 28 April 1974, the team, led by ICJ secretary-general Niall MacDermot, interviewed state officials, members of the bar, the **Supreme Court of Justice**, and the leaders of human rights organizations, among them Cardinal Raúl Silva Henríquez. The team's findings were published in the *Final Report of Mission to Chile, April 1974, to Study the Legal System and the Protection of Human Rights* and in the *Supplemental Report* of January 1975. The reports revealed a pattern of repression that denied such basic rights as freedom of assembly and due process, and criticized the courts for not intervening.

A second supplement to *Final Report of Mission to Chile, Arrests and Detentions and Freedom of Information in Chile*, published in September 1976, included a copy of an "open letter" sent by five prominent Chilean jurists to the the **Organization of American States**, which had met in Santiago earlier in the year. The letter deplored the human rights abuses of the junta and the lack of legal protection. Among the five were the law professor Eugenio Velasco Letelier and former minister of justice and former representative to the **United Nations** Human Rights Commission **Jaime Castillo Velasco.**

–J–

JARA, VICTOR (1938–1973). Chilean composer and folk singer, most closely associated with the *Nueva Canción Chilena* (New Chilean Song). He is best remembered for his song "*Plegaria a un labrador*" ("Prayer to a Laborer"). A former seminarian, he later attended drama school where he trained as an actor and stage director. He joined **Chile**'s Juventud Comunista (Communist Youth) in 1964. In 1966 he joined the Peña de los Parra, a group largely composed of members of the Parra family of songwriters, singers, and poets. A prominent cultural figure under the **Unidad Popular** (UP, Popular Unity) government of **Salvador Allende Gossens**, he was arrested in the days following the 1973 coup against Allende Gossens and brought to the

National Stadium in Santiago, where he was tortured by members of the national police and murdered.

JEWISH MOVEMENT FOR HUMAN RIGHTS. *See* MOVIMIENTO JUDÍO POR LOS DERECHOS HUMANOS.

JOINT COMMAND. *See* DEATH SQUADS.

JUSTICIALISMO. *See* PERONISM.

–K–

KIRKPATRICK, JEANE (1926–). United States ambassador to the United Nations and cabinet member under President **Ronald Reagan** (1981–1989). A political scientist and professor, Kirkpatrick published the controversial article "Dictatorships and Double Standards" in the November 1979 issue of *Commentary* magazine. The article criticized the **human rights** policy of President **Jimmy Carter**, which she argued was applied inconsistently and, therefore, led to hypocrisy. She argued that the policy was directed at right-wing authoritarian allies as opposed to left-wing totalitarian adversaries. In the name of human rights, she said, the policy helped undermine our allies (Anastasio Somoza in Nicaragua, the Shah of Iran), replacing them with regimes unfriendly to the United States and of extremist bent (the Sandinistas, the Ayatollah Khomeini). She was especially troubled when the authoritarians were replaced with regimes having ties to the communist movement. She argued further that, unlike communist regimes, which never evolve into democracies, right-wing authoritarian regimes sometimes do—under the right circumstances. Kirkpatrick concluded that the United States should be more careful about distinguishing between its friends (**Argentina** and **Chile**) and its enemies (the Cuba of Fidel Castro). The article, reflecting Kirkpatrick's strong anticommunist sentiment, impressed the presidential candidate Ronald Reagan, who in 1980 would appoint Kirkpatrick ambassador to the United Nations.

The neoconservative ambassador supported the Reagan administration's policies toward improving U.S. relations with **military** governments in the Southern Cone, including the Chilean dictatorship of General **Augusto Pinochet Ugarte**. **Jaime Castillo Velasco**, a lawyer and human rights activist, noted that after Kirkpatrick commented favorably on the Chilean government during a tour of Latin America in August

1981, Pinochet Ugarte renewed his assault on political dissidents, jailing and exiling members of human rights organizations. Throughout her term, Kirkpatrick accused the UN of applying a double standard. In 1983, when the General Assembly adopted resolutions against **Chile**, El Salvador, and Guatemala for human rights violations, Kirkpatrick protested that the criticism was unwarranted because there were other Latin American countries with worse records of human rights abuse. She noted, for example, that although Chile monitored its **trade unions**, Cuba did not allow trade unions at all.

KISSINGER, HENRY (1923–). **United States** secretary of state and head of the National Security Council under Presidents Richard Nixon (1969–1974) and Gerald Ford (1974–1977). His open dislike for **communism** led him to devise a covert strategy to prevent the election of Marxist presidential candidate **Salvador Allende Gossens** in **Chile**, or, if he was elected, to undermine his government. The operation was coordinated by the "Committee of Forty," a secret group of officials from the Nixon administration, including the director of the **Central Intelligence Agency** (CIA). ("Forty" referred, not to the number of members, but to the directive that established the committee.) The committee, which Kissinger chaired, was responsible for funding opposition parties and anti-Allende Gossens propaganda and for engaging in economic sabotage and other activities designed to destabilize the government. The CIA developed its own strategy for subversion, which included generating economic crises and encouraging civil unrest. Allende Gossens was overthrown in a **military** coup in 1973.

Although there is no evidence that the United States supported the coup that toppled President **Isabel Perón** in **Argentina** in 1976, recently declassified U.S. State Department documents reveal that the military government was convinced it had U.S. approval for its **"dirty war."** In October 1976, at the height of the government's campaign against subversion, U.S. Ambassador Robert Hill reported that Admiral César Guzzetti, the Argentine foreign minister, was in a state of euphoria after meeting in Washington with Kissinger, Vice President Nelson Rockefeller, and other high-ranking state department officials. According to Hill, Guzzetti came away with the understanding that the United States would refrain from criticizing Argentina for **human rights** violations, though Guzzetti was urged to get the "dirty war" over quickly— by December or January. The conservative Hill, a human rights advocate, complained about Kissinger's handling of the issue, arguing that the secretary of state undermined his diplomatic efforts to stop the violations.

KORRY, EDWARD. United States ambassador to **Chile** from 1967 to 1971. Korry was implicated in the covert scheme to prevent the establishment of the leftist-oriented **Unidad Popular** (UP, Popular Unity) government in Chile or to ruin the government if elected. The plan was formed by a secret group of White House officials in the administration of Richard Nixon known as the "Committee of Forty," chaired by **Henry Kissinger**, chair of the National Security Council. Although Korry protested the accusation that he was involved in undermining the UP government of President **Salvador Allende Gossens**, it was not until the discovery of **Central Intelligence Agency** (CIA) documents that the ambassador's claims were substantiated. The documents revealed that despite Korry's direct involvement in anti-Allende Gossens activities such as funding media propaganda and channeling funds to opposition parties, he did not participate in activities leading to the **military** takeover of 11 September 1973. He did, however, keep U.S. officials informed of the situation in Chile through a series of memos dubbed "korrygrams." In September 1971 Korry was replaced as ambassador by Nathaniel Davis.

–L–

LABOR UNIONS. *See* TRADE UNIONS.

LAMBRUSCHINI, ARMANDO. Admiral, commander of the navy, and a member of the second junta (March to December 1981) during the **"dirty war"** in **Argentina**. (The other two junta members were Roberto Viola and **Omar D. Graffigna**.) In the 1985 trial of the nine former junta commanders, Lambruschini was sentenced to eight years in prison for his role in the repression. He had served four when he was released in December 1989 by a blanket pardon by President **Carlos Saúl Menem**.

LAMI DOZO, BASILIO A. I. Brigadier general, commander of the air force, and a member of the third junta (December 1981 to June 1982) during the **"dirty war"** in **Argentina**. Like his fellow members of the third junta, **Jorge I. Anaya** and **Leopoldo Fortunato Galtieri**, he was acquitted in the 1985 trial of the junta commanders—it was thought that the worst of the repression had ended by the time they took office.

LA TABLADA. *See* MOVIMIENTO TODOS POR LA PATRIA (MTP).

LAW 23.049. Military justice reforms passed by the **Argentine** Congress after the country's return to democracy and promulgated on 14 February 1984. The law was largely written by Carlos Santiago Nino, an advisor to President **Raúl Alfonsín** and law school professor at the University of Buenos Aires. Two of the articles state the government's position on the two most sensitive issues related to prosecuting participants in the **"dirty war"**: jurisdiction (whether the defendants should be tried in military or civilian courts) and criminal responsibility. In Article 10 the law assigned original jurisdiction to the Supreme Council of the Armed Forces, the military's highest appellate court, but made the court's decisions subject to automatic civilian review by the Federal Chamber of Appeals. The Supreme Council would have six months to complete its hearing of any case or else explain to the Federal Chamber why it failed to reach a conclusion. The Federal Chamber would then have the option of either sending the case back to the Supreme Council for a fixed period of time or—if it found evidence of delay or negligence—assuming jurisdiction over the case itself. As events turned out, the military court failed to reach a verdict in the cases of the nine commanders of the three juntas, and their cases were handed to the civilian court.

The law also settled the issue of who could be prosecuted. Article 11 declared that, unless there was evidence to the contrary, members of the military who lacked decision-making authority could be absolved of wrongdoing on the assumption that they were following orders they considered legitimate, though exceptions would be made if they had committed atrocities. This meant that high-ranking officers, the decision makers, could be held criminally responsible, since they were not entitled to the defense that they were merely following orders. Junior officers, however, would be entitled to the defense—unless it could be proved that they participated in rape, **torture**, murder, or robbery (abduction was not considered an atrocity).

LEIGH GUZMÁN, GUSTAVO. *See* PINOCHET UGARTE, AUGUSTO.

LETELIER DEL SOLAR, ORLANDO (1932–1976). Foreign minister under President **Salvador Allende Gossens** (1970–1973) of **Chile** and former ambassador to the **United States**. Immediately following the coup of 11 September 1973, Letelier del Solar was detained at **Dawson Island** with other officials from the **Unidad Popular** government. Released, he went into **exile** in Washington, D.C., where he joined the Institute for Policy Studies. He was killed on 21 September 1976 when his car exploded as he was traveling along Washington's Embassy Row. Ronni Karpen Moffitt, a staff member at the institute, also died in the explosion. An investigation revealed that Letelier del Solar, a critic of the **military** dictatorship of **Augusto Pinochet Ugarte**, had been targeted by the **Dirección de Inteligencia Nacional** (DINA, Directorate of National Intelligence), Chile's secret police.

The bomb had been made and planted by Michael V. Townley, a U.S. citizen working for DINA. The story began to unfold in 1978, when a Chilean judge, investigating a case of false passports, discovered a trail leading from Townley to two DINA officials, General **Manuel Contreras Sepúlveda** and Colonel **Pedro Espinoza Bravo**. Turned over to U.S. authorities in 1978, Townley cooperated, confessing to his role in the crime and stating that Contreras Sepúlveda and Espinoza Bravo had ordered the assassination. Townley was convicted and served five years in prison. In 1979 the United States asked Chile to extradite the two DINA officials, but Chile refused, saying that Chilean law did not allow evidence obtained through plea bargains. The United States renewed its extradition request in 1987, prompted by the voluntary confession of Major Armando Fernández Larios, a DINA agent, who told U.S. authorities that he had participated in the assassination by tracking Letelier del Solar's whereabouts in Washington. Again, Chile rejected the request.

A small measure of justice came in 1993, when a Chilean court convicted Contreras Sepúlveda and Espinoza Bravo for their role in the murders of Letelier del Solar and Moffitt. They were sentenced to seven years and six years, respectively, and served time in a special military prison.

LEY DE PRESUNCIÓN DE FALLECIMIENTO / "PRESUMPTION OF DEATH" LAW. *See* MADRES DE PLAZA DE MAYO.

LIBERATION THEOLOGY. A radical theology that arose in the Latin American **Catholic Church** during the 1960s. Unlike the traditional church in the region, which had aligned itself for centuries with the

military and the wealthy elites, practitioners of liberation theology aligned themselves with the region's poor. Liberation theology emerged from the intersection of the social sciences and changes within the wider Catholic Church. Sociology—especially Marxist sociology—provided progressive members of the Latin American Church with the analytical tools to understand the region's economic and social underdevelopment. Out of this analysis came the theory of dependency, which saw Latin America as an economic satellite of the **United States**, just as the region had been a satellite of Spain or Portugal and then, after independence, of other European countries like Great Britain. According to this view, Latin America was not only a source of raw materials and cheap labor for U.S. industry but also a market for its finished products, including arms. U.S. loans and foreign investment were seen as having an opposite effect than the one intended. Instead of leading to an economic boom, which would help prevent the region from falling to **communism**, U.S. involvement brought only dependency and suffering.

Equally important to liberation theology were the changes in Catholicism that emerged out of the Second Ecumenical Council, or Vatican II (1962–1965). Convened in Rome by Pope John XXIII with the intention of modernizing the Church, the Council situated the Church squarely within this world and invited laity to full participation alongside priests and bishops. These wider changes were discussed in a Latin American context in 1963 in Medellín, Colombia, where the region's bishops committed the Church to social justice, breaking the institution's longstanding relationship with the rich and powerful. The Medellín conference had the blessing of the new pope, Paul VI, who had traveled to Colombia to open the discussion and whose encyclical, *Populorum Progressio*, had promoted social, economic, and political rights.

Having charted a new course, the Church in Latin America placed a premium on liberating the masses through education. Drawing on the techniques of Paulo Freire, a noted Brazilian philosopher of education, Church members developed educational programs aimed at helping people understand their plight. *Comunidades de base* (base communities) were formed, where small groups of people (a dozen or so) could live and work together and organize for grassroots change. Although the bishops at Medellín had stopped short of calling for revolution, many young priests and nuns chose to participate in left-wing causes, some even joining armed **guerrilla** organizations. The priest Camilo Torres Restrepo, for example, who had joined the guerrillas in his native Colombia, died in combat on 15 February 1966. The following year a small group of students calling itself the Comando Camilo Torres was formed in **Argentina**. This group would later become the **Montoneros**, one of the most powerful guerrilla organizations in Latin America.

LIGA ARGENTINA POR LOS DERECHOS DEL HOMBRE / ARGENTINE LEAGUE FOR THE RIGHTS OF MAN. The oldest **human rights** nongovernmental organization in **Argentina**. The Liga was founded in 1937 following the overthrow of President Hipólito Yrigoyen and the ensuing political repression. During the dictatorship, it concentrated on providing legal support for political prisoners.

LÓPEZ REGA, JOSÉ. *See* ALIANZA ANTICOMUNISTA ARGENTINA (AAA); PERÓN, ISABEL ("ISABELITA").

–M–

MACDERMOT, NIALL. *See* INTERNATIONAL COMMISSION OF JURISTS (ICJ).

MADRES DE PLAZA DE MAYO / MOTHERS OF THE PLAZA DE MAYO. A **human rights** nongovernmental organization that first appeared on 30 April 1977 in **Argentina**, though it did not become a formal organization until 1979. It arose out of the anger and frustration felt by women in their attempts to gather information about their missing children. A disproportionate number of **desaparecidos** were young, between the ages of 18 and 30. When inquiries at public offices, police precincts, and **military** barracks brought no results, some mothers decided to take their protest to the streets. On Saturday, 30 April 1977, at 11 o'clock in the morning, 14 women led by Azucena Villaflor de Vicenti met at the Plaza de Mayo in the hope of drawing attention to their cause. The plaza, situated next to the Casa Rosada (the Pink House, or presidential residence) had been the site of many political demonstrations, though theirs was the first demonstration since the coup. On this particular day, however, the Plaza was deserted, and they eventually settled on Thursdays at 3:30 in the afternoon for their weekly meetings. At first, the Madres were ignored by the junta, or at most dismissed as *las locas de Plaza de Mayo* (the madwomen of the Plaza de Mayo). They were mothers and hence perceived as politically insignificant. At the same time, their status as mothers afforded them protection. At the request of the Madres, fathers did not march alongside them. It was thought that men would surely be kidnapped and disappeared.

But the Madres' growing number—by June they had reached a hundred—and their increasing activism soon made them a political force. By the end of 1977 they presented writs of habeas corpus on behalf of 159 persons; met with **Patricia Derian**, the coordinator of the Bureau of Human Rights under **Jimmy Carter**; and demonstrated when Terence Todman, assistant secretary of state for inter-American affairs, traveled to Buenos Aires to meet with General **Jorge Rafael Videla**. They had also formed alliances with other human rights groups, such as the **Movimiento Ecuménico por los Derechos Humanos** (MEDH, Ecumenical Movement for Human Rights). As the Madres crossed the boundary between traditional motherhood and political activism, they became targeted as subversives. On 8 December 1977 a task force (kidnapping squad) from the **Escuela Mecánica de la Armada** (ESMA, Navy Mechanics School) broke up a meeting between the Madres and other relatives of the missing, abducting nine women, including Alice Domon, a French nun. Two days later—on 10 December, Human Rights Day—Azucena Villaflor and Léonie Renée Duquet, another French nun, were abducted from their homes. All of them were taken to ESMA and disappeared.

In spite of the loss, the Madres persisted in their protest. In 1978 their marches were largely free of disruption. The junta was preoccupied much of the year with hosting the World Cup soccer tournament and enjoying the national frenzy that followed Argentina's first cup victory. The respite ended on 28 December, when the police took control of the plaza, ejecting about a thousand women by force. The police disrupted the marches throughout 1979 and prevented them outright throughout much of 1980. When the Madres could not march, they gathered in churches. In 1979 they made their organization formal in the hope of keeping the movement intact. Under Hebé Pastor de Bonafini, their first president, they established relationships with other human rights groups both at home and abroad, requested interviews with foreign presidents and legislators, and testified during the hearings held in 1979 by the Inter-American Commission on Human Rights of the **Organization of American States** (OAS).

Although the repression associated with the **"dirty war"** had begun to ease in 1978, the Madres remained a threat to the military government. An improved human rights record could not silence the Madres as long as their children remained unaccounted for and their abductors unpunished. In August 1979 the government attempted to put an end to the matter, announcing the *Ley de Presunción de Fallecimiento* (Presumption of Death Law), which would permit relatives of the missing to seek rulings from judges declaring the missing persons to be dead. The new law would apply to those who had disappeared between November 1975 and the date that the law was promulgated. The Madres, joined by other human rights groups and the governments of several countries, attacked the law as a government effort to sidestep accountability. The fate of the *desaparecidos* remained an issue.

As the government gradually loosened its hold, the Madres continued to demonstrate. On 12 March 1981, 68 mothers were arrested and held for several hours. On 7 July Pastor de Bonafini and María Adela Antokoletz, the president and vice president of the Madres, were detained for two hours at Ezeiza airport; they had arrived from Houston, Texas, where they had accepted the Rothko Chapel award for human rights. (The award was confiscated.) The Madres were one of the few sectors of Argentine society to protest the **Falkland Islands/Islas Malvinas** conflict in 1982, and on 10 December, Human Rights Day, staged a 24-hour march in which hundreds of supporters (men and women) participated.

In 1986 the Madres split into two factions—the Línea Fundadora and the Asociación de las Madres de Plaza de Mayo (the Hebé Pastor de Bonafini line). In addition to the Rothko Chapel award, the Madres have received numerous honors. *See also* ABUELAS DE PLAZA DE MAYO, LAS.

MADRES Y FAMILIARES DE LOS URUGUAYOS DESAPARECIDOS EN ARGENTINA. *See* FAMILIARES.

MALVINAS. *See* FALKLAND ISLANDS / ISLAS MALVINAS.

MANUEL RODRÍGUEZ PATRIOTIC FRONT. *See* FRENTE PATRIÓTICO MANUEL RODRÍGUEZ (FPMR).

MARRA, NELSON (1942–). Uruguayan short-story writer, poet, novelist, and journalist. Born in Montevideo, Nelson Marra alternated the teaching of literature in secondary schools with the practice of literary journalism in publications of various Latin American countries until 1974, when his short narrative "El guardaespaldas" was awarded the first literary prize by the Uruguayan weekly *Marcha*. The work was deemed "pornographic" and "subversive" by a **military** junta that read in it a thinly disguised account of the execution of one of its most notorious members—then recently murdered by the **Tupamaros**, an urban **guerrilla** organization. Marra was condemned to four years in prison. Upon his release, he went into **exile** in Sweden. Among his works— none of which has been translated into English—is *El guardaespaldas y otros cuentos* (1985). In 1981 he settled in Spain, where he still resides.

MARTÍNEZ DE HOZ, JOSÉ ALFREDO. Finance minister in **Argentina** during the first junta (1976–1981). A descendant of the landowning oligarchy and a leading figure in the banking industry, Martínez de Hoz reversed the economic policy of his **Peronist** predecessors, setting the economy on a free-market course. Like the **Chicago Boys** in **Chile**, he lowered protective barriors and opened the economy to outside competition. Implementing the new policy involved repressing organized labor, the traditional Peronist political base. Unions were intervened (placed under **military** control), and many of their leaders and members, labled subversive, were disappeared. Martínez de Hoz kept the peso overvalued, ushering in a period of *plata dulce* (sweet money), when affluent Argentines went abroad for vacation or shopping. Many local companies, however, unable to compete with foreign imports, went bankrupt.

MARXISM. *See* COMMUNISM.

MASSERA, EMILIO (1926–). Admiral, commander of the navy, and member of the first junta (1976–1981) during the **"dirty war"** in **Argentina**. As navy commander, he was responsible for the **torture** and murder of at least 5,000 political prisoners held in the **Escuela Mecánica de la Armada** (ESMA, Navy Mechanics School), an infamous detention center. He was also responsible for appropriating goods—companies and houses, furniture and clothing, television sets and washing machines—stolen from the missing (*desaparecidos*). In the 1985 trial of the nine former junta leaders, Massera was sentenced to life in prison but was released in December 1990 under an amnesty declared by President **Carlos Saúl Menem**.

MENDOZA DURÁN, CÉSAR. *See* PINOCHET UGARTE, AUGUSTO.

MENEM, CARLOS SAÚL (1930–). Peronist politician and president of **Argentina** (1989–1999). Menen's election to the presidency on 14 May 1989 marked the first time since 1928 that one Argentine civilian president succeeded another. In 1995 he won a second term in office, the constitution having been revised the previous year to allow two consecutive presidential terms and to reduce the term from six years to four. Carlos Saúl Menem was born on 2 July 1930 in Anillaco in La Rioja province. His parents were Syrian immigrants, and he and his three brothers were raised as Sunni Muslims, though he would later convert to Roman Catholicism. As a college student he became involved in politics, and in 1955 founded the Juventud Peronista, a Peronist youth group. In 1956 he was jailed briefly for supporting an effort to bring back **Juan Perón.** After earning a law degree from the University of Córdoba in 1958, he practiced law in La Rioja, the provincial capital, and served as advisor to the **Confederación General del Trabajo** (CGT, General Labor Federation), a Peronist stronghold. He was elected governor of La Rioja province in 1973 (the year Juan Perón returned), an office he would win again in 1983 and 1987. After the 1976 **military** coup that removed **Isabel Perón** from power, Menem was imprisoned until 1978, and then kept under house arrest until 1982.

In the presidential election of 1989, Menem, heading a Peronist coalition, defeated Eduardo Angeloz, representing the **Unión Cívica Radical** (UCR, Radical Civic Union). Although Menem was scheduled to take office on 10 December, the incumbent president **Raúl Alfonsín,** facing a severe economic crisis, resigned five months before the end of his six-year term, and Menem assumed the presidency on 8 July. Shortly after taking office, he floated the idea of granting a pardon or an amnesty for military officers and **guerrillas.** Although public opinion polls indicated that a majority of Argentines were opposed to any show of mercy toward the armed forces, on 8 October 1989 Menem pardoned 277 persons, including 64 guerrillas. Among those remaining in prison, however, were the three commanders of the first junta (**Jorge Rafael Videla, Emilio Massera,** and **Orlando Ramón Agosti**) and the **Montonero** leader Mario Firmenich. Despite the pardons, lower-ranking officers, who had rebelled three times under Alfonsín, remained restive. One of the pardoned officers was Colonel Mohammed Alí Seineldín, who had been jailed for leading a rebellion in 1988. Rejecting the army's effort to discipline him for his role in that operation, the charismatic Seineldín urged his many followers to stage still another rebellion, aimed at overthrowing the government. Menem had anticipated the action, however, and had shored up support among loyal-

MOVIMIENTO CONTRA LA TORTURA SEBASTIÁN ACE-VEDO / SEBASTIÁN ACEVEDO MOVEMENT AGAINST TORTURE. A **human rights** nongovernmental organization in **Chile.** It was established in 1983 when the budding Movimiento contra la Tortura (Movement against Torture) renamed itself in memory of a man from Concepción. Unable to bear the thought of his two abducted children being **tortured** by security forces, Sebastián Acevedo set himself on fire outside the city's **Catholic** cathedral. The children were later released.

The Sebastián Acevedo Movement protested torture by staging public performances, sometimes outside known detention centers, fully aware that the **carabineros** (national police) would intervene by beating and arresting them. The intention was to convince bystanders that human rights violations were taking place in Chile.

MOVIMIENTO DE LA IZQUIERDA REVOLUCIONARIA (MIR) / MOVEMENT OF THE REVOLUTIONARY LEFT. Also known as the Movimiento Izquierdista Revolucionario. A leftist urban **guerrilla** organization in **Chile.** The MIR was formed in 1965 by a youthful faction that split from the **Partido Socialista** (PS, Socialist Party). Led by Miguel Enríquez, the group focused on grassroots political activities in the *poblaciones* (shantytowns), as opposed to the progressive reform programs undertaken by the government of **Eduardo Frei Montalva** (1964–1970). When the **Unidad Popular** (UP, Popular Unity) government of **Salvador Allende Gossens** began in 1970, the MIR agreed with much of the UP agenda—particularly land redistribution and the takeover of manufacturing concerns—but rejected the government's main goal of achieving social reforms through democratic means. Like other urban guerrilla organizations in the Southern Cone, the MIR viewed itself as a revolutionary vanguard and advocated armed resistance against government oppression. Yet President Allende Gossens, eager to build a leftist coalition, formally recognized the group and opened a line of communication with its leaders, one of them his own nephew, Andrés Pascal Allende. By 1973 the MIR openly supported the PS and UP. In the violence and chaos that accompanied severe economic recession, however, the MIR went underground, prepared to take up arms. It resisted the coup of 11 September 1973, but was no match for the **military.** Once in power, the junta singled out the MIR for destruction. By 1974 the MIR was decimated—its leaders dead or in **exile.**

MOVIMIENTO DE LIBERACIÓN NACIONAL. *See* TUPAMAROS.

MOVIMIENTO ECUMÉNICO POR LOS DERECHOS HUMANOS (MEDH) / ECUMENICAL MOVEMENT FOR HUMAN RIGHTS. A **human rights** nongovernmental organization in **Argentina**. MEDH was founded in 1976 by progressive members of the **Catholic** clergy (with assistance from **SERPAJ**-Argentina) to give support to victims of the **military** dictatorship. It affiliated itself with the World Council of Churches as opposed to the more conservative Argentine Catholic Church, which during the dictatorship was largely supportive of the military regime.

MOVIMIENTO JUDÍO POR LOS DERECHOS HUMANOS / JEWISH MOVEMENT FOR HUMAN RIGHTS. A **human rights** nongovernmental organization in **Argentina**. It was founded in 1982, though its members had been working together informally since 1977. During the dictatorship, Argentina's Jewish community suffered repression out of all proportion to its numbers. The Movimiento Judío, led by the journalist Herman Schiller, gave a distinctive voice to the resistance, often relating the events of the period to the Holocaust. *See also* ANTI-SEMITISM.

MOVIMIENTO PERONISTA DE LIBERACIÓN. *See* UTURUNCOS.

MOVIMIENTO TODOS POR LA PATRIA (MTP) / EVERYONE FOR THE MOTHERLAND. Also known as Todos por la Patria (TPP). A leftist, grassroots, **human rights** organization in **Argentina**, composed of human rights activists, former members of the **Ejército Revolucionario del Pueblo** (the ERP, or People's Revolutionary Army), and progressive **Catholics** inspired by **liberation theology**. Formed in the 1980s, it began as a peaceful organization, but turned to **guerrilla** warfare after a series of *carapintada* revolts by junior officers threatened either a return to **military** rule or at least a vindication of the military for its role in the **"dirty war."** On 23 January 1989 the MTP attacked and occupied the army garrison at La Tablada. The garrison was retaken the following day after President **Raúl Alfonsín** authorized the army to intervene. The toll was 39 dead (28 of them guerrillas) and 62 wounded.

–N–

NATIONAL COMMISSION ON THE DISAPPEARANCE OF PERSONS. *See* COMISIÓN NACIONAL DE INVESTIGACIÓN DE DESAPARICIÓN DE PERSONAS (CONADEP).

NATIONAL COMMISSION ON TRUTH AND RECONCILIATION. *See* COMISIÓN NACIONAL DE VERDAD Y RECONCILIACIÓN.

NATIONAL INFORMATION CENTER. *See* DIRECCIÓN DE INTELIGENCIA NACIONAL (DINA).

NATIONAL LIBERATION MOVEMENT. *See* TUPAMAROS.

NATIONAL REVOLUTIONARY ARMY. *See* EJÉRCITO NACIONAL REVOLUCIONARIO (ENR).

NAVY MECHANICS SCHOOL. *See* ESCUELA MECÁNICA DE LA ARMADA (ESMA).

NERUDA, PABLO (1904–1973). Chilean poet and political activist. One of the major poets in any language of the 20th century, he was born into a working-class family—his father was a train conductor—in Parral, in the rural center of **Chile**, as Neftalí Ricardo Reyes Basoalto. He spent his childhood in southern Chile, in Temuco, amid railroad workers and miners, an experience he would movingly recount in his memoirs, *Confieso que he vivido*—published posthumously in 1974—and which would fuel his political activism. In Temuco he also established a lifelong friendship with his teacher Gabriela Mistral (nee Lucila Godoy Alcayaga, a poet and the winner of the Nobel Prize for Literature in 1945).

While still in his teens, Neruda was awarded a government scholarship to study French in Santiago, Chile, with the object of becoming a provincial teacher. Instead, the publication of his second book of poetry, *Veinte poemas de amor y una canción desesperada* (1924, translated as *Twenty Love Poems and a Song of Despair* in 1969) anointed him one of Latin America's most famous young poets. He was appointed to the Chilean consular service and served in several Asian capitals from 1927 to 1932. The neo-romanticism of his early poetry was abandoned in favor of surrealist verse of startling imagery and political content. To this period correspond two volumes of *Residencia en la tierra* (1933 and 1935). In 1934 he arrived in Spain as Chilean consul, first in Barcelona and then in Madrid. In Spain he was hailed as one of the most important voices of poetry in Spanish by the most important voices of the Generación del 27, led by Federico García Lorca. With the outbreak of the Spanish Civil War (1936–1939), Neruda identified with the cause of the Spanish Republic. With the publication of *España en mi corazón* (1937), the earlier hermetic verse of his surrealist stage was abandoned in favor of a direct language that identified itself with the politically dispossessed.

Neruda abandoned the diplomatic service in 1944, and in 1945 joined the **Partido Comunista de Chile** (PC, Communist Party of Chile). He served in the Chilean Senate from 1945 to 1948. In 1948 the Communist Party was outlawed in Chile, and Neruda went into **exile**, first in the Soviet Union, then in Europe and Mexico. During this period he published his ambitious—and politically controversial—*Canto general* (1950, translated as *Canto General* in 1991). In a monumental style and with a sonorous voice, Neruda portrayed the history and geography of Latin America in an epic mosaic that extends for a thousand pages and 15 cantos. The publication of *Odas elementales* (1954, translated as *Elementary Odes* in 1961) and *Nuevas odas elementales* (1955) marked yet another stage in the literary trajectory of the poet. Written in direct, lyrical language—bereft of political overtones—the poems hailed the simplicity of such everyday objects as an onion, a dictionary, a tomato, and a pair of socks. Published in the columns of a daily in order to reach a wider readership, the *Odas elementales* won another set of admirers for the poet who was already hailed as "the poet of America."

In 1952, the ban on the Communist Party having ended, Neruda returned to his native Chile. In this final stage of his career, he returned to the love poetry of his youth and adopted an intimate, introspective voice that sometimes gently mocked his public persona. The period saw the publication of *Estravagario* (1958); the love poetry of *Los versos del capitán* (1952) and *Cien sonetos de amor* (1959); and the five-volumes of *Memorial de Isla Negra* (1964), a melancholy return to the places, travels, and political commitment of his youth.

In 1970 Neruda was the Communist Party's candidate for president during the **Unidad Popular** campaign. The resulting election saw the triumph of **Salvador Allende Gossens** as president of Chile. Neruda was appointed ambassador to France from 1970 to 1972. In 1971 he was awarded the Nobel Prize for Literature, the capstone to a distinguished career that saw him receive, among other honors, Chile's Na-

1973, just a week after the **military** coup that ended the Allende Gossens presidency, Neruda died at his house in Isla Negra, Chile.

NEW CHILEAN SONG. *See NUEVA CANCIÓN CHILENA.*

"NIGHT OF THE PENCILS." On 16 September 1976, 10 Argentine high-school students were abducted from their homes by security forces. Labeled subversive for having signed a joint petition in favor of student rate bus fares, the students were taken to secret detention centers and tortured. Three of the students were eventually released; the rest remain among the missing (*desaparecidos*).

NIXON, RICHARD M. *See* HENRY KISSINGER; UNITED STATES.

NUEVA CANCIÓN CHILENA / **NEW CHILEAN SONG.** *Nueva Canción* (New Song), a sociocultural movement with music as its base of **cultural resistance**, began in the early 1960s and continues to evolve with the addition of other Latin American and world music forms. In addition to **Chile**, *Nueva Canción* is found in **Argentina**, Brazil, Cuba, Puerto Rico, and **Uruguay**. The movement in Chile suffered extreme acts of political repression in the years following the **military** coup of 11 September 1973.

The impetus of *Nueva Canción Chilena* was the work of singer and songwriter **Violeta Parra**, credited with reviving Chilean folk music. Particularly important were her political protest songs, embraced by the working classes and reinterpreted by young musicians in the years prior to the coup. Among the musicians and groups influenced by Parra were Rolando Alarcón and **Victor Jara**, Angel and Isabel Parra (Violeta's children), and the folk ensembles Inti-Illimani, Illapu, and Quilapayún. They celebrated the aesthetics of indigenous music while promoting the cultures of the rural peasantry and urban working classes. Social justice was a common theme. The early Violeta Parra song "Yo canto la diferencia" ("I Sing of the Difference")—which influenced Victor Jara's "Miner's Song" (1961) and "The Plow" (1965) and Quilapayún's "La batea" ("The Washboard")—is a common example of how *Nueva Canción* placed social concern ahead of commercialism.

Many political resistance movements adopted elements of *Nueva Canción Chilena* into their social change agendas, notably the *Unidad Popular* (Popular Unity) party led by **Salvador Allende Gossens**. The popularity and political significance of *Nueva Canción Chilena* made it a target of the military junta. *Nueva Canción* music was banned and its creative artists were **exiled** or disappeared. Isabel Parra, who was performing outside the country at the time of the coup, was not allowed to return. Victor Jara, one of the regime's most prominent targets, was murdered shortly after the coup. Personal recordings and published music were destroyed in military raids. Folkloric instruments were destroyed and public play was forbidden. *Nueva Canción* was forced outside Chile, and much of its music was performed by exiles or by artists in Europe and North America. Chilean performers went underground, performing in clandestine locations or impromptu venues such as crowded buses. Even after some of the repressive actions were relaxed in 1983, lyrics and performances were still censored, and *Nueva Canción* did not experience a true revival and growth until the early 1990s.

–O–

***OBEDIENCIA DEBIDA* / DUE OBEDIENCE.** Legislation passed in June 1987 in **Argentina** during the administration of President **Raúl Alfonsín**. The law specified that only commanding officers could be held legally responsible for **human rights** violations committed during the recent **military** dictatorship. Lower-ranking officers (those below brigadier general) were exempt from prosecution on the theory that they were following orders which they took to be legitimate.

ONETTI, JUAN CARLOS (1909–1994). Uruguayan novelist, short-story writer, and journalist. Born in Montevideo, Onetti has often been described as **Uruguay**'s literary master of the 20th century. In his early 20s he moved to Buenos Aires, **Argentina**, where he worked briefly as a movie reviewer for the journal *Crítica* and began publishing in, among other periodicals, the literary supplement of the newspaper *La Nación*. On his return to Montevideo, he became editor of the newly founded journal *Marcha*, a post he held until 1942, and also editor for Reuters News Agency. During a second stay in Buenos Aires, between 1943 and 1955, he continued his work for Reuters and edited the journal *Vea y lea*. In 1957, after a brief stint in an advertising agency, he was named director of the Municipal Libraries of Montevideo.

With the publication of his novel *El pozo* in 1939, Onetti was hailed as a truly original voice in the Latin American literary scene for his fusion of fantasy and realism, though his work attracted little critical attention outside his native **Uruguay**. Critical acclaim would follow, however, with the publication over the years of his *Santa María* saga, a however, with the publication over the years of his *Santa María* saga, a series of short stories and novels set in the fictional city of Santa María. The city is a nightmarish composite of Buenos Aires and Montevideo, fraught with the alienation and chaos of the modern urban experience. The series includes *La vida breve* (1950), *El astillero* (1961), *Juntacadáveres* (1964), and *La muerte y la niña* (1973). Although the political situation of Uruguay is alluded to in many of his works, Onetti made it explicit in the 1978 short story "Presencia," where a coup imposes a **military** presence in the city. The cycle was brought to a conclusion by the destruction by fire of Santa María in his 1979 novel *Dejemos hablar al viento*.

In 1974 Onetti—then Uruguay's most prominent writer—was named a jury member for a literary contest organized each year by *Marcha*, at that time one of the oldest and most highly regarded literary journals in Latin America. The first prize in the short-story category went to "El guardaespaldas," by **Nelson Marra**, a work that the military considered "pornographic" and "subversive." Arrested were Onetti; several members of the jury; Marra; the publisher of the journal, Carlos Quijano; and the editor of the journal, Hugo Alfaro. The journal was confiscated and its publication banned by order of the military. Despite the international outcry that ensued, Onetti was detained in a psychiatric institution for several months.

Upon his release, Onetti went into **exile** in Spain, where he became a citizen in 1975. He was the recipient of several prestigious awards, among them the Uruguayan Premio Nacional de Literatura in 1962, the William Faulkner Foundation Ibero-American Award in 1963, the Casa de las Américas prize in 1965, and the Premio Cervantes, the most prestigious literary award in Spain, in 1980. Onetti died in Madrid in 1994.

OPERACIÓN DIGNIDAD. *See CARAPINTADAS.*

OPERATION CONDOR. A clandestine Latin American **military** network whose principal members were **Argentina**, Bolivia, Brazil, **Chile**, Paraguay, and **Uruguay**. Condor was formed in 1975 by Colonel (later General) **Manuel Contreras Sepúlveda**, head of the **Dirección de Inteligencia Nacional** (DINA, Directorate of National Intelligence), Chile's secret police. Condor allowed the militaries of these countries to share information on political opponents and to cooperate in their capture. Consequently, refugees escaping repression in their own countries could no longer find asylum in neighboring countries. They would be tracked down and either returned to their own countries or executed in the countries to which they fled. In addition, Condor allowed the assassination of high-level political leaders perceived to be a threat to the current military regimes. Among its victims were the Chilean **Orlando Letelier del Solar** and his associate **Ronni Karpen Moffitt**, in Washington, D.C., and the Uruguayan legislators Zelmar Michelini and Héctor Gutiérrez, in Buenos Aires. Although the existence of Condor was long suspected, proof did not emerge until the late 1990s.

OPERATION DIGNITY. *See CARAPINTADAS.*

OPERATION TWENTIETH CENTURY. *See* FRENTE PATRIÓTICO MANUEL RODRÍGUEZ (FPMR).

ORGANIZATION OF AMERICAN STATES (OAS). Chartered in 1948, the OAS in May of that year adopted its American Declaration of the Rights and Duties of Man. Like the Universal Declaration of Human Rights, which the **United Nations** (UN) would adopt a few months later, the American Declaration is based on the principle that individuals derive rights from the fact of being human, not from the fact of being citizens. In other words, states do not grant rights but rather recognize already existing rights. Also like the Universal Declaration, the American Declaration was not legally binding—there was not enough agreement to make it so. In 1967, however, the OAS adopted a protocol making the American Declaration the standard by which member states would be judged. The Inter-American Commission on Human Rights (IACHR), which was formed in 1960 and which became part of the OAS in 1967, was empowered to investigate and report on **human rights** violations committed by OAS member nations. The IACHR visited **Chile** in 1974, **Uruguay** in 1977, and **Argentina** in 1979, publishing its findings in 1974, 1978, and 1980, respectively. Unlike the reports of UN rapporteurs, IACHR reports are not kept confidential.

–P–

PARRA, VIOLETA (1917–1967). Chilean folk singer, songwriter, artist (sculptor, ceramist), and poet whose original songs, modeled after traditional Chilean folk music, served as an influential force in the cultural resistance movement known as *Nueva Canción Chilena* (New Chilean Song). Violeta Parra was internationally recognized as an

Song). Violeta Parra was internationally recognized as an ethnomusicologist who cultivated Chilean folk music, having collected and disseminated over 3,000 examples of genres and traditional styles. Her own original works—infused with democratic ideas and composed in solidarity with the peasant and working classes—became an important part of political resistance both before and after the **military** takeover by **Augusto Pinochet Ugarte** in 1973.

Through her fieldwork and artistic endeavors, Parra gave national consciousness and acceptance to Chilean folk music. Songs such as *"La carta"* ("The Letter") and *"¿Qué dirá el Santo Padre?"* ("What Will the Holy Father Say?") reflected the beauty and simplicity in the lives of ordinary people and the political challenges they faced. Her songs provided the guiding impetus to *Nueva Canción* as it grew under the influence of artists such as **Victor Jara**; the groups Inti-Illimani and Quilapayún; and Violeta's own son and daughter, Angel and Isabel Parra.

Encompassing the themes of social injustice, democratic consciousness, and concern about the future of **Chile**, her songs were performed by artists in cafes and nightclubs and incorporated into the rhetoric of political parties representing the working classes. Because of their popular acceptance, they were, like the songs of other *Nueva Canción* artists, subject to strict censorship during the years of the dictatorship. Her records were destroyed by the military during home raids and were unavailable in record stores. Political lyrics and references to her political activities were expurgated from publications by or about the artist and her works.

Ironically, the most influential and recognizable of her songs was the apolitically themed *"Gracias a la Vida"* (*"Thanks to Life"*), which was recorded on the last album before her death by suicide in 1967. It spoke of gratitude for the simple things in life: love, eyes to enjoy the natural beauty of the Chilean landscape, and words to express that beauty. In later years, Chileans in both rural and urban areas adopted the song as a symbol of solidarity and mass **cultural resistance**. One day in 1984, hundreds of thousands of urban workers stopped at noon to sing it en masse.

Shortly after Parra's death, **Pablo Neruda** wrote a poetic tribute to her, "Elegía para cantar" ("Elegy to Sing"), which described in detail the beauty, power, and fragility of the artist who gave so much to the people of Chile through the study and re-creation of one of its traditional art forms.

PARTIDO COMUNISTA DE CHILE (PC) / COMMUNIST PARTY OF CHILE. Founded in 1922, the PC established a strong electoral base among the working classes. Though the party was subject to repression—it was banned from 1948 to 1952—it had by the 1970s grown to 250,000 members, becoming the largest **communist** party in Latin America. The PC exerted a moderating influence on the **Unidad Popular** (UP, Popular Unity) coalition of President **Salvador Allende Gossens**, and was committed to achieving revolution through peaceful means. After Allende Gossens was deposed in the 1973 coup led by General **Augusto Pinochet Ugarte**, the party debated the reasons for the fall of the UP government. At first it blamed the militant stance of the **Movimiento de la Izquierda Revolucionaria** (MIR, Movement of the Revolutionary Left) and the **Partido Socialista de Chile** (PS, Socialist Party of Chile) for the UP's loss of mainstream support. In 1977, however, it blamed the Allende government itself for not defending itself militarily—a charge leveled by radical leftists and the Soviet Union. Yet the party continued its policy of nonviolence in the belief that the government of Pinochet Ugarte would fall on its own.

That policy would soon change. As senior party leaders were arrested, they were replaced by a younger generation committed to removing Pinochet Ugarte by force. In 1980 the party announced a strategy of popular protest that did not exclude violence. Some members resisted the shift and resigned in protest, but others fell in line, emboldened by the fall of the Shah of Iran and the success of the leftist revolution in Nicaragua, both in 1979. The hardliners were now in command, and in 1983 the party gave rise to the **Frente Patriótico Manuel Rodríguez** (FPMR, Manuel Rodríguez Patriotic Front), an urban **guerrilla** organization. Still, the party recognized the need for a broad alliance and reached out to other opponents of the regime. But its refusal to rule out violence alienated many in the Alianza Democrática (AD, Democratic Alliance), a multiparty coalition formed in 1983 to seek a negotiated return to democracy. Excluded from the AD, the PC formed the Movimiento Democrático Popular (MDP, Popular Democratic Movement), a militant left-wing coalition.

PARTIDO DEMÓCRATA CRISTIANO (PDC) / CHRISTIAN DEMOCRATIC PARTY. A centrist political party in **Chile**. Founded in 1957 from the merger of the National Falange and the Social Christian Conservative Party, the PDC has taken a position between the conservative capitalism of the Chilean right and the social collectivism of the Chilean left. By 1970 it had greatly expanded its membership, attracting a majority of the middle class, professionals, and, in the 1960s, voters from the Partido Radical (Radical Party).

The PDC reform government of President **Eduardo Frei Montalva** initiated social policies that benefited many Chileans, especially the middle class and professionals. The PDC, however, did not anticipate the strength of the **Unidad Popular** (UP, Popular Unity) coalition, which in 1970 helped elect the Marxist president **Salvador Allende Gossens**. The result was a bitter, interparty rivalry that continued over the next three years, the PDC using its majority in the Congreso Nacional (National Congress) to bring legislative pressure on Allende Gossens. During the 1973 congressional election campaigns, the PDC formed a coalition with the Partido Nacional (National Party), a major political organization on the right, and other, smaller opposition parties, creating the Confederación Democrática (CODE, Democratic Confederation). The main objective of CODE was to win enough congressional seats to impeach Allende Gossens or at least block his socialist agenda. The resulting impasse between the executive and legislative branches of government paralyzed the UP in the face of fiscal chaos and civil disorder. Several high-placed PDC officials openly called for **military** intervention to depose the government. When the armed forces rebelled on 11 September 1973, the PDC did not intervene, hoping to fill a leadership role once order was restored. When it became clear, however, that a primary objective of the military regime of General Augusto Pinochet Ugarte was to subvert all political parties, the PDC took a lead role in opposing the dictatorship.

PARTIDO JUSTICIALISTA (PJ). The official name of the Peronist party. *See also* PERÓN, JUAN; PERONISM.

PARTIDO SOCIALISTA DE CHILE (PS) / SOCIALIST PARTY OF CHILE. Founded in 1933, the PS provided an option for leftists opposed to the strong Soviet influence over the **Partido Comunista de Chile** (PC, Communist Party of Chile). The PS was divided from the beginning. Some members were committed to taking power through peaceful means; others called for armed struggle. After the Cuban Revolution, the party drifted to the left, and in 1967 proclaimed itself Marxist-Leninist. Yet divisions persisted into the years of the **Unidad Popular** (UP, Popular Unity) government of President **Salvador Allende Gossens** (1970–1973). Carlos Altamirano, the party secretary-general, advocated mass rebellion; **Clodomiro Almeyda Medina**, a socialist and high official in the UP government, urged moderation. After the 1973 **military** coup, the party, owing to its reputation for militancy, became a target of the **Dirección de Inteligencia Nacional** (DINA, Directorate of National Intelligence), the secret police.

As PS leaders disappeared or were **exiled**, the party broke into more than a dozen factions. Altamirano and Almeyda Medina, both in exile in East Germany, competed for control of the party, and, by the late 1970s, had pulled it in opposite directions. Altamirano, rejecting his earlier militancy, now renounced violence and favored social democracy. Almeyda Medina, in contrast, moved from reformism to militancy. The Altamirano camp—later under the leadership of Carlos Briones, interior minister in the UP government—aligned itself with the mainstream coalition Alianza Democrática (AD, Democratic Alliance); the Almeyda Medina camp, under the Marxist-Leninist banner, aligned itself with the leftist coalition Movimiento Democrático Popular (MDP, Popular Democratic Movement). By 1988 the Almeydistas moved to the center, joining in the "no" vote against eight more years of rule by **Augusto Pinochet Ugarte.**

PASTOR DE BONAFINI, HEBÉ. *See* MADRES DE PLAZA DE MAYO.

PATRIA Y LIBERTAD. *See* DEATH SQUADS.

PEACE AND JUSTICE SERVICE. *See* SERVICIO PAZ Y JUSTICIA (SERPAJ).

PEOPLE'S GUERRILLA ARMY. *See* EJÉRCITO GUERRILLERO DEL PUEBLO (EGP).

PEOPLE'S REVOLUTIONARY ARMY. *See* EJÉRCITO REVOLUCIONARIO DEL PUEBLO (ERP).

PÉREZ ESQUIVEL ADOLFO (1931–). Argentine sculptor, architect, and **human rights** advocate. Pérez Esquivel was born in Buenos Aires and educated at the National School of Fine Arts of Buenos Aires and La Plata. In the 1950s he taught architecture at the Manuel Belgrano National School of Fine Arts. He also produced works of art, and his sculptures were widely exhibited throughout Argentina. In 1971 he joined with liberal **Catholic** clergy and laypersons to found **Servicio Paz y Justicia** (SERPAJ, Peace and Justice Service), an organization that advocated nonviolent social reform. SERPAJ had chapters across

Latin America, and in 1974 he became its general coordinator. After the **military** dictatorship in **Argentina** in 1976, he continued his activism, speaking out against the disappearances. He was imprisoned from April 1977 to May 1978. After his release, he remained under house arrest until 1980. In 1979 he gave testimony to the visiting Inter-American Commission on Human Rights, the investigating arm of the **Organization of American States**, whose report on Argentina appeared in 1980. For his nonviolent struggle Pérez Esquivel was awarded the 1980 Nobel Peace Prize. *See also DESAPARECIDOS.*

PERI ROSSI, CRISTINA (1941–). Uruguayan journalist, poet, and novelist. Born in Montevideo, **Uruguay**, Peri Rossi began her professional life as a middle-school teacher and journalist. She later published several collections of poetry and short stories while in her 20s. She collaborated in the weekly *Marcha,* closed by the **military** in 1970. In 1972, as a member of a coalition of left-wing parties in Montevideo, she was forced into **exile** in Spain, where she still resides. She has been the recipient of several honors, among them the 1992 Ciudad de Barcelona award for *Bábel bárbara,* judged the best volume of poetry published in Spanish in 1991.

A prolific writer of over 18 collections of short stories and poetry, as well as novels, Peri Rossi used symbolism and allegory to explore the repression in Uruguay through such works as *Ship of Fools* (1984), perhaps her best-known novel. In it she examines the fragility of the human psyche and offers a feminist critique of patriarchal society. In works that combine the fantastic, the erotic, and the political, Peri Rossi's narrative suggests the possibility that an escape from the rational might be in itself an escape toward individual freedom.

PERMANENT ASSEMBLY FOR HUMAN RIGHTS. *See* ASAMBLEA PERMANENTE POR LOS DERECHOS HUMANOS (APDH).

PERÓN, EVA DUARTE DE ("EVITA") (1919–1952). Charismatic Argentine political leader and the cofounder of **Peronism**. Evita was born on 7 May 1919 as María Eva Duarte. Her father died when she was seven, and she grew up in poverty. Leaving home at 15, she went to Buenos Aires and found work in radio soap opera and the movies. She soon had her own radio show. At 25 she met **Juan Perón**, a young colonel who, like her, had great ambition. She advised him, in his position as the secretary of labor and welfare, to build a political following among urban workers and **trade unionists**, a relationship that would become the foundation of Peronism. When Perón was jailed by political rivals in October 1945, Evita rallied his supporters and helped set him free. Evita and Perón were soon married, and campaigned together for the presidency the following year. As the president's wife and political partner, she established the Fundación de Ayuda Social María Eva Duarte de Perón (Eva Perón Social Aid Foundation), a welfare fund. She lobbied for women's suffrage, which became a reality in 1947. After the constitution was modified (at Perón's request) to allow presidents to succeed themselves, Peronists made an effort to put Evita on the ballot as a vice-presidential candidate. She had become sick, however, and after Perón was reelected in 1951, Evita Perón died of cancer, on 26 July 1952.

Although the ruling classes despised Evita, the workers venerated her. Indeed, many campaigned to have her canonized as a saint. So strongly did she symbolize Peronism that, following the coup that ousted Perón in 1955, her body disappeared. It was later discovered in Italy and was returned to **Argentina** in 1975. Her memory inspired the **Montoneros** and other Peronist **guerrillas**, who saw her as an example of the revolutionary potential within the movement. Today, the memory of Evita continues to evoke great passions.

PERÓN, ISABEL ("ISABELITA") (1931–). President of **Argentina** (1974–1976) and the first woman president of any country. Born María Estela Martínez Cartas on 4 February 1931 in La Rioja, a provincial capital in northwest Argentina. Her family moved to Buenos Aires when she was very young. She quit school after the sixth grade and studied piano, ballet, and French. She also developed a passion for romantic Spanish poetry. In 1952 she set off on a career as a dancer, taking Isabel as her professional name. Three years later, working as a nightclub dancer in Panama City, Panama, Isabel met **Juan Perón**, who had been overthrown as president of Argentina only a few months before and was now in **exile**. Soon she became his personal secretary and live-in companion, moving with him from country to country before they settled, in 1960, in Madrid. They were married in 1961. From Madrid Perón directed his Peronist movement and plotted his return from exile. Isabel became his envoy and made several trips to Argentina, where she attended rallies, endorsed candidates, and entered talks with the administration of President Alejandro Lanusse. She accompanied her husband on a month-long visit to Argentina in November 1972—legal restrictions against him being temporarily waived—and then returned permanently with him in June 1973 after the restoration of civilian government. The new president, **Héctor José Cámpora**, Perón's stand-in during the recent elections, resigned in July at Perón's behest. New elections were called, and there was little doubt that Perón would be the winning candidate. The only question was whom he would select as his running mate—an important matter considering his advanced age (77) and his poor health.

To everyone's surprise he named Isabel, who told a Peronist convention crowd, "I cannot offer you great things. I am only a disciple of Perón." The couple won by a landslide on 23 September 1973, defeating the Radical party candidate Ricardo Balbín. Many thought Perón the only leader influential enough to solve the country's economic and political problems. The economy improved at first, but by the middle of the following year, it deteriorated amid strikes, high inflation, and a black market. The country's long tradition of political unrest persisted. Right- and left-wing Peronists struggled for control of the movement (Perón sided with the right), and the Marxist **Ejército Revolucionario del Pueblo** (People's Revolutionary Army) continued its campaign of violence. On 1 July 1974 Perón died, and Isabel became president. In September the leftist Peronist **Montoneros**, whose hope for any revolutionary potential in Peronism died with Perón, ended their truce and resumed urban **guerrilla** activities. The country moved further to the right as Isabel came under the influence of José López Rega, her spiritual-advisor-turned-minister-of-social-welfare. Government repression against leftists intensified. Meanwhile, the economy continued to worsen. In 1975, under intense pressure, Isabel took lengthy leaves of absence. Her cabinet resigned in July after labor called a general strike. Soon after, her advisor López Rega was forced into exile by organized labor, old-guard Peronists, and the **military**. In November, convalescing after a gall bladder attack, she faced charges of corruption. Despite repeated calls for her resignation, she remained determined to serve out her term of office, scheduled to end in May 1977.

Few were surprised when the military removed her from power on 24 March 1976 and placed her under house arrest. Released in 1981, she went into exile in Spain. She came back to Argentina in 1983 after the return to civility. She has remained in the background ever since.

PERÓN, JUAN (1895–1974). President of **Argentina** (1946–1955, 1973–1974). Born Juan Domingo Perón Sosa on 8 October 1895 in Lobos, a small town in the province of Buenos Aires. His family was rural middle class. In 1913 he graduated from the Colegio Militar de la Nación, the country's **military** academy, with the rank of sublieutenant. In 1924 he graduated from officers' school and held the rank of captain. He then received advanced training at the Escuela Superior de Guerra, where, from 1930 to 1936, he was a professor of military history. During those years, he wrote several books on military strategy. In 1938 his first wife, Aurelia Tizón, whom he married in 1925, died of cancer. From 1939 to 1941, as head of a military mission, he traveled in Europe and was reported to have become impressed with the regimes of Adolf Hitler and Benito Mussolini.

In 1941 Perón, now a colonel, returned to Argentina. He joined the Grupo de Oficiales Unidos (GOU, Group of United Officers), composed of army officers with fascist sympathies. On 4 June 1943 the GOU deposed President Ramón Castillo. The new president, Arturo Rawson, was ousted a few days later in favor of General Pedro Ramírez, in whose government Perón became undersecretary of war and director of the National Department of Labor. The department—which Perón transformed into the Secretariat of Labor and Welfare—was the key to his rise to power. As Argentina became increasingly industrialized, the working classes became a potential political base. Perón captured that base, bestowing on his *descamisados* ("shirtless ones") pay raises, bonuses, improved working conditions, and other benefits. He also took control of the labor movement. In February 1944 Ramírez resigned at the request of Perón. General Edelmiro Farrell, vice president under Ramírez and a close friend of Perón's, became president. Perón was now vice president, minister of war, and secretary of labor and welfare.

Farrell, though president, was a mere figurehead. Power resided in Perón, who faced opposition both at home and abroad. His opponents in the military feared his popularity with the workers. The country's commercial and industrial elites resented his social reforms. And the Allied powers in World War II were troubled by Perón's pro-Axis leanings. Although Argentina, under Ramírez, had recently severed diplomatic relations with Germany and Japan, the new regime was looked upon with suspicion. Indeed, the Allies concluded that Ramírez was ousted out of fear that he might take the next step and declare war on the Axis. On 9 October 1945 Perón's military rivals, resenting his popularity, forced Perón to resign and put him in jail. When word of his imprisonment got out, thousands of his *descamisados* demonstrated in his behalf in the **Plaza de Mayo**. The generals backed down, and, on 17 October, released him. Soon after, Perón married María Eva Duarte—**Evita**—a young movie actress and radio soap-opera star who had helped organize the demonstrators.

Perón's First and Second Terms as President (1946–1952, 1952–1955)

On 24 February 1946 Perón, buoyed by the display of popular support from the year before, won the presidential election, though by a narrow margin. The charismatic Perón, influenced by his second wife, **Eva Perón ("Evita")**, presided over a period of prosperity. Aided by an economic surplus from the export of foodstuffs during World War II, the couple gained a huge following among the masses, their popularity reaching the point of religious veneration. Perón, following the pattern of Francisco Franco, Adolf Hitler, and Benito Mussolini, transformed Argentina into a corporate state, nationalizing industries and utilities and taking control of the **Confederación General del Trabajo** (General Labor Federation), which coordinated **trade unions** throughout the country. Perón called his political philosophy *justicialismo*, which he described as a "middle way," or a "third way"—an alternative to either capitalism or **communism**. His rule was also characterized by corruption and repression. In 1949 Perón cowed Congress into rewriting the constitution to allow presidents to serve consecutive terms. In November 1951, with the aid of the popular Evita, he won reelection by a wide margin. Repression intensified during his second term in office (1952–1955), when, Evita dead from cancer (1952) and the coffers depleted, the country descended into chaos. When Perón was deposed by the military in 1955, the economy was in ruins, and thousands had been imprisoned and tortured.

Perón in Exile (1955–1972)

Perón spent his first five years of **exile**, successively, in Paraguay, Nicaragua, Panama, Venezuela, and the Dominican Republic. In 1960 he settled in Spain, which was under the dictatorship of Francisco Franco. From his villa in Madrid he led his Peronist movement, which still had many loyal followers in Argentina. This following the military was bent on crushing, first under General Pedro Aramburu (1955–1958) and again—after two intervening civilian administrations that the military deemed too soft on Peronism—under General Juan Carlos Onganía (1966–1970). Peronism, however, proved resilient, largely because of Perón's charasmatic personality and his ideological ambiguity. Belonging neither to the right nor to the left, the movement included supporters across the political spectrum, accommodating both traditional anticommunist labor leaders and a younger generation inspired by the Cuban revolution and the exploits of Ernesto ("Che") Guevara. Perón himself was not above playing one group off against another.

Staying in contact with his traditional support base, he also called for the creation of special formations—revolutionary Peronist **guerrilla** groups that, through force of arms, would strive to return him to power. Among the victims of these special formations were not only longtime enemies of Peronism (General Aramburu, for example, whose execution is commonly ascribed to the **Montonero** urban guerrillas), but also longtime Peronists—for example, the labor chief Augusto Vandor. The assassination of Vandor, carried out in 1969 by the **Ejército Nacional Revolucionario** (National Revolutionary Army), came in response to Vandor's growing independence—his attempts to reach an agreement with the current military regime in the hope of establishing Peronism without Perón. Meanwhile, the governments that ruled Argentina after Perón ironically contributed to a clamoring for his return. None could right the country's economy, and the Onganía regime, which for the time being eliminated any hope that change could be effected through the ballot box, persuaded many young people to follow a revolutionary course. As the economy worsened and guerrilla violence increased, many Argentines from all levels of society came to remember the Perón years with growing nostalgia, and began to see the return of Perón as the country's only hope.

Perón's Third Term as President (1973–1974)

The Peronist party (Partido Justicialista, Justicialist Party) received legal recognition in January 1972, and Perón was allowed to return from exile. To ease the mind of the military, he at first ruled indirectly through President **Héctor José Cámpora**, who was elected in March 1973 under the banner of the Frente Justicialista de Liberación Nacional (FREJULI), a Peronist coalition. From Spain Perón had directed the Cámpora campaign, whose slogan was "Cámpora in government, Perón in power." Before the end of the year, however, Perón forced Cámpora to resign and ran for president himself. With his third wife, **Isabel Perón** ("Isabelita"), as his vice-presidential running mate, he won by a landslide. No longer needing his special formations that helped return him to power, he distanced himself from the revolutionary elements within Peronism and moved the country sharply to the right, a trend that continued after his death on 1 July 1974. The new president, Isabelita, possessing little formal education or political experience, faced serious problems, including an economy near collapse and rise in guerrilla violence. Her administration was characterized by incompetence, corruption, and repression. Still, the military was hesitant about removing her, waiting almost two years before staging a coup. Although she lacked the appeal of Evita, Isabelita was the symbol of Peronism, a movement not easily eclipsed. In 1978, at the World Cup soccer tournament in Buenos Aires, crowds called for its return by chanting, "We want the thieves back!"

Today, Peronism lives on.

PERÓN, MARÍA ESTELA MARTÍNEZ DE. See PERÓN, ISABEL ("ISABELITA").

PERONISM. The political ideology of **Juan Perón**, the president of **Argentina** from 1946 to 1955 and also from 1973 to 1974. *Justicialismo*, its official name, gave rise to a movement and a political party (the Partido Justicialista, PJ) and was described by Perón as a middle way, or third way, between capitalism and **communism**. An amorphous ideology, hard to classify in political terms, Peronism attracted adherents from both the right and the left. Its principal characteristics were populism and nationalism.

PERONIST ARMED FORCES. See FUERZAS ARMADAS PERONISTAS (FAP).

PERONIST LIBERATION MOVEMENT. See UTURUNCOS.

PIGLIA, RICARDO (1941–). Argentine novelist, essayist, literary critic, and screenwriter. Born in Androgué (Buenos Aires), Piglia spent much of his youth in Mar del Plata, where he attended the Universidad de la Plata. In his 20s he worked for several Argentine editorial houses. His first published collection of short stories, *La invasion* (1967), was awarded the prestigious Casa de las Américas prize in Havana, Cuba. After the **military** coup in **Argentina** in 1976, Piglia spent several periods abroad as visiting professor at various U.S. universities. In 1980 he published his first novel, *Respiración artificial*, hailed as one of the most representative narratives of the new Argentine fiction in the last decades of the 20th century. The theme of political repression that is obliquely touched upon in the first novel is openly addressed in *La ciudad ausente* (1992). Shortly after, Piglia adapted *La ciudad ausente* for the opera, with a musical score by Gerardo Gandini. The work had its premier in the famed Teatro Colón of Buenos Aires during the season of 1995.

A prolific literary critic, Piglia has published several studies on Argentine writers as well as edited literary compilations. During the 1960s he edited the Serie Negra series, which introduced to Argentine readers authors such as Dashiel Hammet and Raymond Chandler. On several occasions Piglia has written for the screen. In 1992 he collaborated with Brazilian director Hector Babenco in the script for *Corazón iluminado*, based on boyhood memories the two shared of the seaside resort town of Mar del Plata, where the Argentine-born Babenco lived until his family moved to São Paulo, Brazil. In addition, Piglia collaborated in the script for *Comodines*, by Argentine director Jorge Nisco, one of Argentina's box-office successes in 1997, and *La sonámbula* (1998), by Argentine director Fernando Spiner. He has also adapted works by Julio Cortázar and **Juan Carlos Onetti** for the screen.

In 1990 Piglia returned to Buenos Aires, where he still resides. His latest novel, *Plata quemada*, inspired by an actual police case in Buenos Aires, became a best-seller in **Argentina** and received the Premio Planeta as the best novel of the year. In 1999 he published a compilation of brief narratives entitled *Formas breves*. His works have been translated into several languages, and his latest works have been published simultaneously in U.S. and Brazilian editions. Piglia alternates his duties as professor at the Universidad de Buenos Aires with a visiting professorship at Princeton University in New Jersey.

PINOCHET UGARTE, AUGUSTO (1915–). General, army commander, and head of state in **Chile**. He led the coup that toppled the elected government of the socialist president **Salvador Allende Gossens** on 11 September 1973, establishing a **military** dictatorship that lasted 17 years. His regime deprived thousands of Chileans of their constitutional rights. Although credited with introducing economic reforms, he authorized **human rights** abuses that drew international condemnation.

Augusto Pinochet Ugarte was born on 25 November 1915 into an upper-middle-class family in Valparaíso, Chile. He graduated from the Escuela Militar (military academy) in 1936 with the rank of second lieutenant and from the Academia de Guerra (War College) in 1952. In 1954, then a major, he joined the faculty of the Academia, teaching courses on geography and artillery. He left two years later to serve in the **United States** and in Ecuador. After commanding an infantry regiment in Chile in the early 1960s, he returned to the Academia in 1964, teaching geopolitics and geography and serving as assistant director. He made visits (in 1965, 1968, and 1972) to the U.S. Army's School of the Americas in the Panama Canal Zone, where military personnel from Chile and other Latin American countries were receiving tactical training, especially in counterinsurgency. During the administration of President **Eduardo Frei Montalva** (1964–1970), Pinochet Ugarte became a colonel (1966) and then a brigadier general (1968).

During the administration of President Allende Gossens (1970–1973), Pinochet Ugarte earned a reputation for loyalty. In December 1971 he was in charge of the army garrison in Santiago when rioting broke out between supporters of the **Unidad Popular** (UP) government and opposition groups. Allende Gossens declared a state of emergency. General Pinochet Ugarte ordered a curfew and arrested more than a hundred people. He threatened to use violence if necessary, declaring that "coups do not occur in Chile." In November 1972, following a strike by independent truck owners, Allende Gossens attempted to stabilize his government by appointing several military officers to his cabinet. General **Carlos Prats González**, commander in chief of the army, was named minister of the interior, and Pinochet Ugarte was named Prats González's temporary replacement. On 24 August 1973 the president made Pinochet Ugarte's appointment permanent. Prats González, a long-time friend of Pinochet Ugarte's, assured the president that Pinochet Ugarte was loyal to the constitution. A strict constitutionalist, Prats González had defeated Colonel Roberto Souper's tank rebellion (*tancazo*) of 29 June. Neither Prats González nor Pinochet Ugarte was aware of the plot for a military coup being planned by the remaining commanders of the armed forces: General Gustavo Leigh Guzmán of the air force, General César Mendoza of the **Carabineros** (national police), and Admiral José Toribio Merino Castro of the navy. Pinochet Ugarte was informed of the plans less than a week before the proposed coup of 11 September 1973.

Although Pinochet Ugarte was the last man to sign on to the coup, on 11 September he directed the ground and air assault on the presidential palace, La Moneda. Within a few hours La Moneda was destroyed, Allende Gossens was dead, and UP officials were captured as they left the burning building. In a radio broadcast, Pinochet Ugarte claimed victory, declaring that order had been restored. Two days later, the four generals established the ruling junta. Pinochet Ugarte was named president, an office that—according to plan, at least—each of the four was to occupy in turn.

Pinochet Ugarte and the junta believed they had rescued Chile from social and economic chaos. Pinochet Ugarte declared a stage of siege, dispensed with the rule of law, issued decrees, suspended all political parties, and declared war on communists. The extirpation of Marxism from Chile had been the main objective of the coup. The government systematized a plan to identify, arrest, and execute or force into **exile** all opponents of the ruling junta, especially members of the UP government and leftist sympathizers. Pinochet Ugarte then applied himself to a plan to restore the country's economy. He put together a team of consultants who advocated the free-market policies espoused by the University of Chicago economics professor Milton Friedman. The group, known as the **Chicago Boys**, developed a program that included cutting many of the social service programs instituted by the Allende Gossens government, returning expropriated businesses to their previous owners, removing price controls, and—all union activity having been disbanded by the junta—holding down wage levels. These policies revived the economy and benefited the upper and middle classes, who, in turn, gave the junta their support.

Although Pinochet Ugarte's military regime had achieved local success, it was condemned by foreign governments and human rights organizations. These "interventionists"—as Pinochet Ugarte described them—were concerned the abuse of political prisoners, many of whom were in clandestine detention centers and whose numbers had reached as high as 10,000 at the end of 1973. In June 1974 Pinochet Ugarte organized a covert intelligence agency to eliminate his opponents at home and abroad. He trusted the command of the **Dirección de Inteligencia Nacional** (DINA, Directorate of National Intelligence) to one of his former students from military school, Colonel **Manuel Contreras Sepúlveda**. Contreras reported directly to Pinochet Ugarte, bypassing the other junta commanders. Although based in Chile, DINA operated abroad through the terrorist network known as **Operation Condor**.

Within a year following the coup, Pinochet Ugarte floated the idea of taking full control of the nation, arguing that he commanded the largest branch of the armed forces, the army. The idea met great resistance from Leigh Guzmán, the senior member of the junta. Yet on 20 June 1974 Pinochet Ugarte signed Decree 527, granting himself supreme authority. The decree, which did not require the approval of the other junta commanders, relegated them to subordinate roles. He would now rule as *jefe supremo de la nación* (supreme chief of the nation), while remaining head of the junta.

With the assistance of DINA, Pinochet Ugarte continued his plans to eliminate Marxist influences from Chile. After decimating the **Partido Socialista** (PS, Socialist Party) and the **Partido Comunista de Chile** (PC, Communist Party of Chile), he turned his attention to other political opponents, including the members of local human rights groups like the **Vicaría de la Solidaridad** (Vicariate of Solidarity). Civilians who were merely suspected of political activity were detained, tortured, and released as examples to would-be dissidents. Pinochet Ugarte also enlisted the help of DINA in eliminating his three greatest political opponents living in exile: Bernardo Leighton, one of the founders of the **Partido Demócrata Cristiano** (PDC, Christian Democratic Party) and former official in the Frei Montalva government; **Orlando Letelier del Solar**, a lawyer who had served as defense minister in the Allende Gossens government and who was now working in the United States; and his old friend and colleague Prats González. Pinochet Ugarte assigned the task to Contreras, who coordinated the assassinations: Letelier del Solar and Prats González were killed; Leighton was severely incapacitated.

In December 1977 the **United Nations** passed a resolution condemning the military government for human rights abuses. Pinochet Ugarte responded by calling a referendum in January 1978 to seek support for his policies. He received the endorsement of more than 75 percent of the voters, though opponents claimed the results were fraudulent. He then assigned a committee the task of drafting a new constitution, which would contain provisions guaranteeing his future leadership. Approved in a 1980 referendum (also considered fraudulent) and taking effect the following year, the **constitution of 1981** designated Pinochet Ugarte president for eight years following his swearing in on March 1981. The constitution called for a plebiscite in 1989 (the date would later be moved forward to 1988). A yes vote would award a junta-appointed presidential candidate (most likely Pinochet Ugarte) an eight-year term in office; a no vote would give rise to general elections with a slate of candidates.

The **plebiscite of 1988** would be Pinochet Ugarte's downfall. In the 1980s, economic decline contributed to a growing demand for a return to democracy, and state repression, which had subsided after the 1978 referendum, increased in response to protest movements. Although DINA had been replaced in 1977 with the low-key Centro Nacional de Información (CNI, National Information Center), human rights abuses continued. In 1986, for example, CNI agents seized and tortured hundreds of leftists following the attempted assassination of Pinochet

Ugarte by the urban **guerrilla** group **Frente Patriótico Manuel Rodríguez** (FPMR, Manuel Rodríguez Patriotic Front). In 1988 a group of some 16 political parties formed a coalition, the Comando por el No (Command for the No), to lead the opposition against Pinochet Ugarte, who had been named the sole presidential candidate.

Pinochet Ugarte was surprised by his defeat in the plebiscite of 5 October 1988. He was even more surprised when he was not allowed to run as a presidential candidate in the elections of 1989. In March 1990 he handed the presidency over to **Patricio Alywin Azócar**, a Christian Democrat. Despite losing his seat of authority, he was in position to wield considerable power, which would protect both him and the military from prosecution. The constitution of 1981 allowed him to remain commander in chief of the army for eight more years and then, upon his retirement from active duty, to assume the position of senator for life. His lifetime appointment began in March 1998, but he would soon discover that his legal defenses did not protect him abroad. In October 1998 he traveled to London for back surgery. The Spanish Judge **Baltasar Garzón** asked British authorities to arrest Pinochet Ugarte and extradite him to Spain for crimes against humanity. Pinochet Ugarte was under house arrest while British courts debated whether he was immune from prosecution as a former head of state. Although the extradition order was finally upheld, Pinochet Ugarte was allowed to return to Chile in March 2000 after independent doctors reported that his health was too poor for him to stand trial.

Supporters of Pinochet Ugarte were elated—the likelihood of his facing prosecution in Chile seemed remote. Yet a new generation of judges began removing obstacles to putting him on trial. In June 2000 he was stripped of his parliamentary immunity, a decision later confirmed by the Supreme Court. Judges also began arguing, like judges in Argentina, that amnesty laws did not cover cases in which the missing (*desaparecidos*) were still missing: if the remains have not been discovered, the crime is still being committed. On 1 December 2000 Juan Guzmán Tapia indicted Pinochet Ugarte on charges of kidnapping and murder in connection with the **caravan of death**, a 1973 helicopter tour that resulted in the deaths of 75 political prisoners. The charges were reduced the following March—from responsibility for the episode to conspiracy to conceal it. The case never went to trial. An appeals court ruled on 9 July 2001 that Pinochet Ugarte was mentally unfit to face prosecution.

PLAN Z. (Also, Plan Zeta.) One of five alleged conspiracies that the **military** regime of **Augusto Pinochet Ugarte** claimed to have uncovered. Plan Z was supposedly a plot by the **Unidad Popular** (Popular Unity), government of **Salvador Allende Gossens** to assassinate military leaders and form a dictatorship. The regime cited the plan as justification for its coup of 11 September 1973.

PLAZA DE MAYO. The main public square in Buenos Aires, the capital city of **Argentina**. Situated near the Casa Rosada, or presidential palace, the plaza has been the traditional spot for listening to presidential speeches and making public protests. It was there in October 1945 that thousands of demonstrators gathered in support of the jailed **Juan Perón**. The **Madres** (Mothers) and **Abuelas de Plaza de Mayo** (Grandmothers of the Plaza de Mayo) chose to demonstrate there as well.

PLEBISCITE OF 1988. A referendum that was conducted in **Chile** on 5 October 1988. As stipulated in the Chilean **constitution of 1981**, voters were asked whether they would approve an eight-year presidential term for the candidate put forward by the **military** government. The candidate was General **Augusto Pinochet Ugarte**, who had ruled the country since 1973. Voters voted against Pinochet Ugarte. Instead, an open presidential election was held in December 1989, won by **Patricio Aylwin Azócar**.

POPPER, DAVID H. United States Ambassador to **Chile** during the regime of **Augusto Pinochet Ugarte**. Although the administration of President Richard Nixon was generally supportive of Pinochet Ugarte and communicated this policy to its embassy in Santiago, Popper is remembered for publicly denouncing the Chilean government's treatment of its citizens. His remarks earned him a written rebuke from Secretary of State **Henry Kissinger**, who advised him to stop the "political science lectures." The Chilean government responded to the "lectures," not by easing repression, but by initiating a propaganda campaign.

POPULAR UNITY. *See* UNIDAD POPULAR (UP).

PRATS GONZÁLEZ, CARLOS (1915–1974). Chilean general, commander in chief of the army under President **Salvador Allende Gossens** (1970–1973), and a constitutionalist who opposed the coup of 11 September 1973. In June 1973 Prats González had demonstrated his commitment to constitutional government by putting down a tank rebellion (*tancazo*) led by Colonel Roberto Souper, thereby earning the enmity of anti-Allende Gossens forces within the **military**. The victim of a right-wing propaganda campaign, he was forced to resign as commander in chief in August 1973, replaced by General **Augusto Pinochet Ugarte**, a longtime friend and colleague. After the coup, Prats González went into **exile** in **Argentina**, where he worked on his memoirs. On 29 September 1974 he and his wife, Sofía, were murdered by a car bomb planted by agents of the **Dirección de Inteligencia Nacional** (DINA, Directorate of National Intelligence), **Chile**'s secret police. The operation, which reached across the border, prefigured the high-level political assassinations carried out by **Operation Condor**, a Latin American military network formed in 1975. Pinochet Ugarte, the head of the Chilean junta, denied involvement in the murder, despite the threat that Prats González posed to the military regime. In 1998, however, it became known that Pinochet Ugarte ordered the assassination of Prats González and two other rivals, Bernardo Leighton and **Orlando Letelier del Solar**.

"PRESUMPTION OF DEATH" LAW. *See* MADRES DE PLAZA DE MAYO.

PROCESO DE REORGANIZACIÓN NACIONAL / PROCESS OF NATIONAL REORGANIZATION. The term, often shortened to "Proceso," refers to the **military** regime that ruled **Argentina** from 1976 to 1983. The Proceso was a program designed to transform the country politically, economically, and culturally. The regime repressed any resistance to its rule and anything not in keeping with free-market capitalism and "Western Christian" civilization.

PROCESS OF NATIONAL REORGANIZATION. *See* **PROCESO DE REORGANIZACIÓN NACIONAL.**

PUIG, MANUEL (1932–1990). Argentine novelist, playwright, scriptwriter, and assistant director. Born in the town of General Villegas, in the province of Buenos Aires, a town often described as a remote backwater in the arid pampas. His lifelong fascination with movies began early, when the young Puig and his mother attended the cinema to escape the boredom of provincial life under the early regime of **Juan Perón**, a period he would later satirize in his first novel, *La traición de Rita Hayworth* (1965, translated as *Betrayed by Rita Hayworth* in

1971). In 1946 Puig moved to Buenos Aires to attend an American boarding school. He enrolled at the University of Buenos Aires in 1951, first as a student of architecture and later as a philosophy major. In 1955 he was awarded a scholarship to study movie directing with Vittorio De Sica and Cesare Zavattini at the Centro Sperimentale di Cinematografia in Rome. Puig would later describe himself as disenchanted with the filmmaking process at Cinecitta and would abandon his studies. Between 1957 and 1961 he worked as an assistant film director and translator of subtitles in Rome, Paris, and Buenos Aires, with a brief stay in Stockholm. He later moved to New York City, where he worked for Air France.

In 1967 Puig returned to his native **Argentina**. His novel *La traición de Rita Hayworth* had been panned by Argentine critics and had problems with local censors, but was later acclaimed by literary critics in the **United States** and France. Upon his return, the openly gay Puig soon came under attack by a hostile press as an enemy of "family, religion and class structure," according to his biographer and translator, Suzanne Jill Levine. The hostility against the author continued with the publication of his second novel, *Boquitas pintadas* (1969, translated as *Heartbreak Tango: A Serial* in 1973), which became an instant bestseller in Argentina, and culminated with the publication in 1973 of *The Buenos Aires Affair*. Repeated telephone threats and the return of **Juan Perón** to power in 1973—**Isabel Perón**, Perón's third wife and successor, was, according to some accounts, an implacable foe of the writer—sent Puig into **exile**, where he finished *El beso de la mujer araña* in 1976 (translated as *Kiss of the Spider Woman* in 1979).

This novel, Puig's best-known work, tells the story of two cellmates, the gay window dresser Molina and the young Marxist revolutionary Valentín in an unnamed Latin American country, clearly identifiable as Argentina. In the story, cast as a series of dialogues overheard by an unseen and anonymous listener, Molina attempts to distract the young Valentín, suffering from the effects of **torture**, by retelling and sometimes inventing improbable Hollywood plots, all featuring enigmatic heroines, including the Spider Woman of the title. A story of love, loss, and redemption through the artificiality of the movies, the novel was filmed in 1985 under the direction of Hector Babenco, with a screenplay by Leonard Schrader and the participation of William Hurt, Raul Julia, and Sonia Braga. The movie won a Best Actor Oscar for William Hurt. The novel was later adapted for the stage with a libretto by Terrence McNally, score by John Kander and Fred Ebb. After an initial debut off Broadway, where it was met by lukewarm reviews, the

Hayworth was named the best novel of 1968–1969 by the French newspaper *Le Monde*; earlier, it had been a finalist in the Seix Barrar Editorial Biblioteca Breve award. He received the Curzio Malaparte Film Prize in 1966 and the San Sebastian Festival Jury Prize in 1978. Puig died in Cuernavaca in 1990.

PUNTO FINAL / FULL STOP. Legislation passed in **Argentina** on 24 December 1986, intended to impose a limit on the number of officers prosecuted for **human rights** violations. *Punto Final* specified that only those indicted within the next 60 days could be put on trial; it set 22 February 1987 as the cutoff date. Despite the deadline, about 400 officers were indicted.

–R–

RADICAL CIVIC UNION. *See* UNIÓN CÍVICA RADICAL (UCR).

REAGAN, RONALD (1911–). President of the **United States** (1981–1989). In the presidential election of November 1980, Reagan, a conservative Republican, defeated **Jimmy Carter**, the incumbent Democratic president. Reagan attacked Carter's **human rights** policy, blaming it for weakening the United States in relation to international **communism**. The Carter policy, Reagan charged, was not sufficiently aimed at human rights violations committed by communist nations. Instead, the policy focused on and helped undermine regimes in Iran and Nicaragua, for example, regimes that, however authoritarian and repressive, had been friendly to the United States. Reagan placed the concept of human rights within the context of the Cold War. To the Reagan administration, protecting human rights was equated with fighting communism. To personify this shift in policy, Reagan appointed **Jeane Kirkpatrick** to be U.S. ambassador to the **United Nations** (UN) and nominated Ernest Lefever to be assistant secretary of state for Human Rights and Humanitarian affairs, a post occupied by **Patricia Derian** during the Carter administration. Lefever's nomination failed to win confirmation in Congress: his views on human rights were too conservative—and his personality too abrasive—for both Republicans and Democrats alike. **Elliott Abrams** was confirmed to the post instead. Like Lefever, Abrams saw communist regimes to be the main target of U.S. human rights policy. Unlike Lefever, he advanced an argument confirmation in Congress: his views on human rights were too conservative—and his personality too abrasive—for both Republicans and Democrats alike. **Elliott Abrams** was confirmed to the post instead. Like Lefever, Abrams saw communist regimes to be the main target of U.S. human rights policy. Unlike Lefever, he advanced an argument that was much more nuanced, speaking of the need to criticize violations committed by U.S. allies.

At the UN Kirkpatrick attacked the human rights records of communist nations while defending the records of its authoritarian allies, including the **military** regimes of the Southern Cone. Yet by 1980 the generals in **Uruguay** had already begun lengthy negotiations with civilian leaders, the result of which were national elections in 1984 and a return to democracy a year later. **Argentina** returned to democratic rule in 1983, the collapse of the military due in large part to its defeat in the **Falkland Islands/Islas Malvinas** war, in which Reagan sided with Great Britain. **Chile** would remain under military rule until the end of the decade, but by 1985, the beginning of Reagan's second term in office, U.S. policy toward authoritarian allies began to shift. Kirkpatrick was no longer at the UN, and Richard Schifter, a moderate, had replaced Abrams. Although its policy was still centered on anticommunism, the Reagan administration began to realize that government oppression was not so much eliminating opposition forces as sustaining them. Hence it began to apply pressure for change on authoritarian regimes like Chile.

RELATIVES OF THE DETAINED AND MISSING FOR POLITICAL REASONS. *See* FAMILIARES DE DESAPARECIDOS Y DETENIDOS POR RAZONES POLÍTICOS.

RELEGACIÓN. Also called internal **exile.** A repressive system of police control in **Chile** whereby dissident individuals were picked up and taken to temporary prison camps in remote areas or abandoned in desolate, hostile environments. A provision of the transitional government allowed police to dispatch *relegados* (usually opposition leaders or students) to locations in the mountains or deserts for periods lasting up to three months, but judicial internal banishments could last for years and were to more permanent locations such as **Dawson Island**. The system was harshly punitive and efficient. Seldom were *relegados* formally charged with a crime or tried in the courts. Those abandoned in remote areas were forbidden assistance from local townspeople or villagers, though members of the **Catholic Church** often disobeyed this edict.

Because *relegados* were picked up and dispatched to undisclosed locations that cut them off from society, the **military** government was able to effectively dissipate opposition.

RETTIG REPORT. See COMISIÓN NACIONAL DE VERDAD Y RECONCILIACIÓN.

REVOLUTIONARY ARMED FORCES. See FUERZAS ARMADAS REVOLUCIONARIAS (FAR).

RICO, ALDO. See *CARAPINTADAS.*

ROCK MUSIC. See CULTURAL RESISTANCE.

ROMAN CATHOLIC CHURCH. See CATHOLIC CHURCH.

–S–

SÁBATO, ERNESTO (1911–). Argentine physicist, novelist, and essayist. Born in Rojas (Buenos Aires), into a large Italian-Albanian family. An early militancy in the Juventud Comunista during the years of the dictatorship of General José Félix Uriburu was disowned in the 1930s following accounts of Stalinist atrocities in the Soviet Union. Later he earned a doctorate in physics from the Universidad de La Plata (1938), where he also studied philosophy and literature under the noted educator and humanist Pedro Henriquez Ureña (Dominican Republic, 1884– 1946). Upon graduation, Sábato was awarded a fellowship at the Joliot Curie Laboratory in Paris to pursue studies in nuclear physics. In 1940 he returned to **Argentina** as professor at the Universidad Nacional de Buenos Aires. During this period, he also wrote for the literary journal *Sur* and the daily *La Nación.* A series of articles published in *La Nación* attacking the regime of **Juan Perón** forced him to abandon his post at the university in 1945.

That year also marked the publication of his first collection of essays, *Uno y el universo* (1945), a critique of moral relativism and logical positivism inherited from another century. He would revisit this theme in *Hombres y engranajes* (1951), one of the most influential collections of essays in Latin America in the 1950s. A writer of great literary influence in his native Argentina and abroad, Sábato has published three novels: *El tunnel* (1948); *Sobre héroes y tumbas* (1961), considered one of the most important novels in Latin America in the 20th century; and *Abaddón, el exterminador* (1974), which presents a universe dominated by forces of evil, where resistance seems futile. A recipient of several important awards, Sábato received in 1984 the Premio Cervantes, the most prestigious literary award in Spain.

In 1983 Sábato was named to the presidency of the Comisión Nacional sobre la Desaparición de Personas (CONADEP, National Commission on the Missing), and directed the compilation of the report *Nunca más*, which detailed the atrocities perpetrated by the Argentine **military** against the civilian population.

SÁBATO COMMISSION. *See* COMISIÓN NACIONAL SOBRE LA DESAPARICIÓN DE PERSONAS (CONADEP).

SAER, JUAN JOSÉ (1937–). Argentine narrator, journalist, scriptwriter, literary critic, and professor of film and Latin American literature. Born in the small town of Serondino, into a working-class family of Syrian immigrants from Damascus. His family moved to Santa Fé, in the littoral of the Paraná River, when Saer was 11. Some of his poems were published in a local newspaper, where he began working as a journalist at age 19. In 1960 he published his first collection of short stories and soon began teaching courses in film and literary criticism at the Instituto de Cinematografía of the Universidad Nacional del Litoral at Santa Fé. In 1968 Saer was awarded a fellowship by the French government to study film. He settled in Paris, where he has lived ever since. He has made annual visits to this native **Argentina** except during the period of the **military** regime. He received the Premio Nadal, awarded by Editorial Nadal in Spain, for his novel *La ocasión* (1968, translated as *The Event* in 1995) and the Prix de Nantes for *El entenado* (1983), judged the best novel in French translation in 1988. He is a professor of Latin American literature at the University of Rennes in France. In 1993 he was a teaching fellow at Princeton University. He is a frequent lecturer on literary topics in the **United States** and Argentina.

Saer is the author of several novels and volumes of short stories centered on the fictional town of Colastine and peopled by a cast of regular characters. He is also the author of several works of literary criticism that examine the literary tradition of the Southern Cone. Saer works associated with the period of the **"dirty war"** are *Nadie nada nunca* (1980, translated as *Nobody Nothing Never* in 1993) and *Glosa* (1986). *Nadie nada nunca* is a haunting story that portrays a string of several killings and mutilations of horses—a crime, unexplained and never solved, that mimics the climate of fear during the political repression. *Glosa* presents two conflicting choices—suicide or **exile**—as the only options open to two young friends in the Argentina of 1978.

His narrative, described by a critic as "rooted . . . in a nonmagical brand of realism almost Balzacian in scope," has also dealt with the power of memory and remembering. In an interview published in English in 1999, Saer is quoted as saying, "there can be no doubt that when we forget, it is not so much a memory we lose as our desire to remember it."

SAINT JEAN, IBÉRICO. Argentine general, governor of Buenos Aires during the first junta, and minister of the interior under the third. In her book *Children of Cain: Violence and the Violent in Latin America*, Tina Rosenberg quotes General Saint Jean as saying, "First, we must kill all subversives, then their sympathizers; then those who are indifferent; and finally, we must kill all those who are timid."

SANGUINETTI, JULIO MARÍA. President of **Uruguay** (1985–1990), the first civilian president following the end of the **military** dictatorship (1973–1985). Representing the Colorado political party, Sanguinetti managed the country's return to democracy and restored civil and **human rights**. He freed all political prisoners within a month of taking office on 1 March 1985. His presidency was weakened, however, by sponsoring an amnesty for military and police officials accused of human rights violations during the dictatorship. About 160 officers were affected by the amnesty. Despite much popular support for bringing officers to trial, a referendum in 1989 upheld the amnesty. Sanguinetti was voted out of office in November of that year, when the Blancos political party, led by Luis Alberto Lacalle, returned to power for the first time in 23 years.

SANTUCHO, MARIO ROBERTO ("ROBI") (1936–1976). Leader of the **Ejército Revolucionario del Pueblo** (ERP, People's Revolutionary Army), a **guerrilla** movement in **Argentina**. Santucho was born into a large, prosperous family in the city of Santiago del Estero. He became interested in political ideas as an adolescent, having grown up in a household accustomed to debate. In the late 1950s he studied accounting at the University of Tucumán, and became active in student politics. In 1961 he spent several months in Cuba, for whose socialist revolution he had already declared his support. While there, he received guerrilla training. In July 1961, during his absence, his brothers Francisco René and Oscar Asdrubal founded the Frente Revolucionario Indoamericano Popular (FRIP, Indo-American Popular Revolutionary Front). On his return, Santucho envisioned FRIP as the beginning of a revolutionary party. He began to recruit members in Tucumán province, where he was working as an accountant for the sugar workers' union. The workers were receptive to his message—the local economy was dependent on sugar subsidies, which the federal government continually threatened to cut off. Santucho was active in the union's many protests. In 1965 FRIP merged with Palabra Obrera (PO, Workers' Word), a Trotskyist party, to form the Partido Revolucionario de los Trabajadores (PRT, Workers' Revolutionary Party). The PO had been embroiled in an internal dispute over whether to engage in armed conflict. The dispute continued after the merger. Nahuel Moreno, the PO leader, opposed guerrilla warfare; Santucho—urged on by his friends Luis Pujals and Enrique Gorriarán Merlo—promoted it. In January 1968 Moreno was forced out, and Santucho, now head of the PRT, set the organization on a revolutionary course. The ERP, the armed branch of the PRT, was established in 1970.

Over the next four years, Santucho led an urban guerrilla campaign of bank robberies, kidnappings, and assassinations. In 1974, frustrated by the ERP's inability to win the support of urban workers, Santucho set up a rural front in Tucumán province. By then, the sugar industry had collapsed, and the many unemployed were eager to support a revolutionary cause. The rural front was defeated a year later, when President **Isabel Perón** sent in the army. By mid-1976 (four months after the coup that ushered in the **"dirty war"**), the ERP was in ruins, and Santucho was prepared to go to Cuba. In July, however, the army mounted a surprise attack on a house where he was to meet with other guerrilla leaders, including the **Montonero** chief Mario Firmenich. Santucho died in the resulting gunfight.

SCHOOL OF THE AMERICAS. *See* UNITED STATES.

SCILINGO, ADOLFO FRANCISCO. Navy captain and member of the notorious **Escuela Mecánica de la Armada** (ESMA, Navy Mechanics School) during the **"dirty war"** in **Argentina**. Ending almost 20 years of silence, Scilingo confessed to participating in the disappearance of political prisoners. He said that from 1976 to 1983, thousands of prisoners were thrown alive into the Atlantic Ocean from navy aircraft after being stripped, drugged, and weighted down. His story is told in a book, *El vuelo*, by the writer and **human rights** activist **Horacio Ver-**

bitsky. Published in 1995, *El vuelo* was translated in 1996 as *The Flight: Confessions of an Argentine Dirty Warrior.*

SEBASTIÁN ACEVEDO MOVEMENT AGAINST TORTURE. *See* MOVIMIENTO CONTRA LA TORTURA SEBASTIÁN ACEVEDO.

SEINELDÍN, MOHAMMED ALÍ. *See CARAPINTADAS.*

SEMANA SANTA. See CARAPINTADAS.

SENDIC ANTONACCIO, RAÚL (c. 1925–1989). Founder of the **Tupamaros**, a leftist **guerrilla** movement in **Uruguay**. Sendic Antonaccio dropped out of law school in the late 1950s to become an activist among sugar workers in the northern province of Artigas. In 1963 he founded the Tupamaros, who made their public appearance in 1967 and began a campaign of bombings, robberies, and kidnappings against the **military** and police. First captured in 1970, he led a prison breakout a year later, freeing himself and 105 other guerrillas. He was captured again in September 1972. After his release in 1985 under an amnesty announced by the civilian government of President **Julio María Sanguinetti**, Sendic Antonaccio remade the Tupamaros into a legal political party. His health declined rapidly, however, from the **torture** and other harsh treatment he suffered during his 14 years as a political prisoner. He died on 27 April 1989.

SERVICIO ECUMÉNICO DE REINTEGRACIÓN (SER) / ECUMENICAL SERVICE FOR REINTEGRATION. A **human rights** nongovernmental organization in **Uruguay**. Founded by church groups in 1984, SER provided material, psychological, and social assistance to those released from prison and returning from **exile**. In 1990 SER became the Servicio Ecuménico por la Dignidad Humana (SEDHU, Ecumenical Service for Human Dignity), an organization involved in rural development and in assistance to poor immigrants.

SERVICIO ECUMÉNICO POR LA DIGNIDAD HUMANA. *See* SERVICIO ECUMÉNICO DE REINTEGRACIÓN (SER).

SERVICIO PAZ Y JUSTICIA (SERPAJ) / PEACE AND JUSTICE SERVICE. A pan-Latin American **human rights** organization founded in 1971. Since 1974, it has been led by **Adolfo Pérez Esquivel**, an Argentine and winner of the Nobel Peace Prize. Although committed to social justice and **liberation theology**, SERPAJ is ecumenical and not affiliated with any church. It has branches in **Argentina, Chile, Uruguay**, and other countries of Latin America. During the years of **military** rule, SERPAJ-Argentina provided material and legal support to the victims of state violence, especially the poor. SERPAJ-Chile, founded in 1977, concentrated on organizing at the grassroots level, promoting nonviolent action through workshops and seminars, neighborhood groups, and networks. Its efforts helped form the **Movimiento contra la Tortura Sebastián Acevedo** (Sebastián Acevedo Movement against Torture). SERPAJ-Uruguay, founded in 1981, gained international attention for promoting human rights throughout the region. Although closed by the military in 1983, SERPAJ-Uruguay continued its work, helping to form other human rights groups and participating in the **Concertación Nacional Programática** (CONAPRO), a 1984 joint party agreement calling for truth and justice upon the country's return to democratic rule. The promise of CONAPRO was never fulfilled—President **Julio María Sanguinetti** did not sign it. Nevertheless, SERPAJ-Uruguay joined with the **Instituto de Estudios Legales y Sociales** (IELSUR), another Uruguayan human rights group, to produce the report *Uruguay nunca más* (1989), an account human rights violations committed from 1972 to 1985.

SILVA HENRÍQUEZ, RAÚL. *See* CATHOLIC CHURCH; COMITÉ DE LA PAZ (COPACHI); VICARÍA DE LA SOLIDARIDAD.

SUÁREZ MASÓN, CARLOS. Also known as *Pajarito* (Birdie) and *El Cacique* (Chief). **Argentine** general and commander of the First Army Corps in Buenos Aires. He was a hardliner during the repression, and wanted the **military** to hold power indefinitely. After the return to civilian rule, he fled to California to escape prosecution, but was discovered in 1987 and extradited to Argentina. Convicted of **human rights** crimes, he was released in October 1989 in a blanket pardon declared by President **Carlos Saúl Menem**.

SUPREME COURT OF JUSTICE (CHILE). Also known as the High Court. The Supreme Court and the courts of appeals are composed of justices and prosecutors appointed by the president. The court prepares the list of nominees from which the president makes a selection. During the **military** dictatorship, **Augusto Pinochet Ugarte** packed the court with conservatives, and the **constitution of 1981** made his appointments unimpeachable. The court thus remained loyal to the military after the country returned to democracy in 1990.

–T–

TERUGGI, FRANK, JR. *See* CHARLES HORMAN.

THEBERGE, JAMES. A career diplomat with experience in Latin America, Theberge was appointed by President **Ronald Reagan** to serve as **United States** ambassador to **Chile** in 1982. While under service in Chile, Theberge developed such a strong association with the **military** government of General **Augusto Pinochet Ugarte** that he was widely referred to as the junta's "fifth man." In 1986 Ambassador Theberge was replaced by **Harry Barnes**, a man who shared the U.S. government's growing receptivity to the idea of redemocratization in Chile and other South American countries. Barnes, in turn, would become a hated figure of the military dictatorship.

TIMERMAN, JACOBO (1923–1999). Argentine journalist. Born in the Ukraine, he fled with his family to **Argentina** in 1928 to escape persecution against Jews. In his 20s Timerman began work as a journalist in Buenos Aires for publications such as *El Mundo* and *La Nación*. Censured during the regime of **Juan Perón**, he worked then for the Agence France Press. He first achieved professional success in 1962 with the publication of *Primera Plana*, a weekly news magazine inspired by U.S. models. In 1971 he founded *La Opinión*, a newspaper in the style of the French *Le Monde*. During the period of the **"dirty war,"** *La Opinión* became one of the strongest critics of the **military** dictatorship. It campaigned against arrests and disappearances, publishing in its pages the habeas corpus brought to the courts by the families of the missing (*desaparecidos*). After numerous anonymous death threats to Timerman and the bombing of his house and the editorial offices of the newspaper, he was arrested in 1977 by military intelligence agents under the command of General **Ramón Juan Alberto Camps**. While in military custody, Timerman was repeatedly **tortured** and held incommunicado. Upon his release, he was held under house arrest for two years. Soon after, he was stripped of his citizenship and property and put aboard a plane to Israel.

Timerman returned to Argentina in 1984 and became editor of the newspaper *La Razón*. In 1988, then presidential candidate **Carlos Saúl**

Menem sued Timerman for libel and defamation. He was acquitted following two separate trials, but the charges were not finally dropped until 1996, following Timerman's flight to **Uruguay** and an international outcry. An outspoken and at times controversial figure in Latin American journalism, Timerman was a founding member of the press freedom group Asociación para la Defensa del Periodismo Independiente. In 1981 he received the Maria Moors Cabot journalism award by Columbia University in New York.

His best-known work is *Prisoner without a Name, Cell without a Number* (1980), an account of his imprisonment and the abuses of the military dictatorship. A controversial screen version of this work—the screenwriter asked that his name be removed from the credits—was filmed in 1983 by the director Linda Yellen as *Jacobo Timerman: Prisoner without a Name, Cell without a Number*. Timerman is also the author of *Chile: Death in the South* (1987), where he provides testimony from prisoners of the regime of **Augusto Pinochet Ugarte** in **Chile**. *See also* ANTI-SEMITISM.

TODOS POR LA PATRIA (TPP). *See* MOVIMIENTO TODOS POR LA PATRIA.

TORTURE. Those abducted by the **military** and security forces during the **"dirty wars"** were routinely subjected to torture, both physical and psychological. Common methods of physical torture were beatings, electric shocks to sensitive areas of the body, repeated submersion, sexual violation, and prolonged suspension. Methods of psychological torture included threats, insults, humiliation, and mock executions. Among the thousands who suffered torture were the journalist **Jacobo Timerman**, in **Argentina**, and the **guerrilla** leader **Raúl Sendic Antonaccio**, in **Uruguay**.

Torturers were generally members of the military and police. Each of the service branches and police organizations had its own intelligence operation, and courses on torture were often included in counterinsurgency training. In 1974 a secret police organization appeared in **Chile**, the **Dirección de Inteligencia Nacional** (DINA, Directorate of National Intelligence), which drew not only from the military and police but also from civilian extremist groups. After the return to democracy, torturers largely escaped punishment, the beneficiaries of amnesty laws protecting the police and military from prosecution. In Argentina the law *Obediencia debida* (Due Obedience) exempted all but the most senior officers from facing charges for **human rights** violations.

The most infamous torture site in Argentina was the **Escuela Mecánica de la Armada** (ESMA, Navy Mecanics School), in Buenos Aires. In Chile DINA operated out of a number of places around Santiago, including **Villa Grimaldi** and Londres 38. In Uruguay a torture site often recalled is 300 Karl (named for 300 Karl Marx, a military operation directed at members of the Communist Party). Housed in an army base, 300 Karl was referred to by both prisoners and jailers alike as *el infierno* (hell).

Although torture was often used to extract information from prisoners—new suspects were kidnapped because their names were spoken during interrogation sessions—gathering information seems not to have been the primary aim. Indeed, health professionals who specialize in treating torture victims say that information extracted by torture is often unreliable—victims report having blurted out anything they thought might satisfy their tormentors. Instead, specialists say, the primary aim of torture is to dominate victims by breaking down their personalities and destroying their identities and self-esteem. Many torture victims suffer from depression, guilt, and powerlessness. Many fear authority figures, mistrust strangers, and have difficulty holding on to jobs. They often experience sleeplessness, flashbacks, and nightmares. Some turn to drugs and alcohol or commit suicide.

Some victims have received help from nonprofit organizations that have arisen worldwide during the past 20 years to rehabilitate torture survivors. Today there are more than 200 organizations, about two dozen of them in the **United States**. Not all of the patients are from Latin America; some are from Africa, Asia, and Eastern Europe. Working often on shoestring budgets, volunteer doctors and therapists interview patients gently, listen to their stories, and attempt to treat their physical and psychological wounds. By interacting with others who share similar experiences, patients receive emotional support.

Health professionals agree that societies as well as individuals are affected by torture and need to recover. Since examining a torture-filled past is painful, a lingering concern among these professionals is how long such a process of societal healing will take.

TRADE UNIONS. The history of trade unionism in the Southern Cone is entwined with the history of **communism** in the region. In **Argentina** the **Confederación General del Trabajo** (CGT, General Labor Confederation), an umbrella organization, was under leftist control before becoming the backbone of the **Peronist** movement during the 1940s. The CGT's counterpart in **Chile** was the Central Única de Trabajadores

(CUT, Unified Workers' Central), dominated by the **Partido Comunista** (PC, Communist Party) and the **Partido Socialista** (PS, Socialist Party). In **Uruguay** the Convención Nacional de Trabajadores (CNT, National Convention of Workers) was under communist leadership.

Though radical in origin, unions in these countries had reached an understanding with the mainstream political parties by the 1930s or 1940s. Unions bargained with the state rather than with individual employers, and workers benefited from welfare reforms and from economies based on manufacturing for domestic consumption. In Argentina **Juan Perón** forged a relationship between industry and labor, incorporating both within his movement. In Chile and Uruguay, leftists controlled unions but not national politics, and workers looked to centrist parties to satisfy their demands.

In the 1960s these arrangements began to unravel. As economies slumped, states could no longer reconcile the competing interests of labor and industry. Class conflict emerged, exacerbated by the effects of the Cuban Revolution, which led younger workers to reject reformism and embrace radicalism. In Argentina left-wing followers of Perón began to see Peronism as a means of achieving socialism. In Chile the Marxist **Salvador Allende Gossens**, following three failed presidential attempts, captured the presidency in 1970. And in Uruguay the leftist coalition Frente Amplio (FA, Broad Front) emerged to challenge the traditional Colorado (Red) and Blanco (White) parties.

Socialist aspirations in these countries contributed to the social unrest that provoked **military** coups in the 1970s. In the repression that followed, trade unionists were often targeted—especially leaders and radical members. Having silenced labor, the military governments proceded to institute free-market economic reforms such as those recommended by the **Chicago Boys** in Chile. By the early 1980s, however, unions began to recover, working with international organizations, **human rights** groups, and political parties to create pressure for a return to democracy. Yet labor was by no means homogeneous, and some unionists chose to negotiate with the military regimes.

With the return to democracy in the region, trade unions were inclined to be more moderate and reformist than they had been before military rule, having become less anticapitalist and more antidictatorship.

TRIPLE A. *See* ALIANZA ANTICOMUNISTA ARGENTINA (AAA).

TUPAMAROS. The popular name for the Movimiento de Liberación Nacional (MLN, Movement for National Liberation), an urban **guerrilla** organization active in **Uruguay** in the 1960s and 1970s. The name is a contraction of Tupac Amaro (the organization's spelling of Tupac Amaru [José Gabriel Condorcanqui]), the Inca who in 1780–1781 led a revolt against the Spanish in Peru. The Tupamaros were a colorful group, earning a reputation for carrying out operations with precision and panache. Although often described as a middle-class movement (reflecting Uruguay itself), they recruited men and women from all classes and sectors of society. Recruiting took place within networks of family and friends, each recruit known to someone already in the movement. As a further precaution against betrayal and leaks of information, the movement (below the executive level) was divided into columns, which, in turn, were divided into cells. Each column was a replica of the movement as a whole.

The movement's origins can be traced to 31 July 1963, when a group of leftists raided the Swiss Rifle Club in Colonia, a town 80 miles from Montevideo. At the center of the group was a band of Socialists led by **Raúl Sendic Antonaccio**, a former law student who had organized sugar workers in northern Uruguay. But the group also attracted leftists of other persuasions (Anarchists, Maoists, Trotskyists)—all committed to bringing about change through armed insurrection. The guerrillas spent several years in preparation—recruiting and training, gathering weapons, and establishing safe houses. In 1965 they adopted the name Movimiento de Liberación Nacional (Tupamaros) and in 1967—following some premature encounters with the police—published their first communiqué, declaring themselves outside the law.

Their first two years of public activity are often described as their "Robin Hood" period, in which they attracted attention to themselves and discredited the government rather than attack the government head on. In 1969 they made a leap to another level of guerrilla warfare, seizing the town of Pando on 8 October. When it was learned that captured guerrillas were being tortured by the police, the Tupamaros responded by assassinating the torturers. On 31 July 1970 the Tupamaros made an international statement by abducting Daniel Mitrione, a USAID police advisor whom they accused of being a **Central Intelligence Agency** (CIA) member and **torture** instructor. They demanded as ransom the release of 150 political prisoners. As the government was about to give in, the police captured several Tupamaro leaders in the process of planning their next move. The government broke off negotiations, thinking it had gained the upper hand. On 8 August 1970 Mitrione was found dead.

After the Mitrione killing, the Tupamaros—who until then had enjoyed much public support—lost some of their mystique. They also lost many of their members to capture. They were far from defeated, however, conducting an enormous bank heist in November 1970 and kidnapping British Ambassador Sir Geoffrey Jackson in January 1971. On 9 September Sendic Antonaccio (captured the year before) led 105 other Tupamaros in a daring escape from Punta Carretas Prison, tunneling to a nearby house. They conducted the operation with Tupamaro flair: a sign left in the tunnel read, "Movement for National Liberation Transit Authority—Please keep to your left." The organization, triumphant, released Sir Geoffrey unharmed. The government, embarrassed, put antiguerrilla operations in control of the **military**. The Tupamaros, however, had called a truce, having decided to support a leftist coalition—the Frente Amplio (Broad Front)—in the election scheduled for November 1971. After **Juan María Bordaberry**, a staunch conservative, won the presidency in a controversial election, they ended their truce, assaulting and abducting police officers suspected of participating in **death squads** during the election period. On 14 April 1972 they assassinated four government officials in Montevideo, provoking the government to declare a "state of internal war" (martial law). The military seized the opportunity to escalate its counterinsurgency campaign, and by the end of the year the Tupamaros were crushed. Guerrilla hideouts were discovered, scores of prisoners rounded up, weapons captured, and "people's prisons" liberated. In September 1972 Sendic Antonaccio was shot in the face during a gun battle and recaptured.

In 1973 the military took control of the weakened government and held power for 12 years. When civilian rule returned in March 1985, the Tupamaros and other political prisoners were released under an amnesty. Sendic Antonaccio remade the Tupamaros into a legal political party, which joined the Frente Amplio. In February 1987 they began a campaign—joined by **trade unions**, **human rights** organizations, and other leftist political parties—to force a referendum on whether to overturn an amnesty that had been granted to the police and military in December 1996. The issue was put to a vote in 1989, and the amnesty law was upheld.

The actions of the Tupamaro guerrillas—especially the Mitrione killing—were the subject of the **Costa-Gavras** film *State of Siege* and the novel *El color que el infierno me escondiera* (published in English as *El infierno*), by Carlos Martínez Moreno.

–U–

UNIDAD POPULAR (UP) / POPULAR UNITY. A coalition of five leftist political parties in **Chile**, including the **Partido Comunista** (PC, **Communist** Party) and the **Partido Socialista** (PS, Socialist Party). Formed in 1969, the UP helped elect **Salvador Allende Gossens** to the presidency in 1970. The UP enjoyed the broad support of the Chilean working class, many of whom were urban workers who had been traditionally excluded from the democratic process. UP leader Salvador Allende Gossens presented a party platform advocating reform, not revolution—a "peaceful road" toward a democratically based socialist government.

Once in office, the UP tried to fulfill its main objective of redistributing wealth and power. Its program was vigorously opposed by the right and center party representatives in the legislature, particulary the Christian Democrats, and by the upper and middle classes. Attempts to circumvent the opposition resulted in economic and social chaos. In the end, the UP fell victim to elements from both inside and outside the country. Protests were organized by conservative women's groups, professional guilds (*gremios*), and business and landowners associations. Meanwhile, through economic blockades and political conspiracies, the **United States**, under the administration of President Richard Nixon, sought to destabilize the economy and discredit the government. The UP was overthrown in a coup led by General **Augusto Pinochet Ugarte** on 11 September 1973.

UNIÓN CÍVICA RADICAL (UCR) / RADICAL CIVIC UNION. A centrist, primarily middle-class political party in **Argentina**. By no means radical in the sense that the word is usually understood in Anglo-American politics, the UCR is committed to the rule of law. President **Raúl Alfonsín** (1983–1989), representing the UCR, oversaw the country's transition to democratic rule. *See also* PERONISM.

UNITED NATIONS. The UN Charter, drawn up in 1945 in the wake of the Holocaust, committed the organization and its members to the protection of **human rights**. The Universal Declaration of Human Rights, adopted by the UN General Assembly on 10 December 1948, recognized two categories. Civil and political rights include freedom from arbitrary arrest (Article 9) and freedom from torture (Article 5); economic, social, and cultural rights include the right to an adequate standard of living for individuals and their families (Article 25). When the

Declaration was first adopted, there was not enough agreement among members to make it legally binding. Later, however, the two categories of rights were separated into two documents: The International Covenant on Civil and Political Rights came into effect on 23 March 1976; the International Covenant on Economic, Social and Cultural Rights came into effect on 3 January 1976.

The UN established agencies and procedures to address human rights concerns. Primary responsibility fell to the Human Rights Commission (UNHRC) and its Sub-Commission on Prevention of Discrimination and Protection of Minorities (renamed in 1999 the Sub-Commission on Discrimination and Protection of Human Rights). One difficulty lay in deciding how to protect human rights without interfering in the domestic affairs of a nation—interference was prohibited by the charter. For many years, there was no procedure in place for acting on complaints. In 1967 the UN introduced resolution 1235, which allowed the Commission to review complaints for consistent patterns of "gross violations." In 1970 a new resolution, 1503, took the procedure a step further, allowing for the preparation of a confidential blacklist of offending governments. Under 1503, complaints received by the UN would first undergo a general review. Those revealing a consistent pattern would be passed on to a group of five subcommissioners, who would compile a preliminary blacklist. After being voted on by the full subommission, the list would go to the commission, where a similar process took place. Blacklisted governments would first be reprimanded in private. If they did not improve, the procedure called for them to be reprimanded in public. The offending governments, however, were themselves members of the UN and went to considerable efforts to avoid censure; hence the importance within the UN of international nongovernmental organizations (NGOs) such as **Amnesty International** (AI) and the **International Commission of Jurists** (ICJ). Free of governmental constraints, NGOs documented human rights abuses and issued reports suggesting the actual scope of the problem. Still, the NGOs had to abide by strict rules. In order to participate in the UN—to speak at meetings and distribute documents—they had to become accredited, proving their financial independence and promising to refrain from "politically motivated" attacks on governments.

This was the context in the 1970s in which the UN examined human rights situations in **Argentina**, **Chile**, and **Uruguay**.

Argentina

After the **military** coup of March 1976, Gabriel Martínez, Argentina's ambassador to the UN, turned his attention from trade (his specialty) to the defense of the junta's human rights record. As early as August 1976, the UN subcommission, meeting in Geneva, drafted a resolution in behalf of two thousand political refugees—mostly leftists—who had escaped military regimes in their own countries and were now at risk in Argentina. The resolution had been prompted by the deaths of Héctor Gutiérrez Ruiz and Zelmar Michelina, Uruguayan legislators who disappeared in Buenos Aires in May. The resolution passed despite Martínez's objections, and Argentina was well on its way to making the blacklist.

The case against the junta began to build. In November a team from AI went on a fact-finding mission to Argentina. The team's report, published on 23 March 1977 (on the eve of the first anniversary of the coup), contained a clear record of political abductions and won AI the Nobel Peace Prize for 1977. The junta, however, took the offensive. It accused four NGOs of making politically motivated attacks, citing a long-neglected UN rule requiring NGOs to renew their accreditation, or consultative status, every four years. The UN called a special meeting early in 1978 to consider the charge. Nothing definitive came out of the meeting, but Martínez claimed victory, noting that from then on the NGOs would have to act with more caution. Meanwhile, in 1977, Argentina had avoided the preliminary blacklist by the narrowest of margins. Given a year's reprieve, Martínez set out to pack the subcommission, his own role on the commission being limited to that of observer. In 1978 he engineered the election of Mario Amadeo, a fellow Argentine, and the defeat of several of Argentina's most vocal critics. Martínez's efforts paid off for the junta. When Argentina made the preliminary list in 1978 and the case advanced to the full subcommission, Amadeo asked for one more year, arguing that the abductions had ceased and that the government needed more time to examine individual complaints. The subcommission voted to spare the junta once again.

The junta's reprieve was short-lived. On 20 December 1978 the UN General Assembly passed a resolution condemning disappearances (*desaparecidos*), citing excesses committed by police and security forces. The resolution did not mention any country, but was clearly aimed at Argentina. An even stronger statement—this time naming Argentina—came in February 1979 at the session of the UNHRC in Geneva. Delegates from Western Europe and North America proposed that complaints about disappearances be collected and analyzed by the secretary general. The proposal carried a strong threat of establishing a working group like the one sent to Chile. Martínez answered the threat using a variety of methods. He drafted an alternative proposal, lobbied Socialist and non-Western delegates for support, filibustered, and at a crucial moment in the negotiations walked out of a UNHRC meeting. The issue was tabled until the 1980 session.

For three years Martínez had managed to keep Argentina off the blacklist. In 1979 he conceived a plan to buy even more time. He decided to stop fighting the inevitable and to allow the blacklisting, knowing that the case would be kept confidential for a year. Both the five subcommissioners and the full subcommission voted to forward the name of Argentina on to the UNHRC, which would meet the following February. On 28 January 1980 Martínez appeared before a group of five Commission delegates and presented a 92-page response to concerns raised at the 1979 session of the UNHRC. The delegates found the response lacking and put tough questions to Martínez. The implication was that a failure to answer the questions would open the case to the public the following year. The next month, at the UNHRC meeting, Jerome Shestack, the delegate from the **United States** and a **Jimmy Carter** appointee, maintained the tough line of questioning despite the Carter administration's softened stance toward Argentina. His efforts earned him a rebuff from the State Department, but moved the case of Argentina forward at the UN. The French renewed the call for a working group on disappearances in response to the 1977 abduction and murder of two French nuns who had been working with the **Madres de Plaza de Mayo** (Mothers of the Plaza de Mayo).

Martínez was in retreat—so much so that in August 1980 an Argentine foreign ministry official advised the junta to put an end to the disappearances and return the country to civilian rule. Meanwhile, the UN formed the Working Group on Disappearances and, over the objections of Martínez, authorized it to intervene in behalf of individuals and to collect information from nonaccredited NGOs, a category that would include most of the NGOs in Argentina. The junta received a public reprimand in December 1980 when the UN working group released its report on disappearances (the group had visited Argentina in October). By then, however, **Ronald Reagan** had been elected president, and the junta gained renewed life.

Chile

In 1975 the UN established a working group to visit Chile. It was not until July 1978, however, that the regime of **Augusto Pinochet Ugarte** allowed a visit to take place. The group, led by Theo van Boven, the director of the Human Rights Division of the UN, met with Pinochet Ugarte, with former democratically elected Chilean presidents, and with relatives of people who disappeared. It visited prisons as well, including **Villa Grimaldi**, a detention center where the **Dirección de Inteligencia Nacional** (DINA, Directorate of National Intelligence), the secret police, once tortured its prisoners. Although Chilean officials denied that the villa had been put to that use—it was now an officers' club—prisoners previously held there convinced team members of its former porpose. Many believe that Pinochet Ugarte permitted the visit in the hope of being rewarded for his cooperation. After all, Chile was the first country to allow a human rights investigation by the UN. The group's report, however, provided a comprehensive look at the human rights situation in Chile, covering not only **torture** and disappearance but also such issues as health care, unemployment, child welfare, and labor laws. Although Pinochet Ugarte argued that the group had overstepped its bounds, the visit helped direct the attention of van Boven—and the UN—to Latin America in general.

Uruguay

Uruguay was placed on the UNHRC confidential blacklist in 1976. For three years, however, the case was kept under review without any improvement in the country's human rights record. The commission's failure to make the case public during that period is attributed to the personality of its Uruguayan delegate, Carlos Giumbruno, whose emotional displays in defense of his country were effective and mistaken for cooperation. In 1979 the commission, faced with a decision, opted to send an envoy to Uruguay. UN Secretary General Kurt Waldheim appointed for this task the Peruvian-born Javier Pérez de Cuéllar, an experienced diplomat, the current undersecretary general for political affairs, and the future secretary general.

Pérez de Cuéllar traveled to Montevideo in December 1979, accompanied by Carlos Giumbruno. His 1980 report, sympathetic with the military regime, was leaked, and proved embarrassing to the UN. Its conclusions—that prison conditions were reasonable and that no one was imprisoned because of his or her ideas—were flatly contradicted by those of another report, also leaked, issued about the same time by the Red Cross. The commission, which could neither reject the report of its own envoy nor embrace its findings, decided to keep the case of Uruguay under review and to ask Secretary General Waldheim to make additional efforts the following year. *See also* ORGANIZATION OF AMERICAN STATES.

UNITED STATES. U.S. involvement in the **"dirty wars"** can be traced to the advent of the Cold War. From the 1950s onward, the United States trained thousands of Latin American **military** students at its School of the Americas (at such locations as the Panama Canal Zone and Fort Benning in Columbus, Georgia) and other army facilities like the **Inter-American Defense College** (IADC) at Fort Lesley J. McNair in Washington, D.C. In the absence of any external threat, the primary concern of this military cooperation was to combat communist subversion, the fear of which became more pronounced after Fidel Castro came to power in Cuba in 1959. Students at the U.S. facilities were trained in counterinsurgency and anticommunism and were immersed in North American culture and values. Some were groomed for leadership: the IADC curriculum included courses in financial management, communications, and international finance. The result was the creation in each country of a military that equated its interests with those of the United States and could be expected to maintain stability. Among the graduates of the IADC, for example, were Admiral **Emilio Massera** of **Argentina** and General **Gustavo Leigh Guzmán** of **Chile**, both of whom were members of ruling juntas, and General José Cardozo of Uruguay, who headed the antisubversives board. This military cross-fertilization—Argentina drew also upon the advice of French officers who had fought in Algeria—led to a rethinking of the primary role of the armed forces in Latin America. War, it was argued, was no longer against external forces but against internal "subversives." The new enemy did not line up across a battlefield but blended in with everyday society. An unconventional enemy called for unconventional warfare; the enemy, therefore, had to be rooted out, even in disregard of internationally recognized **human rights**.

Although the United States supported the 1948 Universal Declaration of Human Rights, for much of the Cold War the country's foreign policy ignored or paid little attention to human rights. During the administration of President Dwight D. Eisenhower (1953–1961), Secretary of State John Foster Dulles equated the support of human rights with the containment of Soviet-led communism. The short-lived administration of John F. Kennedy (1961–1963) continued the anticommunist approach to policy. To that end, it unveiled the Alliance for Progress, a program aimed at promoting economic development and rescuing people from poverty and repression. The assumption was that flourishing economies were the best defense against communist aggression. A bureaucracy was needed to administer U.S. assistance, and the Agency for International Development (AID) was created. The problem was how to keep communism away until prosperity took hold. The answer was to use military aid to bolster countries' national security. Out of this concern arose the **guerrilla**-fighting U.S. Army Special Forces (Green Berets) and a wide range of military support to Latin American and other countries—advisors, engineers, and increased training.

When Kennedy was assassinated in 1963, optimism died with him. Under the administrations of Presidents Lyndon Johnson, Richard Nixon, and Gerald Ford, foreign policy settled into maintaining the status quo. During the Johnson years (1963–1969), an increasing number of AID personnel received military training, and a large share of the economic aid budget for Latin America went for counterinsurgency training. During the Nixon years (1969–1974), human rights—secondary considerations under Kennedy and Johnson—were devalued even further. Nixon's secretary of state, **Henry Kissinger**, made no secret of his belief that human rights often interfered with other foreign-policy objectives.

In the early 1970s, political fallout from the Vietnam War and the Watergate scandal led to a questioning of a foreign policy preoccupied with anticommunism and the status quo. The impetus came from Congress, especially the efforts of Representative Donald M. Fraser, whose Subcommittee on International Organizations and Movements of the Committee of Foreign Affairs conducted a series of human rights hearings beginning in 1973. As the hearings continued over the next three years, the countries of the Southern Cone fell under scrutiny. Congress was outraged by what it heard to the point of legislating against continued assistance. Congress had been especially shocked by growing evidence of U.S. involvement in the overthrow of **Salvador Allende Gossens's** elected government in **Chile**. The administration of President **Jimmy Carter** (1977–1981) built on congressional efforts and gave the issue of human rights an independent status, separating it from what Carter called America's "inordinate" fear of communism. The enforcement of his human rights policy, however, was inconsistent. Even in the Southern Cone, where administration pressure was credited with saving many lives, the policy succumbed to pragmatism over time.

With the administration of President **Ronald Reagan** (1981–1989), Cold War policy returned. The protection of human rights was once again reduced to the fight against communism. Leading the attack on Carter's human rights record was **Jeane Kirkpatrick**, the U.S. ambassador to the UN. By the beginning of Reagan's second term, however, Kirkpatrick's ideas had fallen out of favor. Overlooking human rights abuses committed by anticommunist allies was seen as counterproductive, since repression often provokes unrest. In Chile, the Reagan administration feared a resurgence of the left, and began to persuade the military regime to move the country toward democracy.

URUGUAY (1973–1985). Uruguay, like **Chile**, fell under **military** control in 1973. Until then, both countries had been admired for their strong democratic institutions—Uruguay having earned such nicknames as "the Switzerland of America" and "the Sweden of the South." Unlike Chile and **Argentina**, however, whose transitions to military rule occurred suddenly on dates etched in collective memory, Uruguay's descent into dictatorship was long and drawn out. Another important difference is that whereas fewer people died in Uruguay than in either Chile or Argentina, Uruguay had a larger percentage of political prisoners—more per capita than in any other country in the world. One out of every 500 prisoners was a victim of **torture**. Under military rule, the once "Switzerland of America" was transformed into what **Eduardo Galeano** would call "a vast torture chamber."

Background to the "Dirty War"

Two political parties have dominated Uruguayan politics for most of the country's history, emerging out of a power struggle following Uruguay's declaration of independence in 1825. In April of that year 33 Uruguayan **exiles** crossed the river from Argentina and regained control of their homeland, which had been annexed by Brazil five years before. A treaty signed in 1828 between Argentina and Brazil (brokered by England) established the buffer state known as the República Oriental del Uruguay (taking its name from its location on the east side of the Uruguay River). One of the leaders of the "treinta y tres orientales" (the "Thirty-Three Immortals," or "Thirty-Three Easterners") was General José Fructuoso Rivera, who, following the adoption of a constitution in 1830, became the country's first president. He was succeeded in the presidency in 1835 by General Manuel Oribe, another leader of the "treinta y tres." Rivera, however, staged an armed revolt, defeating

Oribe and his supporters in 1838 and reestablishing himself as president. The two sides set themselves apart by the color of their flags and hatbands. Rivera's forces, whose political sympathies were urban and liberal, were the Colorados (Reds); Oribe's forces, rural and conservative, were the Blancos (Whites, later becoming the Partido Nacional, or National Party). Rivera's recapturing of the presidency touched off more than a decade of civil war, the Guerra Grande (Great War), which ended in 1852 with the defeat of the Blancos along with their Argentine allies. Out of these warring bands rose the Colorado and Blanco political parties.

Over the next 10 years the two parties traded political power, but in 1865 the Colorados gained the upper hand, capturing the presidency in a rebellion and retaining control of the country until 1958. Still, the remainder of the 19th century was characterized by political unrest—governments were racked with assassination, infighting, and revolt. Instability also marked the first years of the 20th century. The election in 1903 of the reformer José Batlle y Ordóñez ignited a civil war a year later with those Blanco leaders opposed to his plans to unite the country under a strong federal government. The Colorados quickly won the war, creating a political stability that would last into the 1960s. During his two terms in office (1903–1907 and 1911–1915), Batlle y Ordóñez transformed the country into a welfare state, enacting labor reforms such as the eight-hour workday, the right to strike, and workmen's compensation. He passed social legislation, legalizing divorce and advancing the rights of women. And he brought the economy under government control by nationalizing important industries—utilities, banking, insurance, and transportation. The results of his actions and policies were national stability and an increased standard of living.

Despite the dominance of the Colorados, the idea had taken hold toward the end of the 19th century that the two major political parties should share power. This concept of *coparticipación* (coparticipation) was reflected in legislation that allowed minority factions within each party an opportunity to be represented in Congress. Under the "double simultaneous ballot," passed in 1907, each faction fielded its own candidates for office. Votes for individual "lists" contributed to the total number of votes for each party. Since this legislation meant that primary elections and regular elections took place simultaneously, the two parties found themselves fragmented. *Coparticipación* was also reflected in changes at the executive level. Batlle y Ordóñez had originally proposed in 1913 that the executive branch be modeled after the collegial executive of Switzerland's, a system he admired. His proposal called for replacing the office of president with an elected nine-member *Junta de Gobierno*. The suggested reform faced opposition from both the Colorados and the Blancos, the latter seeing it as a ploy by Batlle y Ordóñez to retain political influence after his retirement in 1915, for he could not succeed himself. Compromise with the Blancos, however, created a bicephalous executive instead, which went into effect with a new constitution in 1919. The new system retained the office of the president, but placed alongside it a Consejo Nacional de Adminis-tración (National Council of Administration). The Consejo was com-posed of nine elected members—six from the majority party, three from the minority. The president was principally responsible for for-eign policy, national security, and internal order. The Consejo assumed all other executive functions.

Batllismo (as Batlle y Ordóñez's reformist ideas were called) did not sit well with some sectors of Uruguayan society. Many thought his ideas too far to the left (though there is no evidence that Batlle y Ordóñez was a socialist). As early as 1916 anti-Batllista Colorados had called for an end to social and economic activism. Pro-urban and pro-welfare, Batllismo also exacerbated the longstanding tensions between the liberal capital city of Montevideo and the conservative countryside. Many in this predominantly Catholic country resented Batlle y Ordóñez's atheism, opposing his legalization of divorce and seculariza-tion of education. Nevertheless, the welfare programs already in place—combined with a healthy export economy—maintained political stability throughout most of the 1920s.

In 1929, the death of Batlle y Ordóñez and the start of the Great Depression brought dissension in both parties as well as economic cri-sis. The situation resulted in a coup, the first in Uruguay in the 20th century—the second would come in 1973. The coup took place on 31 March 1933, when the president, Gabriel Terra, dissolved parliament and altered the constitution, abolishing the Consejo and limiting Senate membership to those belonging to the dominant factions of the two par-ties. By 1938, elections were allowed, and by 1942, the changes to the constitution were reversed. Although the period from 1933 to 1942 could be described as a dictatorship, it was a dictatorship of politicians, not of the military. The dictatorial interlude (known as the *dictablanda*, or "soft" dictatorship) was free of torture, execution, and political pris-oners, and there was little censorship. Constitutional rule returned as quietly as it left, bringing with it the civil liberties, distributive policies, and stability that characterized the Batlle y Ordóñez years.

This stability was financed by the robust export economy the country enjoyed during World War II and the Korean War. By the early 1950s Uruguay—then a prosperous, middle-class welfare state—had reached the height of what many consider its golden age. Eager to share in the spoils, the Blancos joined forces with the Colorados in realizing Batlle y Ordóñez's vision of a completely collegial executive. A special incentive for the Blancos was their inability to capture the presidency, a failure largely due to the *ley de lemas* (the law of party titles). The law allowed the factions in each party to pool their votes, the leading candidate in the winning party being awarded the presidency. In the 1950 election, for example, Luis Alberto de Herrera, the leading Blanco, drew 92,000 more votes than any other contestant, but lost the presidency to a Colorado—the Colorado factions together having amassed 433,000 votes to the Blanco's 255,000. A collegial executive guaranteed the Blancos a share of executive power. The constitution of 1952 eliminated the office of president and packed all executive functions into a nine-member Colegiado—six seats for the winning party, three for the runner-up. The new constitution also legitimized a patronage system begun in 1931 by what was jocularly known as the Pacto de Chinchulín (Pork Barrel Pact), which ensured each party a share in public employment.

By the mid-1950s declining exports and a poor domestic economy contributed to a period of economic stagnation that was to play an important role in the coming social unrest and later military intervention. In 1958 the economic crisis, combined with strong antiurban sentiment among ranchers and farmers, helped the Blancos accomplish what had eluded them for 93 years—victory in a national election. It was widely hoped that a change in the majority party would return the country to happier days. What the change actually meant was that the Blancos would be entitled to a larger share of a dwindling amount of patronage. The economy continued to stagnate under new leadership, and although the Blancos won the next presidential election in 1962, they did so by a much smaller margin than in 1958. The Colegiado was widely blamed for the crisis, and people began to clamor for a president—for a strong leader who could take decisive action.

The election of 1966 included a plebiscite that returned the country to a presidential system, abolishing the Colegiado. It created an Office of Planning and Budget and gave the president control over the economy. The election also returned the Colorados to power in the form of a right-wing faction led by Oscar Gestido, a retired general. President Gestido died within a year, and Jorge Pacheco Areco, his vice president, succeeded him. President Pacheco faced a worsening economy, labor unrest, and the exploits of an urban **guerrilla** group called the **Tupamaros**. He used his executive powers to repress opposition, arguing that constitutional liberties had to be sacrificed in the name of internal order. Labor leaders and other activists were arrested, and there were reports of beatings and torture. Many legislators objected to the strong measures, but the threat of military intervention on Pacheco's behalf forced them to back down.

The Tupamaros, officially known as the Movimiento de Liberación Nacional (MLN, Movement for National Liberation), did not back down. They increased their activities in response to the harsh campaign waged against them by Pacheco. Formed in 1963, the Tupamaros spent the first few years carrying out operations of the Robin Hood variety. In 1969, however, they turned to the main task at hand—to undermine the government. Despite taking their guerrilla warfare to the next level, they managed to retain public support until 1970, when they executed Daniel Mitrione. Mitrione, a retired police chief from Muncie, Indiana, was a police advisor provided through the United States Agency for International Development (AID). According to the Tupamaros and others, he was also an agent of the **Central Intelligence Agency** (CIA) and **torture** instructor. Abducted on 31 July, he was found dead on 8 August after the government refused to fulfill the terms of his ransom—the release of all guerrilla prisoners.

The Mitrione killing not only tarnished the Tupamaros' image but escalated the government's campaign against them, an escalation that led to the capture of many guerrillas within the following year. The imprisoned guerrillas responded by staging a dramatic escape on 9 September 1971, freeing 106 of their comrades. The Tupamaros released a prisoner of their own, Sir Geoffrey Jackson, the British ambassador to Uruguay, whom they had abducted eight months earlier. For the government, the prison breakout was embarrassing and came at the worst possible time. Not only was the national election only two months away; it was an election in which the dominant parties faced their first serious challenger, a left-wing coalition endorsed by the Tupamaros.

The Frente Amplio (Broad Front) coalition comprised the Communists, the Christian Democrats, the Socialists, and two leftist factions from the Colorados and Blancos. Although the Frente's presidential candidate, Liber Seregni, a retired general, was not a Marxist, the coalition's leftist platform appealed to the Tupamaros, who participated in the election through a front organization. A Gallup poll in August had predicted a close race among the three major contestants. On election day the Colorados narrowly defeated the Blancos, and both parties gained more than twice as many votes as the Frente. The new Colorado president, a wealthy rancher named **Juan María Bordaberry**, took office on 1 March 1972 for a five-year term. A former member of Pacheco's cabinet, Bordaberry was determined to continue the previous president's campaign against the Tupamaros. But first he had to get past Congress, which objected to the intensity of the campaign. Meanwhile, the Tupamaros ended the informal truce they had called a month before the election. On 14 April 1972 they assassinated several government officials throughout Montevideo. Congress granted Bordaberry's request for a declaration of a "state of internal war"—but only for 30 days. Suspending all constitutional liberties, "internal war" essentially amounted to martial law. Thirty days later, Congress extended the decree for 45 days following much spirited debate. By June the internal war had become so intense that Congress—over the objections of the Frente representatives—extended the decree indefinitely.

The state of internal war meant that the military was in full control of antiguerrilla operations, essentially allowed to combat subversion as it saw fit. By the middle of 1972 the guerrilla movement was in disarray, most of its members either in jail or in exile. The international press reported very few guerrilla casualties (about 30) but many guerrilla prisoners (about 1,600 in August). Charges had began to surface that prisoners were regularly tortured, reports that led the Uruguayan Roman **Catholic Church** in June to issue a 16-point declaration urging a return to peace. Not only did the government ignore the plea to reverse its course toward militarization, but the military, now politicized, began the long process of taking full control of the government.

The "Dirty War": Uruguay under Dictatorship

The coup stretched out over a four-month period. The first step began on 12 February 1973 when officers from the army and air force rebelled against President Bordaberry, insisting that the military be given a voice in setting national policy. Bordaberry was allowed to remain president, but was instructed to create a Consejo de Seguridad Nacional (COSENA, National Security Council), which would be dominated by the military and would oversee policy. Next, the military took aim at Congress. It viewed the body as obstructionist and was especially angered by the refusal of Congress to lift the immunity of Senator Enrique Erro, whom it charged with aiding and abetting the Tupamaros. Erro had also voted for an investigation into the alleged use of torture by the military. On 27 June 1973, Bordaberry, with the support of the military, dissolved Congress and replaced it with a Council of State, which was composed of 25 appointed civilians. He also dissolved the communist-controlled Convención Nacional de Trabajadores (CNT, National Convention of Workers), which had called a general strike to protest the closing of Congress. The CNT, ignoring the order to dissolve, continued to strike. Students joined workers in an angry demonstration that racked Montevideo for two weeks. The police and military finally quashed the uprising, making mass arrests of demonstrators as well as labor and political leaders, among them General Liber Seregni.

With the Tupamaros defeated, Congress closed, and the labor movement destroyed, the military consolidated its rule. It banned leftist political parties, took control of the university and secondary schools, and silenced the press. It then turned its attention to the economy, adopting a free-market approach like that taken by the military government in Brazil. Although the military was now firmly established, Uruguay was still, technically, a *civilian* dictatorship, since a constitutionally elected president remained in office. In June 1976 the military removed this pretense, deposing Bordaberry and suspending national elections. The newly created Council of the Nation (composed of the Council of State and the 21-member Junta of Generals) was charged with appointing the president and formulating general policy. Executive power resided in COSENA (composed of the president, his ministers, and the commanders of the three armed services). Meanwhile, thousands of Uruguayans lost their political rights, forbidden from taking part in political activity or from holding office. This group included those who had been put on trial for political crimes or had participated in the elections of 1966 and 1971 as either office holders or candidates.

In July 1976 the Council of the Nation elected Dr. Aparicio Méndez Manfredini to the presidency for a five-year term. By this time, plans were under way for a gradual return of the country to civilian government—but on the military's terms. Repression, however, continued. **Human rights** groups estimated the number of political prisoners to have reached 6,000. Meanwhile, tens of thousands of Uruguayans had fled the country, many of them academics and artists. In August 1977 the government announced its *cronograma* (timetable), which called for a plebiscite in November 1980 on a constitution drafted by the military. The draft constitution permitted the military to intervene in civilian governments—to suspend constitutional liberties in the name of national security. The draft also severely limited the authority of a legislative body to lift a state of emergency, and allowed for the trying of civilians in military courts. If approved, the new constitution would write into law the extra-legal acts committed by the dictatorship. On 30 November 1980 the constitution was rejected by 57 percent of the voters.

The military, repudiated, settled in for a lengthy negotiation toward civilian rule. In September 1981 General Gregorio Alvarez Armellino became president, and the government announced a new *cronograma*. The plan called for the reorganization of political parties, the drafting of a new constitution by party leaders and the military, a vote on the constitution in a combined plebiscite election in November 1984, and finally the transition to a civilian government on 1 March 1985. The party reorganization, however, was subject to guidelines set down in a law passed by the Council of State on 3 June 1982. The law banned Marxist parties as well as parties that had made up the Frente Amplio in 1971. The only parties allowed were the Colorados, the Blancos, and a Christian-democratic party called Unión Cívica (Civic Union). The election held in November 1982 to determine party leadership delivered another serious blow to the military. Not only did antimilitary candidates win by a landslide; the top vote getter was Wilson Ferreira Aldunate ("Wilson"), a charismatic Blanco leader.

Rebuffed again, the military employed a delaying tactic, not entering into negotiations until well into 1983. But talks with the opposition parties broke down in July over the issue of national security. The military continued to insist on a national security council, which would allow the generals to intervene in a civilian government and to try civilians in military courts. In September the generals banned all political activity, and in late October announced that they would bring a constitution to a vote in November 1984 as scheduled—with or without negotiations. The three legal parties, forming a coalition called the Interpartidaria, responded to this pressure by applying pressure of their own, organizing demonstrations that continued into the following year. The demonstrations were met in turn by continued government force, which added new political prisoners to the hundreds remaining in detention. Popular unrest was increased by a rapidly declining economy—the country in the midst of a deep recession. The labor movement, reorganized, joined the fray. A new (but illegal) confederation, the Plenario Intersindical de Trabajadores (PIT, Interunion Plenary of Workers) supported the demonstrators and applied additional pressure in the form of work stoppages and demands for higher pay. It was also in late 1983 that the opposition gained an important international ally. **Raúl Alson-**

sín, the newly elected president of Argentina, made it clear to Uruguay that it should join his country in a return to civilian rule.

By 1984 the military, politically isolated, was eager for a negotiated exit. In anticipation of the elections scheduled for later that year, it passed a law that restored legal status to all leftist parties except the communists. With this move, the generals were determined to avoid a repeat of the 1983 party election, when leftists, unable to slate their own candidates, cast their votes for Wilson. Political tensions increased on 16 June 1984 when Wilson himself returned to Uruguay after 11 years in exile. He was immediately arrested. When talks resumed in July, the Blancos boycotted negotiations in protest of their jailed leader. The remaining opposition parties, negotiating from a position of strength, won important concessions. Most notably, the military dropped its demand for a national security council in return for representation on an advisory body. Despite these gains, Wilson remained in jail (though he was released five days after the election), and neither he nor Seregni would be allowed to run for office.

The Colorados won a narrow victory in the November 1984 elections, receiving 41 percent of the vote. The Blancos received 35 percent; the Frente Amplio, 22 percent; and Unión Cívica, 2 percent. Each party was awarded a proportional number of seats in a newly installed legislature. The leading Colorado candidate, **Julio María Sanguinetti**, became president. According to schedule, he was inaugurated on .1 March 1985.

The Aftermath of the "Dirty War"

By the end of March 1985, all political prisoners were released under an amnesty law passed by Congress. About 200 prisoners received a general amnesty; the sentences of about 60 other prisoners—those who had participated in assassination and kidnapping—were commuted following reviews by civilian courts. One of those receiving a commuted sentence was **Raúl Sendic Antonaccio**, the founder of the Tupamaros. President Sanguinetti approved of the distinction, arguing that those convicted of violent acts were being released, not out of forgiveness, but in the interest of peace and national reconciliation.

Sanguinetti argued also that national reconciliation should include an amnesty for the military as well. He contended that the guerrillas were chiefly to blame for the politicization of the military. Besides, he pointed out, the number of missing (*desaparecidos*) was much smaller in Uruguay than in Argentina—about 170 as opposed to 9,000–30,000, though allegations of torture numbered in the thousands. (Of the 170 disappeared Uruguayans, about 140 vanished in Argentina, Chile, and Paraguay as part of **Operation Condor**.) In August 1986 the government proposed legislation that would grant an amnesty to all military and police personnel accused of human rights abuses. The opposition parties rejected the draft legislation, but on 22 December approved a revised version (*Punto Final*) that put an end to human rights trials and placed the responsibility for further investigations on the president. The law provoked widespread opposition from human rights groups, torture victims, civil-rights lawyers, center-left political parties, **trade unions**, and students. In February 1987 they began a campaign to collect signatures from 25 percent of the registered voters, the number that the constitution required to force a referendum on legislation. Needing at least 555,701 signatures, they had collected 634,702 by December, despite opposition to the process from the military and elites. It was not until the end of 1988, however, that the electoral court completed its charge of verifying signatures.

The referendum was scheduled for 16 April 1989. Sanguinetti campaigned in favor of the amnesty, arguing that dredging up the past would threaten the country's fragile democracy by provoking a coup. Opponents of the legislation argued that the only basis for democracy is justice. In the end, the amnesty law called *Ley de Caducidad* (Law of Caducity, or Impunity Law) was upheld by 53 percent of the voters, though people in Montevideo voted strongly against it, as did young people.

Although the amnesty law remained in effect, one of its clauses supplied an opening for human rights activism. Article 4 directed the government to determine the fate of the disappeared, including the 12 children kidnapped with their parents or born in prison and illegally adopted by military families. Over the next 15 years, however, despite protests and petitions, three democratic administrations ignored the mandate. Not until March 2000, with the inauguration of President Jorge Batlle Ibáñez, did investigations begin. Almost as soon as he took office, Batlle Ibáñez led the search for the granddaughter of the Argentine poet **Juan Gelman**. She had been born 24 years before in a Uruguayan prison. Within a month, Gelman and his granddaughter were reunited. In August he created the Comisión para la Paz (Peace Commission), whose charge was to uncover the fate of the missing and to share this information with victims' relatives. Led by Archbishop Nicolás Cotugno, the commission issued a preliminary report in October 2002. It found evidence that the military dictatorship had been responsible for the disappearance of 26 Uruguayans. All the victims were alleged to have died under torture and been cremated, their ashes thrown into the Atlantic Ocean.

Having assumed responsibility for the deaths, the government is looking into reparations. Meanwhile, the Peace Commission report has stirred debate over whether the government should seek to punish those responsible.

UTURUNCOS. The word means "Tigermen" in Quechua. It was the popular name for the Movimiento Peronista de Liberación (MPL, Peronist Liberation Movement), a **guerrilla** organization that appeared in **Argentina** in 1959. Inspired by the success of the Cuban revolution, the MPL took up arms in rural Tucumán Province. The 20 guerrillas, mostly urbanites and students, were unprepared for armed insurrection. A few weeks into their campaign, they were surrounded and captured.

–V–

VALENZUELA, LUISA (1938–). Argentine journalist and novelist. Born in Buenos Aires, Valenzuela is the daughter of the Argentine novelist Luisa Mercedes Levinson. Early collaborations in her career included the literary supplement of *La Nación* and *El Mundo*, both in Buenos Aires, as well as a stint at Radio Télévision Française in Paris, where she lived for three years. Her first novel, *Hay que sonreír*, was published in 1966. Between 1969 and 1978 Valenzuela spent many periods abroad, staying in Mexico, Spain, and the United States. During the **"dirty war"** in **Argentina**, she resided in the United States, where she taught at Columbia University and New York University. She has been the recipient of many honors, among them a Guggenheim Fellowship in 1982.

Valenzuela's fiction often seeks to liberate language from the constraints imposed on individuals, particularly women, by patriarchy and political power. Sexual relationships are often examined and configured as relationships of power. Translated into several languages, the works most associated with the "dirty war" are the short-story collections *Strange Things Happen Here: Twenty-Six Short Stories and a Novel* (1975) and *Other Weapons* (1982), as well as the novel *The Lizard's Tail* (1983). An account of the life of José López Rega ("*El brujo*," "the sorcerer"), private secretary to **Juan Perón**, *The Lizard's Tail* is often read as a thinly disguised rendering of the dislocation and horror of Argentine society during the repression. A later novel, *Black Novel with Argentines* (1990), explores the conditions that gave rise to the "dirty war" in an apparently "civilized" society.

In 1989, after the restoration of democracy, Valenzuela returned to Argentina.

VERBITSKY, HORACIO (1942–). Argentine journalist. Possibly the best-known newspaper columnist in **Argentina**. Since 1987 Verbitsky has published a weekly political commentary in the alternative daily *Página/12* of Buenos Aires. He was awarded the Latin American Studies Association (LASA) Media Award in 1996 and the International Press Freedom Award in 2001. A member of the executive board of the **Human Rights** Watch/Americas, he is also one of the founding members of the Latin American press freedom organization Periodistas.

Born into a family of journalists—his father and several uncles and cousins were all members of the Argentine press—Verbitsky began his career while still in high school as a movie reviewer for several Buenos Aires publications. In his early years he wrote for the dailies *El Siglo* and *El Mundo* as well as for radio and television programs. During the last two years of the government of **Juan Perón** (1973–1974), Verbitsky joined the **Montoneros** and wrote for the leftist press, including the weekly *CGT*, published by the Argentine General Confederation of Labor, in collaboration with the journalists Rogelio García Lupo and **Rodolfo Walsh**. He combined his clandestine activities with work in mainstream publications such as *Confirmado, Primera Plana, La Opinión,* and *Clarín*. Between 1974 and 1975 he lived in **exile** in Peru. During the last years of the **military** regime—and after the closing of several publications and the disappearance of fellow journalists—he made a living as a translator for a small agency.

He is the author of several books on Argentine political and economic affairs. His best-known work is *El vuelo* (1995), published in 1996 as *The Flight: Confessions of an Argentine Dirty Warrior.* In it Verbitsky transcribed a series of interviews with **Adolfo Francisco Scilingo**, a former navy captain and member of the notorious **Escuela Mecánica de la Armada** (ESMA, Navy Mechanics School). In the first public admission of guilt by a member of the military, Scilingo detailed how, between 1976 and 1983, thousands of political detainees were drugged, stripped naked, and thrown from navy aircraft into the waters of the Atlantic Ocean.

Nicknamed "el perro" ("the dog") for his relentless reporting style, Verbitsky is a frequent contributor to *El País*, the *New York Times*, and the *Wall Street Journal.*

VERDUGO, PATRICIA. Chilean journalist. One of the best-known journalists in Latin America, Verdugo has been widely published in Latin America and Europe. She is the recipient of the Maria Moors Cabot Award from Columbia University in 1993, the National Journalism Award of Chile in 1997, and the Latin American Studies Association (LASA) Media Award in 2000.

Verdugo is the author of 11 books, among them *Chile, Pinochet and the Caravan of Death*, published in 1989 as *Los zarpazos del puma*. The book, which holds the best-seller record in **Chile**, is a detailed account of the **caravan of death** ordered by General **Augusto Pinochet Ugarte** and carried out by General Arellano Stark in Chile in 1973. The evidence collected in this book is considered one of the key elements that led to Pinochet Ugarte's arrest in London in 1998 and to eventual hearings in Chile in which the former dictator was stripped of prosecutorial immunity and ordered to be held under house arrest.

In July 1976 her father, Sergio Verdugo Herrera, a member of the Christian Democratic Party and a union leader, was abducted from his home. His tortured body was later discovered drowned in the Mapocho River in Santiago. Verdugo has written extensively of his disappearance and death, most notably in her 1999 book *Bucharest 187*—titled after her father's house in the Providencia neighborhood of Santiago—in which she detailed her family's unsuccessful attempts to determine his whereabouts and to bring his murderers to justice. Previously Verdugo published *Interferencia secreta* (1998), which offered transcripts of the radio communiqués between Pinochet Ugarte and **military** officers involved in the coup, which had been recorded by an unnamed Chilean radio aficionado. The book, with its accompanying compact disc of the actual radio transmissions, was widely distributed in Latin America and Europe.

In *Bucharest 187* Verdugo described her work as one of remembrance, an act both "sacred" and "subversive," in opposition to a prevailing social discourse that would demand collective amnesia.

VICARÍA DE LA SOLIDARIDAD / VICARIATE OF SOLIDARITY. A human rights nongovernmental organization in **Chile**. Established in 1976 by Cardinal Raúl Silva Henríquez, the Vicaría documented **human rights** violations and distributed humanitarian aid during the **mili-**

tary government of General **Augusto Pinochet Ugarte**. It replaced the **Comité de la Paz** (COPACHI, Committee for Peace), which had been formed in 1973. Like COPACHI, the Vicaría was affiliated with the **Catholic Church**. Unlike COPACHI, however, the Vicaría enjoyed the full protection of the Church, having been created under the auspices of the Archdiocese of Santiago.

Since repression affected all aspects of Chilean life, the Vicaría addressed a wide range of problems—legal, medical, and social. Its legal program centered on collecting evidence of detention, **torture**, political execution, and disappearance. Its medical program provided health care to the poor as well as treatment for torture victims and those injured during demonstrations against the government. Indeed, torture victims were often left outside the Vicaría's door. Its social programs gave material support both to human rights victims and to workers displaced by the shock-treatment economics of Pinochet Ugarte's **Chicago Boys**. Daily means were provided by *ollas comunes* (literally, "common pots," or soup kitchens).

The Vicaría's activities, especially its efforts at documentation, antagonized the military. Unlike other human rights organizations, which lost records to security raids, the Vicaría had the advantage of Church protection. The military did, however, wage a campaign of harassment and terror against the legal staff. Lawyers were especially vulnerable because of their filings of *amparos*, or writs of habeas corpus, and were subject to arrest, **exile**, and *relegación* (internal exile).

Throughout the dictatorship, the Vicaría was a source of inspiration to many Chilenas. After the return to democrary in 1990, its legacy continued in the **Comisión Nacional de Verdad y Reconciliación** (National Commission on Truth and Reconcilation), which was charged with investigating human rights abuses.

VICARIATE OF SOLIDARITY. *See* VICARÍA DE LA SOLIDARIDAD.

VIDELA, JORGE RAFAEL (1925–). Nicknamed "the Bone," because of his lean and hard-muscled physique. General, commander of the army, and leader of the first junta (1976–1981) during the **"dirty war"** period in **Argentina**. (The other members of the first junta were **Emilio Massera** and **Orlando Ramón Agosti**.) Videla was born on 2 August 1925 in Mercedes, a city in Buenos Aires Province. His father, Rafael Videla, was an army colonel who commanded the Sixth Infantry Regiment. His mother, María Redondo, came from a Mercedes family of long standing. He graduated from the Colegio Militar (Military Academy) in 1944 as an infantry lieutenant and from the Senior War College in 1954. He devoted a large portion of his career to the Colegio Militar, training future officers in his roles as instructor, professor, and (from 1971 to 1973) commandant. In 1973 he was promoted to chief of the General Staff (second in the army chain of command) and, in August 1975, commander in chief.

The promotion of Lieutenant General Videla to the top position came when the army rejected an effort by President **Isabel Perón** to bring the service under the control of **Peronists**. He had a reputation for being a political moderate—neither a Peronist nor an avowed anti-Peronist. He also knew and had the respect of officers in the field, having taught many of them. And like most other officers, he was a strong anticommunist, his distaste for Marxism reinforced by a traditional Roman Catholicism. Under his leadership, the army waged "war"—its first war of the century—against left-wing **guerrillas**, who had been conducting a campaign of kidnappings, assassinations, and bombings. Following the **military** coup of 24 March 1976, he emerged as the leader of a three-man junta and was named president. He presided over a "dirty war" against subversives. His definition of "subversive" included anyone promoting ideas alien to "Western, Christian values." He retired in 1981, replaced as president by General Roberto Viola, the new army commander in chief and leader of the second junta.

On 22 April 1985, after the return to civility, Videla was put on trial with the eight other service commanders who had made up the three juntas of the "dirty war" period. The defendants were charged with murder, kidnapping, illegal detention, **torture**, and robbery. The six-member Federal Court of Appeals delivered its verdict on 9 December 1985. Videla, as the leader of the army during the worst years of government repression, was convicted and sentenced to life in prison. In late December 1990 he was pardoned and released, along with Massera and Viola, under a controversial amnesty. In June 1998 Videla was placed under house arrest for ordering the traffic of babies born to detained mothers. (The abduction and illegal adoption of children are crimes not covered in the earlier amnesty.) He remains under house arrest.

VILAS, ACDEL EDGARDO. *See* EJÉRCITO REVOLUCIONARIO DEL PUEBLO (ERP) / PEOPLE'S REVOLUTIONARY ARMY.

VILLAFLOR DE VICENTI, AZUCENA. *See* MADRES DE PLAZA DE MAYO.

VILLA GRIMALDI. A palatial estate at the foot of the Andes mountains that served as the main **torture** and detention center for the **Dirección de Inteligencia Nacional** (DINA, Directorate of National Intelligence), the Chilean secret police. More than 200 political prisoners were detained there from 1974 until 1977, when DINA was officially dissolved. After the return to civilian rule, Villa Grimaldi was razed, and **human rights** groups converted the space into a "Park of Memory" in honor of the thousands who disappeared during the **military** regime of **Augusto Pinochet Ugarte**.

VILLA MARTELLI. *See* CARAPINTADAS.

–W–

WALSH, RODOLFO (1927–1977?). Argentine journalist and writer. Born in Choele-Choel, in Río Negro province, into a family of Irish immigrants. Walsh abandoned his studies at 16 and soon became a translator and proofreader for the editorial house Hachette. In 1951 he began working as a journalist, collaborating with the magazines *Leoplan* and *Vea y Lea*. In 1959 he traveled to Cuba, where he was one of the founders of the news agency Prensa Latina. Back in his native **Argentina**, Walsh worked for the daily *Noticias* as well as for several weeklies: *Panorama, Primera Plana, Villero*, and the *CGT* (a publication of the Argentine General Confederation of Labor). Many of these publications were later closed by the **military** regime during the **"dirty war."** In 1976 Walsh founded the Agencia de Noticias Clandestinas (ANCLA), a clandestine network aimed at disseminating news about Argentina to national and international media. According to the journalist **Horacio Verbitsky**, a participant in another clandestine news service called Information Chain, one-page newsletters were secretly circulated and handed to people who were asked to make copies and distribute them in turn.

Between 1969 and 1973, Walsh published several books that won him a reputation as a daring investigative reporter: *¿Quién mató a Rosendo?* (1969), *Un oscuro día de justicia* (1973), and *El caso Satanovsky* (1973). He was also an award-winning author of works for the stage—his 1965 play *La granada*, for example—and short stories. His short story "Esa mujer" has often been singled out as one of the most innovative short narratives of Argentine literature in the 20th century. His best-known work, however, remains the "Carta abierta de Rodolfo Walsh a la Junta Militar" of 24 March 1977, marking the first anniversary of the coup. In this open letter to the military junta, Walsh denounced the political repression, murders, **torture**, and disappearances that had taken place in Argentina during the junta's first year in power, a period that saw his daughter, María Victoria Walsh, assassinated by members of the military and his house in Tigre Delta raided and ransacked.

On 25 March 1977, the day after "Carta abierta" was circulated, Walsh was abducted by security forces near the Constitución station in Buenos Aires. The previous evening, his house in San Vicente, in Buenos Aires province, had been under attack for more than two hours by about 40 heavily armed men who later ransacked the place, according to eyewitness reports. Walsh remains among the *desaparecidos*.

WAR TRIBUNALS. Wartime courts established by the **Junta** in **Chile** to try and convict its political opponents. The trial and sentencing procedures violated the basic **human rights** of the accused. Meanwhile, the lower courts and the **Supreme Court of Justice** claimed to have no jurisdiction during a "state of siege" or "state of war." Although the law clearly established the independence of the courts under such conditions, the lower and high courts remained loyal to the **military** government. Jurists who challenged the courts' pro-government stance were censured or removed.

Bibliography

Contents

Introduction

The most important primary sources documenting human rights violations committed during the "dirty wars" are the reports issued by government truth commissions: *Nunca Más* [*Never Again*], listed in the "Argentina—Aftermath" section (under the corporate author Argentina. Comisión Nacional sobre la Desaparición de Personas), and the *Report of the Chilean National Commission on Truth and Reconciliation,* two volumes, listed in the "Chile—Aftermath" section (under the corporate author Chile. Comisión Nacional de Verdad y Reconciliación). No government truth-commission report exists for Uruguay; however, the human rights nongovernmental organization Servicio Paz y Justicia-Uruguay produced its own report, *Uruguay Nunca Más: Human Rights Violations, 1972–1985,* listed in the "Aftermath" section for that country. Reports issued by regional and international human rights organizations—especially following site visits—are important sources as well, having directed international attention to the region and the offending countries. Among those organizations whose policy it was to publish reports were the Organization of American States Inter-American Commission on Human Rights, which visited Argentina, Chile, and Uruguay; the International Commission of Jurists, which visited Chile; and Amnesty International, which visited Argentina and Chile (listed in the "dirty war" sections under the countries involved). In addition, the Inter-Church Committee on Chile published *One Gigantic Prison,* a report of a fact-finding mission to all three countries ("General Works—Nonfiction" section under the authors Andrew Brewin, Louis Ducios, and David MacDonald). Although it is not the policy of the Red Cross to publish reports, its report on Uruguay was leaked; it appeared in the *New York Review of Books* under the title "In Libertad Prison" ("Dirty War—Nonfiction" section under the author J. F. LaBarthe). If items in the bibliography are available in both English and Spanish—and most of the reports are—both versions are listed.

At the local level, human rights nongovernmental organizations (HRNGOs)—the Vicaría de la Solidaridad in Chile, for example—were instrumental not only in providing assistance to victims but also in documenting cases of abuse. Many testified before truth commissions and visiting human rights organizations. Almost all maintain collections of documents, some of which are made available to visiting scholars. For a good overview of what is housed in these collections, see the article by Louis Bickford entitled "Human Rights Archives and Research on Historical Memory: Argentina, Chile, and Uruguay" ("General Works—Nonfiction" section).

Victims' testimonials, or *testimonios*, are listed in the "'Dirty War'—Nonfiction" section under the countries involved. Perhaps the best known of these is *Prisoner without a Name, Cell without a Number* (*Preso sin nombre, celda sin número*), in which the Argentine journalist Jacobo Timerman relates his detention and torture under General Ramón Camps. Many *testimonios*, however—like the three-volume *Las manos en el fuego*, by the Uruguayan Ernesto González Bermejo—remain untranslated.

Another category of works describing the effects of a particular "dirty war" on the general population is literature, or what has become known as the literature of the dictatorship. Some of the works included are symbolic and allegorical, such as Cristina Peri Rossi's novel *Ship of Fools* (*La nave de los locos*), which examines the dictatorship in Uruguay. A few are set in a different time period from that of the "dirty wars." The events in Isabel Allende's *Portrait in Sepia* (*Retrato en sepia*), for example, seem to presage the social dislocation found in her earlier novel the *House of the Spirits* (*La casa de los espíritus*), which traces events leading up to and directly following the coup in Chile. Many readers may already be familiar with these works, as well as those of other authors who have been translated into English—Marta Traba and Luisa Valenzuela, Manuel Puig and Ricardo Piglia, and José Donoso and Ariel Dorfman. There are, however, many works, in Spanish, that remain untranslated. The short stories of Nelson Marra and the novella *Un viaje a Salto*, by Circe Maia, are only two examples, both from Uruguay. It is hoped that their inclusion will stimulate the interest of readers and scholars in bringing these texts to the attention of the English-speaking public.

Movies are another way to document the past, and like works of literature, items in this category may be allegorical, set in a different time period, or even set in a different country. *Sweet Country* (*Dulce país*), directed by Michael Cacoyannis and based on the novel of the same title by Caroline Richards, is ostensibly about Chile, though may apply equally to Greece, which went through its own period of dictatorship. *Camila*, directed by María Luisa Bemberg, is set in Argentina during an earlier repressive period, but could be taken as a statement about the most recent one. *Il postino* (*The Postman*), based on the novel *Ardiente paciencia*, by Antonio Skármeta of Chile, is set in Italy. Among the major feature films are the *Kiss of the Spider Woman* (on Argentina), *Missing* (on Chile), and *State of Siege* (on Uruguay). Important documentaries include *La historia official* (*The Official Story*), on Argentina, and the series of films directed by Patricio Guzmán: *La batalla de Chile* (parts one, two, and three) and *Le cas Pinochet* (*El caso Pinochet, The Pinochet Case*).

Among secondary sources, good general overviews are *Guerrillas and*

Generals: The "Dirty War" in Argentina (2002), by Paul H. Lewis; *Dossier Secreto: Argentina's Desaparecidos and the Myth of the "Dirty War"* (1993), by Martin Edwin Andersen; *Chile Under Pinochet: Uncovering the Truth* (2000), by Mark Ensalaco; *Soldiers in a Narrow Land: The Pinochet Regime in Chile* (1994), by Mary Helen Spooner (listed in the "Dirty War—Nonfiction" sections); two books by Martin Weinstein, *Uruguay: The Politics of Failure* and *Uruguay: Democracy at the Crossroads* (1988) ("Aftermath" section); and *A Miracle, a Universe: Settling Accounts with Torturers* (1998), by Lawrence Weschler ("Aftermath" section). For more concise overviews, consult the *Europa Year Book*, a standard reference encyclopedia that offers up-to-date political histories for all the countries of the world. For an in-depth discussion of the role of the United Nations in the region, see *Behind the Disappearances: Argentina's Dirty War against Human Rights and the United Nations*, by Iain Guest ("Dirty War—Nonfiction" section).

The bibliography does not attempt to list critical and interpretive works on the literature of dictatorship. The following titles, however, can be mentioned as examples of secondary sources available to the literary critic: Jorgelina Corbatta's *Narrativas de la guerra sucia en Argentina: Piglia, Saer, Valenzuela, Puig* ("Argentina—Aftermath" section) and Jorge Ruffinelli's "Uruguay: Dictadura y re-democratización: Un informe sobre la literatura, 1973–1989" ("Uruguay—Aftermath" section). The body of critical material on the topic is vast, and the Modern Language Association database remains an excellent tool for identifying additional titles.

The World Wide Web is helpful in various ways. First, the open web can be used to consult truth commission reports, as well as the recently declassified U.S. State Department documents on Argentina and Chile (www.foia.state.gov [4 September 2002]). Second, it can be used to find information on human rights organizations. After all, what more authoritative source on, for example, the Madres de Plaza de Mayo than their very own website? Third, it can be used to find biographical information, supplementing information found in such traditional works as *Current Biography* (H.W. Wilson Company, various years), biographical dictionaries, newspaper articles, and secondary sources. Sites on the open web, however, need to be evaluated carefully—for currency, authority, and objectivity.

Although the bibliography comprises mostly books, book chapters, and articles in scholarly journals, it also references significant magazine and newspaper articles. The following news sources were consulted as well to track down an elusive fact or clear up a discrepancy between other sources:

Agence France Presse
Associated Press
EFE News Services
Guardian (London)
Independent (London)
Inter Press Service
Los Angeles Times
New York Times
San Francisco Chronicle
Washington Post

General Works

Nonfiction

Agee, Philip. *Inside the Company: CIA Diary.* New York: Stonehill, 1975.

Agosin, Marjorie, and Monica Bruno, eds. *Surviving beyond Fear: Women, Children, and Human Rights in Latin America.* Fredonia, N.Y.: White Pine Press, 1993.

Amnesty International USA. *Disappearances: A Workbook.* New York: Amnesty International USA, 1981.

Andrew, Christopher. *For the President's Eyes Only: Secret Intelligence and the American Presidency from Washington to Bush.* New York: HarperCollins, 1995.

Baumgartner, José Luis. *Mamá Julien.* Montevideo: Ediciones Trilce, 1988.

Bickford, Louis. "Human Rights Archives and Research on Historical Memory: Argentina, Chile, and Uruguay." *Latin American Research Review* 35, no. 2 (2000): 160–82.

Brewin, Andrew, Louis Ducios, and David MacDonald, Members of the Canadian Parliament. *One Gigantic Prison: the Report of the Fact-Finding Mission to Chile, Argentina, and Uruguay, September 30 to October 10, 1976.* Toronto: Inter-Church Committee on Chile, 1976.

Brito, Alexandra Barahona de. *Human Rights and Democratization in Latin America: Uruguay and Chile.* Oxford: Oxford University Press, 1997.

Bunster-Burotto, Ximena. "Surviving beyond Fear: Women and Torture in Latin America." In *Women and Change in Latin America,* June Nash, Helen Safa, and contributors, 297–325. South Hadley, Mass.: Bergin & Garvey, 1985.

Carothers, Thomas. *In the Name of Democracy: U.S. Politics towards Latin America in the Reagan Years.* Berkeley: University of California Press, 1991.

Corradi, Juan E., Patricia Weiss Fagan, and Manuel Antonio Garretón, eds. *Fear at the Edge: State Terror and Resistance in Latin America.* Berkeley: University of California Press, 1992.

Davis, William Columbus. *Warnings from the Far South: Democracy versus Dictatorship in Uruguay, Argentina, and Chile.* Westport, Conn.: Praeger, 1995.

Deming, Angus, and Scott Sullivan. "Carter's Point Woman" [Patricia Derian]. *Newsweek* (16 May 1977): 70.

Drake, Paul W. *Labor Movements and Dictatorships: The Southern Cone in Comparative Perspective.* Baltimore: Johns Hopkins University Press, 1996.

Dussell, Enrique, ed. *The Church in Latin America, 1492–1992.* A History of the Church in the Third World, vol. 1. Tunbridge Wells, Kent: Burns & Oates; Maryknoll, N.Y.: Orbis Books, 1992.

Encyclopedia of Genocide. 2 vols. Santa Barbara, Calif.: ABC-CLIO, 1999.

Forsythe, David P. "Human Rights in U.S. Foreign Policy: Retrospect and Prospect." *Political Science Quarterly* 105, no. 3 (1990): 435–454.

Frankel, Marvin E., with Ellen Saidman. *Out of the Shadows of Night: The Struggle for International Human Rights.* New York: Delacorte Press, 1989.

Guiraldes, Juan José. "Saving the Western Hemisphere: The Threat to the Americas." *Vital Speeches of the Day* (1 October 1979): 756–61.

Gunson, Phil, Andrew Thompson, and Greg Chamberlain. *The Dictionary of Contemporary Politics of South America.* New York: Macmillan, 1989.

King, Peter John. "Comparative Analysis of Human Rights Violations under Military Rule in Argentina, Brazil, Chile, and Uruguay." *Statistical Abstract of Latin America* 27 (1989): 1043–65.

Klaiber, Jeffrey L. *The Church, Dictatorships, and Democracy in Latin America.* Maryknoll, N.Y.: Orbis Books, 1998.

Kohl, James, and John Litt. *Urban Guerrilla Warfare in Latin America.* Cambridge, Mass.: MIT Press, 1974.

Lernoux, Penny. *Cry of the People: United States Involvement in the Rise of Fascism, Torture, and Murder and the Persecution of the Catholic Church in Latin America.* Garden City, N.Y.: Doubleday, 1980.

McSherry, J. Patrice. "Operation Condor: Clandestine Inter-American System." *Social Justice* 26, no. 4 (1999): 144–74.

Muravchik, Joshua. *The Uncertain Crusade: Jimmy Carter and the Dilemmas of Human Rights Policy.* Lanham, Md.: Hamilton Press, 1986.

O'Connor, Anne-Marie. "Out of the Ashes: Helping Torture Survivors Heal is Becoming a Public Health Specialty, with the U.S. Moving to Subsidize Programs in L.A. and Elsewhere." *Los Angeles Times,* 22 October 2000, home edition.

O'Donnell, Guillermo, Philippe C. Schmitter, and Laurence Whitehead, eds. *Transitions from Authoritarian Rule: Latin America.* Baltimore: Johns Hopkins University Press, 1986.

Perelli, Carina. "From Counterrevolutionary Warfare to Political Awakening: The Uruguyan and Argentine Armed Forces in the 1970s." *Armed Forces and Society* 20, no. 1 (1993): 25–49.

Ranelagh, John. *The Agency: The Rise and Decline of the CIA.* Revised and updated. New York: Simon and Schuster, 1987.

Rojo, Ricardo. *My Friend Ché.* Translated by Julian Casart. New York: Dial Press, 1968. Translation of *Mi amigo el Ché* (Buenos Aires: Editorial Jorge Alvarez, 1968).

Roniger, Luis, and Mario Sznajder. *The Legacy of Human-Rights Violations in the Southern Cone: Argentina, Chile, and Uruguay.* Oxford: Oxford University Press, 1999.

Rouquié, Alain. *El estado militar en América Latina.* Buenos Aires: Emecé, 1984.

Schneider, Cathy Lisa. "Violence, Identity and Spaces of Contention in Chile, Argentina, and Colombia." *Social Research* 67, no. 3 (2000): 773–802.

Schoultz, Lars. *Human Rights and United States Policy toward Latin America.* Princeton, N.J.: Princeton University Press, 1981.

State Crimes: Punishment or Pardon: Papers and Report of the Conference, November 4–6, 1988, Wye Center, Maryland. Queenstown, Md.: Justice and Society Program of the Aspen Institute, 1989.

Waldmann, Peter. "Guerrilla Movements in Argentina, Guatemala, Nicaragua, and Uruguay." In *Political Violence and Terror: Motifs and Motivations,* edited by Peter H. Merkl, 257–81. Berkeley: University of California Press, 1986.

Whitaker, Arthur P. *The United States and the Southern Cone: Argentina, Chile, and Uruguay.* Cambridge, Mass.: Harvard University Press, 1976.

Wiarda, Howard J., and Harvey F. Kline, eds. *Latin American Politics and Development,* 2d ed. Boulder, Co.: Westview Press, 1985.

Wren, Christopher. "Salvaging Lives after Torture." *New York Times Magazine* (17 August 1986): 18–20.

Zlotchew, Clark M., and Paul David Seldis, eds. *Voices of the River Plate: Interviews with Writers of Argentina and Uruguay.* San Bernadino, Calif.: Borgo Press, 1993.

Literature

Albán, Laureano. *Biografías del terror.* San José: Editorial Costa Rica, 1987.
Breaking Free: An Anthology of Human Rights Poetry. Selected by Robert Hull. New York: Thomson Learning, 1995.
Partnoy, Alicia, ed. *You Can't Drown the Fire: Latin American Women Writing in Exile.* Pittsburgh, Pa.: Cleis, 1988.

Films and Documentaries

Down Came a Blackbird. Directed by Jonathan Sanger. 112 minutes. Viacom Pictures, 1995.
Esperanza incierta, La (Uncertain Hope). Directed by Fernando Sanatoro. 52 minutes. 1991.
Father Roy: Inside the School of the Americas. Directed by Robert Richter. 60 minutes. Richter Productions, 1997.
School of the Assassins. Narrated by Susan Sarandon. 18 minutes. Maryknoll World Productions, 1994.

Argentina

Background to the "Dirty War"

Carlson, Eric Stener. "The Influence of French "Revolutionary War" Ideology on the Use of Torture in Argentina's "Dirty War."" *Human Rights Review* 1, no. 4 (2000): 71–84.
Cavarozzi, Marcelo. "Political Cycles in Argentina since 1955." In *Transitions from Authoritarian Rule: Latin America,* edited by Guillermo O'Donnell, Philippe C. Schmitter, and Laurence Whitehead, 19–48. Baltimore: Johns Hopkins University Press, 1986.
Cox, Robert. "The Second Death of Perón?" *New York Review of Books* 30 (8 December 1983): 18–22.
———. "Total Terrorism: Argentina, 1969 to 1979." In *Terrorism, Legitimacy, and Power: The Consequences of Political Violence,* edited

by Martha Crenshaw, 124–42. Middletown, Conn.: Wesleyan University Press, 1983.

Crawley, Eduardo. *A House Divided, Argentina 1880–1980.* London: Hurst, 1984.

Davis, William Columbus. "Argentina: A Divided Land." Chap. 3 in *Warnings from the Far South: Democracy versus Dictatorship in Uruguay, Argentina, and Chile, 71–149.* Westport, Conn.: Praeger, 1995.

"Edging Closer to Open Chaos." *Time* (29 March 1976): 42.

"The Generals Call a Clockwork Coup." *Time* (5 April 1976): 32.

Gillespie, Richard. "Armed Struggle in Argentina." *New Scholar* 8, nos. 1 and 2 (1982): 387–427.

———. "Political Violence in Argentina: Guerrillas, Terrorists, and *Carapintadas.*" In *Terrorism in Context,* edited by Martha Crenshaw, 211–48. University Park: Pennsylvania State University Press, 1995.

———. *Soldiers of Perón: Argentina's Montoneros.* Oxford: Clarendon Press, 1982.

Hodges, Donald Clark. *Argentina, 1943–1987: The National Revolution and Resistance.* Rev. ed. Albuquerque: University of New Mexico Press, 1988.

———. *Argentina's "Dirty War": An Intellectual Biography.* Austin: University of Texas Press, 1991.

Lewis, Paul. "The Right and Military, 1955–1983." In *The Argentine Right: Its History and Intellectual Origins, 1910 to the Present,* edited by Sandra McGee Deutsch and Ronald H. Dolkart, 147–80. Wilmington, Del.: SR Books, 1993.

Moyano, María José. *Argentina's Lost Patrol: Armed Struggle, 1969–1979.* New Haven, Conn.: Yale University Press, 1995.

Opfell, Olga S. "Isabel Perón: President of Argentina." In *Women Prime Ministers and Presidents.*" Jefferson, N.C.: McFarland, 1993.

Potash, Robert A.. *The Army and Politics in Argentina.* Vol. 3, *1962–1973: From Frondizi's Fall to the Peronist Restoration.* Stanford, Calif.: Stanford University Press, 1996.

Rock, David. *Argentina 1516–1987: From Spanish Colonization to Alfonsín.* Rev. ed. Berkeley: University of California Press, 1987.

———. *Authoritarian Argentina: The Nationalist Movement, Its History, and Its Impact.* Berkeley: University of California Press, 1993. Published in Spanish under the title *La Argentina autoritaria: los nacionalistas, su historia y su influencia en la vida pública* (Buenos Aires: Ariel, 1993.)

Snow, Peter G. "Argentina: Politics in a Conflict Society." In *Latin American Politics and Development,* 2d ed., edited by Howard J. Wiarda and

Harvey F. Kline, 123–59. Boulder, Colo.: Westview Press, 1985.

Verbitsky, Horacio. *Ezeiza.* Buenos Aires: Editorial Contrapunto, 1985.

Walsh, Rodolfo. *Caso Satanowski.* 2d ed. Buenos Aires: Ediciones de la Flor, 1986.

———. *Operación masacre.* 22nd ed. Buenos Aires: Ediciones de la Flor, 2001.

———. *¿Quién mató a Rosendo?* 7th ed. Buenos Aires: Ediciones de la Flor, 1997.

The "Dirty War," 1976–1983

Nonfiction and Testimonios

Amnesty International. *Report of the Mission to Argentina, November 6– 15, 1976.* London: Amnesty International, 1977.

———. *Testimony on Secret Detention Camps in Argentina.* London: Amnesty International, 1980.

Andersen, Martin Edwin. *Dossier Secreto: Argentina's Desaparecidos and the Myth of the "Dirty War."* Boulder, Colo.: Westview Press, 1993.

———. "Kissinger Had a Hand in "Dirty War." *Insight on the News* (28 January 2002): 24–25+.

Arditti, Rita. *Searching for Life: The Grandmothers of the Plaza de Mayo and the Disappeared Children of Argentina.* Berkeley: University of California Press, 1999.

Arditti, Rita, and M. Brinton Lykes. "The Disappeared Children of Argentina: The Work of the Grandmothers of Plaza de Mayo. In *Surviving beyond Fear: Women, Children, and Human Rights in Latin America,* edited by Marjorie Agosin and Monica Bruno, 168–75. Fredonia, N.Y.: White Pine Press, 1993.

Armony, Ariel C. *Argentina, the United States, and the Anti-Communist Crusade in Central America.* Athens: Ohio University Center for International Studies, 1997.

Asociación de Periodistas de Buenos Aires. *Con vida los queremos: periodistas desaparecidos.* Buenos Aires: La Asociación, 1986.

Bonasso, Miguel. *Recuerdo de la muerte.* Buenos Aires: Bruguera, 1984.

Bondone, José Luis. *Con mis hijos en las cárceles del Proceso.* Buenos Aires: Ediciones Dialéctica, 1988.

Bousquet, Jean Pierre. *Las locas de Plaza de Mayo.* Translated by Jacques Despres. Buenos Aires: El Cid Editor, 1983. Translation of *Les folles de la place de Mai* (Paris: Stock, 1982).

Bouvard, Marguerite Guzman. *Revolutionizing Motherhood: The Mothers of the Plaza de Mayo.* Wilmington, Del.: Scholarly Resources, 1994.

Camps, Ramón J. A. *El poder en la sombra.* Buenos Aires: RO. CA. Producciones S.R.L., 1983.

Carlson, Marifran. "A Tragedy and a Miracle: Leonar Alonso and the Human Cost of State Terrorism in Argentina. In *Surviving beyond Fear: Women, Children, and Human Rights in Latin America*, edited by Marjorie Agosin and Monica Bruno, 71–85. Fredonia, N.Y.: White Pine Press, 1993.

Catholic Church. Conferencia Argentina. *Documentos del Episcopado Argentino sobre la violencia, 1970–1977.* Buenos Aires: Editorial Claretina, 1977.

Centro de Estudios Legales y Sociales. *Testimonio sobre el centro clandestino de detención de la Escuela de Mecánica de la Armada Argentina, ESMA.* Buenos Aires: Centro de Estudios Legales y Sociales, 1984.

Chaffee, Lyman. "Poster Art and Political Propaganda in Argentina." *Studies in Latin American Popular Culture* 5 (1986): 78–89.

Chelala, César A. "Women of Valor: An Interview with the Mothers of Plaza de Mayo." In *Surviving beyond Fear: Women, Children, and Human Rights in Latin America*, edited by Marjorie Agosin and Monica Bruno, 58–70. Fredonia, N.Y.: White Pine Press, 1993.

Ciancaglini, Sergio, and Martín Granovsky. *Crónicas del apocalipsis.* Buenos Aires: Editorial Contrapunto, 1985.

Cohen, Roberta. "Human Rights Diplomacy: The Carter Administration and the Southern Cone." *Human Rights Quarterly* 4, no. 2 (1982): 212–42.

Contepomi, Gustavo, Patricia Contepomi, and Roberto Raúl Reyna. *La perla 2.* Córdoba, Argentina: El Cid Editor, 1984. Sequel to *La perla*, by Roberto Raúl Reyna.

Corradi, Juan E. "The Mode of Destruction: Terror in Argentina." *Telos* 54 (Winter 1982–83): 61–76.

Diago, Alejandro. *Hebe, memoria y esperanza: Conversando con las Madres de Plaza de Mayo.* Buenos Aires: Ediciones Dialéctica, 1988.

DuBois, Lindsay. "Torture and the Construction of an Enemy: The Example of Argentina." *Dialectical Anthropology* 15, no. 4 (1990): 317–28.

Duhalde, Eduardo. *El estado terrorista argentino.* Buenos Aires: Ediciones El Caballito, 1983.

———. *El estado terrorista argentino: Quince años después, una mirada crítica.* Buenos Aires: Eudeba, 1999.

Escudé, Carlos. *La Argentina:¿paria internacional?* Buenos Aires: Editorial de Belgrano, 1984.

Familiares de Desaparecidos y Detenidos por Razones Políticas. *Abogados desaparecidos: República Argentina.* Buenos Aires: Familiares de Desaparecidos y Detenidos por Razones Políticas, 1988.

Fisher, Jo. *Mothers of the Disappeared.* Boston: South End Press, 1989.

Frontalini, Daniel, and María Cristina Caiati. *El mito de la guerra sucia.* Buenos Aires: Centro de Estudios Legales y Sociales, 1984.

Gabetta, Carlos. *Todos somos subversivos.* Buenos Aires: Bruguera, 1983.

Gasparini, Juan. *Montoneros: Final de cuentas.* Ed. Ampliada. La Plata Argentina: De La Campana, 1999.

Gelman, Juan, and Mara la Madrid. *Ni el flaco perdón de Diós: hijos de desaparecidos.* Buenos Aires: Planeta, 1997.

Giussani, Pablo. *Montoneros: la soberbia armada.* Buenos Aires: Sudamericana/Planeta, 1984.

Goñi, Uki. *Judas: La verdadera historia de Alfredo Astiz, el infiltrado.* 2d ed. Buenos Aires: Editorial Sudamericana, 1996.

González Janzen, Ignacio. *La Triple-A.* Buenos Aires: Editorial Contrapunto, 1986.

Graham-Yooll, Andrew. *A State of Fear: Memories of Argentina's Nightmare.* London: Eland, 1986.

Graziano, Frank. *Divine Violence: Spectacle, Psychosexuality, and Radical Christianity in the Argentine "Dirty War."* Boulder, Colo.: Westview, 1982.

Guest, Iain. *Behind the Disappearances: Argentina's Dirty War against Human Rights and the United Nations.* Philadelphia: University of Pennsylvania Press, 1990.

Gutiérrez, María Alicia. *Iglesia Católica, estado y democracia.* Serie Documentos de trabajo /EURAL, no. 52. Buenos Aires: EURAL, 1993.

Hagelin, Ragnar. *Mi hija Dagmar (My Daughter Dagmar).* Buenos Aires: Sudamericana, 1984.

Jordán, Alberto R. *El proceso: 1976/1983.* Buenos Aires: Emecé Editores, 1993.

Kaufman, Victor S. "The Bureau of Human Rights during the Carter Administration." *Historian* 61, no. 1 (1998): 51–66.

Kon, Daniel. *Los chicos de la guerra = The Boys of the War.* Dunton Green, England: New English Library, 1983. Translation of *Los chicos de la guerra: hablan los soldados que estuvieron en Malvinas*, 1982. The basis of the film *Los chicos de la guerra.*

Lernoux, Penny. "Blood Taints Church in Argentina." *National Catholic Reporter* (12 April 1985): 1, 4–5.

Lewis, Paul H. *Guerrillas and Generals: The "Dirty War" in Argentina.* Westport, Conn.: Praeger, 2002.

López Echagüe, Hernán. *El enigma del general Bussi: de la Operación Independencia a la Operación Retorno.* Buenos Aires: Editorial Sudamericana, 1991.

Marchak, M. Patricia. *God's Assassins: State Terrorism in Argentina in the 1970s.* Montreal: McGill-Queen's University Press, 1999.

Martín de Pozuelo, Eduardo, and Santiago Tarín. *España acusa.* Barcelona: Plaza & Janés, 1999.

Maurer, Harry. "Anti-Semitism in Argentina." *Nation* (12 February 1977): 170–3.

Mellibovsky, Matilde. *Circle of Love over Death: Testimonies of the Mothers of the Plaza de Mayo.* Translated by Maria and Matthew Proser. Willimantic, Conn.: Curbstone Press, 1997. Translation of *Círculo de amor sobre la muerte* (Buenos Aires: Ediciones de Pensamiento Nacional, 1990).

Memoria activa: 5 años de impunidad. Buenos Aires: Editorial La Página, 1999.

Metres, Katherine. "U.S. and U.N. Human Rights Policy toward Argentina, 1977–1980." *Michigan Journal of Political Science* 19 (1995): 93–153.

Mignone, Emilio Fermín. *Witness to the Truth: The Complicity of Church and Dictatorship in Argentina, 1976–1983.* Translated by Phillip Berryman. Maryknoll, N.Y. Orbis Books, 1988. Translation of *Iglesia y dictadura* (Buenos Aires: Ediciones de Pensamiento Nacional, 1986).

Miguens, José Enrique. *Honor militar, violencia terrorista y conciencia moral.* Buenos Aires: Sudamericana/Planeta, 1986.

Mittlebach, Federico, and Jorge Luis Mittlebach. *Sobre áreas y tumbas: Informe sobre desaparecedores.* Buenos Aires: Editorial Sudamericana, 2000.

Monteleone, Jorge. "Cuerpo constelado: Sobre la poesía de rock argentina." *Cuadernos Hispanoamericanos*, nos. 517–519 (1993): 401–20.

Naipaul, V.S. "Argentina: Living with Cruelty." *New York Review of Books* 39, no. 3 (30 January 1992): 13–18.

Navarro, Marysa. "The Personal is Political: Las Madres de Plaza de Mayo." In *Power and Popular Protest: Latin American Social Movements*, edited by Susan Eckstein, 241–58. Berkeley: University of California Press, 1989.

Nosiglia, Julio E. *Botín de guerra.* Buenos Aires: Cooperativa Tierra Fértil, 1985.

Ogando, Ariel. *Latinoamérica lucha: Entrevistas a Hebe de Bonafini, Javier Calderón, Ivo Ribeira de Avila y Adelmar Cibulski.* Jujuy, Argentina: Ediciones Wayruro, 1998.

Organization of American States, Inter-American Commission on Human Rights. *Report on the Situation of Human Rights in Argentina.* Washington, D.C.: General Secretariat of the Organization of American States, 1980. Published in Spanish as *Informe sobre la situación de los derechos humanos en Argentina* (Washington, D.C.: Secretaría General de la Organización de los Estados Americanos, 1980).

Oria, Piera Paola. *De la casa a la plaza.* Buenos Aires: Editorial Nueva America, 1987.

Paoletti, Alipio. *Como los Nazis, como en Vietnam.* Buenos Aires: Editorial Contrapunto, 1987.

Partnoy, Alicia. *The Little School: Tales of Disappearance and Survival in Argentina.* Translated by Alicia Partnoy with Lois Athey and Sandra Braunstein. Pittsburgh, Pa.: Cleis, 1986. Translation of *La escuelita* (no publication information available).

———. *Revenge of the Apple = Venganza de la manzana.* Translated by Richard Schaaf, Regina Kreger, and Alicia Partnoy. Pittsburgh, Pa.: Cleis Press, 1992.

Peregrino Fernández, Rodolfo. *Autocrítica policial.* Buenos Aires: Fundación para la Democracia en Argentina: El Cid Editor, 1983.

Reyna, Roberto Raúl. *La perla.* Cordoba, Argentina: El Cid Editor, 1984.

Robben, Antonius C. G. M. "State Terror in the Netherworld: Disappearance and Reburial in Argentina." In *Death Squad: The Anthropology of State Terror,* edited by Jeffrey A. Sluka, 91–113. Philadelphia: University of Pennsylvania Press, 2000.

Rodríguez, Andrea. *Nacidos en la sombra: la historia secreta de los mellizos Reggiardo Tolosa y el subcomisario Miara.* Buenos Aires: Sudamericana, 1996.

Rodríguez Molas, Ricardo. *Historias de la tortura y el orden represivo en la Argentina.* Buenos Aires: Eudebe, 1985.

Rosenberg, Tina. *Children of Cain: Violence and the Violent in Latin America.* New York: Penguin Books, 1991.

Sánchez, Matilde. *Historias de vida: Hebe de Bonafini.* Buenos Aires: Fraterna/Del Nuevo Extremo, 1985.

Seisdedos, Gabriel. *El honor de Dios: mártires palotinos: la historia silenciada de un crimen impune.* Buenos Aires: San Pablo, 1996.

Seoane, María, and Hector Ruíz Núñez. *La noche de los lápices.* Buenos Aires: Editorial Contrapunto, 1986.

Simpson, John, and Jana Bennett. *The Disappeared and the Mothers of the Plaza: The Story of the 11,000 Argentinians Who Vanished.* New York: St. Martin's, 1985.

Solanas, Fernando. *Otro país es possible: La alternativa que somos.* Buenos Aires: Editorial 19 de Julio, 1992.

Solari Yrigoyen, Hipólito. *Los años crueles.* Buenos Aires: Bruguera, 1983.

Taylor, Diana. "Spectacular Bodies: Gender, Terror, and Argentina's 'Dirty War.'" In *Gendering War Talk,* edited by Miriam Cooke and Angela Woollacott, 20–40. Princeton, N.J.: Princeton University Press, 1993.

Timerman, Jacobo. *Prisoner without a Name, Cell without a Number.* Translated by Toby Tolbot. New York: Knopf, 1981. Translation of *Preso sin nombre, celda sin número* (New York: Random Editores, 1981).

Uriarte, Claudio. *Almirante Cero: biografía no autorizada de Emilio Eduardo Massera.* Espejo de la Argentina. Buenos Aires: Planeta, 1992.

Verbitsky, Horacio. *The Flight: Confessions of an Argentine Dirty Warrior* [Confessions of Francisco Scilingo]. Translated by Esther Allen. New York: New Press, 1996. Translation of *El vuelo* (Barcelona: Seix Barral, 1995).

———. *Open Letter to the Argentine Military Junta March 24, 1977.* Washington, D.C.: Argentine Commission for Human Rights Washington Information Bureau, 1977. Translation of "Carta abierta de Rodolfo Walsh a la Junta Militar."

———. *Rodolfo Walsh y la prensa clandestina.* Buenos Aires: Ediciones de la Urraca, 1985.

———. *La última batalla de la Tercera Guerra Mundial.* Buenos Aires: Editorial Legasa, 1984.

Videla, Jorge Rafael, Emilio Eduardo Massera, and Orlando Ramón Agosti. "Proceso de Reorganización Nacional." In *El proceso de reorganización nacional: cronología y documentación,* compiled by Oscar Troncoso. Vol. 1: 107–14. Buenos Aires: Centro Editor de América Latina, 1984.

Vila, Pablo. "*Rock Nacional* and Dictatorship in Argentina." In *Rockin' the Boat: Mass Music and Mass Movements,* edited by Reebee Garofalo, 209–29. Boston: South End Press, 1992.

———. "Tango, folklore y rock: Apuntes sobre música, política y sociedad en Argentina." *Caravelle,* no. 48 (1987): 81–93.

Walsh, Rodolfo. *Yo también fui fusilado.* Buenos Aires: Gente Sur, 1990.

Zamorano, Carlos M. *Prisionero político: Testimonio sobre las cárceles políticas argentinas.* Buenos Aires: Ediciones Estudio, 1983.

Literature

Asís, Jorge. *La calle de los caballos muertos.* Buenos Aires: Legasa Literaria, 1982.

———. *Flores robadas en los jardines de Quilmes.* Buenos Aires: Losada, 1982.

Battista, Vicente. *El libro de todos los engaños.* Buenos Aires: Bruguera, 1984.

Caparrós, Martín. *No velas a tus muertos.* Buenos Aires: Ediciones de la Flor, 1986.

Castex, Mariano. *El otro.* Buenos Aires: Ediciones de Rocío, 1983.

Catania, Carlos. *El pintadedos.* Buenos Aires: Legasa Literaria, 1984.

Cedrón, Aníbal. *La memoria extraviada.* Buenos Aires: Editorial Cartago, 1985.

Cortázar, Julio. *We Love Glenda So Much, and Other Tales.* Translated by Gregory Rabassa. New York: Knopf, 1983. Translation of *Queremos tanto a Glenda y otros relatos* (Mexico City: Editorial Nueva Imagen, 1980).

Costantini, Humberto. *The Gods, the Little Guys, and the Police.* Translated by Toby Talbot. New York: Harper & Row, 1984. Translation of *De dioses, hombrecitos, y policías* (Mexico City: Editorial Nueva Imagen, 1979).

———. *The long night of Francisco Sanctis.* Translated by Norman Thomas di Giovanni. New York: Harper & Row, 1985. Translation of *La larga noche de Francisco Sanctis* (Buenos Aires: Bruguera, 1984).

Dal Masetto, Antonio. *Fuego a discreción.* Buenos Aires: Folios Ediciones, 1983.

Denevi, Marco. *Manual de historia.* Buenos Aires: Ediciones Corregidor, 1985.

Domínguez, Carlos María. *Pozo de Vargas.* Buenos Aires: Emecé Editores, 1985.

Fernández Tiscornia, Nelly. *Made in Lanús = Made in Buenos Aires.* Spanish and English. Translated into English by Raúl Moncada. Buenos Aires: Editorial Legasa, 1990.

Firpo, Norberto. *Cuerpo a tierra.* Buenos Aires: Editorial Galerna, 1984.

———. *Grandísimo idiota.* Buenos Aires: Editorial Galerna, 1984.

Foguet, Hugo. *Pretérito perfecto.* Buenos Aires: Legasa Literaria, 1983.

Gambaro, Griselda. *El campo. Dos actos.* Buenos Aires: Ediciones Insurrexit, 1968.

———. *Los siameses. Dos actos.* Buenos Aires: Ediciones Insurrexit, 1967.

————. *Teatro 1: Real envido; La malasangre; Del sol naciente.* Buenos Aires: Ediciones de la Flor, 1984.

Gelman, Juan. *Unthinkable Tenderness: Selected Poems.* Translated by Joan Lindgren. Berkeley: University of California Press, 1997.

Giardinelli, Mempo. *Qué solos se quedan los muertos.* Buenos Aires: Editorial Latinoamericana, 1985.

————. *La revolución en bicicleta.* Barcelona: Editorial Pomaire, 1980.

————. *Santo oficio de la memoria.* Barcelona: Grupo Editorial Norma, 1991.

————. *Sultry Moon.* Translated by Patricia J. Duncan. Pittsburgh, Pa.: Latin American Literary Review Press, 1988. Translation of *Luna caliente* (Buenos Aires: Bruguera, 1984).

Goloboff, Gerardo Mario. *Criador de palomas.* Buenos Aires: Bruguera, 1984.

Gorostiza, Carlos. *Los cuartos oscuros.* Buenos Aires: Editorial Sudamericana, 1976.

Heker, Liliana. *El fin de la historia.* Buenos Aires: Alfaguara, 1996.

Kociancich, Vlady. *La octava maravilla.* Madrid: Alianza Editorial, 1982.

Kozameh, Alicia. *Steps under Water: A Novel.* Translated by David E. Davis. Berkeley: University of California Press, 1996. Translation of *Pasos bajo el agua* (Buenos Aires: Editorial Contrapunto, 1987).

Landaburu, Jorge. *Se lo tragó la tierra.* Buenos Aires: Sudamericana/Planeta, 1984.

Larra, Raúl. *La conspiración del gran Bonete.* Buenos Aires: Ediciones Dirple, 1984.

Levinson, Luisa Mercedes. *El último Zelofonte.* Buenos Aires: Sudamericana/Planteta, 1984.

López Fernando. *Arde aún sobre los años.* Buenos Aires: Editorial Sudamericana, 1986.

————. *El mejor enemigo.* Cordoba, Argentina: El Cid Editor, 1984.

Lynch, Marta. *Informe bajo llave.* Buenos Aires: Editorial Sudamericana, 1983.

————. *La penúltima versión de la Colorada Villanueva.* 4th ed. Buenos Aires: Editorial Sudamericana, 1979.

Manzur, Jorge. *Tinta roja.* Barcelona: Legasa Literaria, 1981.

Martínez, Tomás Eloy. *The Perón Novel.* Translated by Asa Zatz. New York: Pantheon, 1988. Translation of *La novela de Perón* (Buenos Aires: Editorial Legasa, 1985).

————. *Santa Evita.* Buenos Aires: Planeta, 1995.

Martini, Juan Carlos. *El cerco.* Barcelona: Bruguera, 1977.

————. *La vida entera.* Barcelona: Bruguera, 1981.

Masciángioli, Jorge. *Buenaventura, nunca más.* Buenos Aires: Bruguera, 1983.

Medina, Enrique. *Los asesinos.* Buenos Aires: Editores Milton, 1984.

———. *Buscando a Madonna.* Buenos Aires: Milton Editores, 1987.

———. *Con el trapo en la boca.* Buenos Aires: Editorial Galerna, 1983.

———. *Desde un mundo civilizado.* Buenos Aires: Editores Milton, 1987.

———. *The Duke: Memories and Anti-Memories of a Participant in the Repression.* Translated by David William Foster. London: Zed Books, 1985. Translation of *El Duke: Memorias y anti-memorias de un participante en la represión* (Buenos Aires: Editorial Eskol, 1976).

———. *Las muecas del miedo.* Buenos Aires: Editorial Galerna, 1981.

———. *Transparente.* Buenos Aires: Editorial Sudamericana, 1975.

———. *Las tumbas (The Tombs).* Translated by David William Foster. New York: Garland, 1993. Translation of *Las tumbas* (Buenos Aires: Ediciones de Flor, 1972).

Mercader, Martha. *La chuña de los huevos de oro.* Buenos Aires: Legasa Literaria, 1982.

Mercado, Tununa. *In a State of Memory.* Translated by Peter Kahn. Lincoln: University of Nebraska Press, 2001. Translation of *En estado de memoria* (Buenos Aires: A. Korn Editora, 1990).

Moreyra, Federico. *Balada de un sargento.* Buenos Aires: Editorial Galerna, 1985.

———. *El desangradero.* Buenos Aires: Editorial Legasa, 1984.

———. *Solamente ella.* Buenos Aires: Editorial Bruguera, 1981.

Moyano, Daniel. *The Flight of the Tiger.* Translated by Norman Thomas di Giovanni. London: Serpent's Tail, 1995. Translation of *El vuelo del tigre* (Buenos Aires: Legasa Literaria, 1981).

———. *Libro de navíos y borrascas.* Buenos Aires: Editorial Legasa, 1983. Orphée, Elvira. *El Angel's Last Conquest.* Translated by Magda Bogin. New York: Available Press, 1985. Translation of *La última conquista de El Angel* (Caracas: Monte Avila, 1977).

———. *Las viejecitas fantasiosas.* Buenos Aires: Emecé Editores, 1981.

Pavlovsky, Eduardo A. *La mueca; El Señor Galíndez; Telarañas.* Madrid: Editorial Fundamentos, 1973.

———. *El Sr. Laforgue.* Buenos Aires: Ediciones Búsqueda, 1983.

Piglia, Ricardo. *The Absent City.* Translated and introduced by Sergio Waisman. Durham, N.C.: Duke University Press, 1992. Translation of *La ciudad ausente* (Buenos Aires: Editorial Sudamericana, 1992).

———. *Artificial Respiration.* Translated by Daniel Balderston. Durham, N.C.: Duke University Press, 1994. Translation of *Respiración artificial* (Buenos Aires: Pomaire, 1980).

————, comp. *La Argentina en pedazos*. Buenos Aires: Ediciones de la Urraca, 1993.

Pizarnik, Alejandra. *La condesa sangrienta*. Buenos Aires: López Crespo, 1976.

Puig, Manuel. *The Buenos Aires Affair: A Detective Novel*. Translated by Suzanne Jill Levine. New York: Vintage Books, 1980. Translation of *The Buenos Aires Affair: Novela policial* (Buenos Aires: Editorial Sudamericana, 1973).

————. *Eternal Curse on the Reader of These Pages*. Minneapolis: University of Minnesota Press, 1999. Translation of *Maldición eterna a quien lea estas páginas* (Barcelona: Seix Barral, 1980).

————. *Kiss of the Spider Woman*. Translated by Allan Baker. Oxford, England: Amber Lane, 1987. Translation of *El beso de la mujer araña* (Barcelona: Seix Barral, 1976).

————. *Kiss of the Spider Woman*. Translated by Thomas Colchie. New York: Knopf, 1979. Translation of *El beso de la mujer araña* (Barcelona: Seix Barral, 1976). The basis of a film of the same title.

————. *Pubis Angelical*. Translated by Elena Brunet. Minneapolis: University of Minnesota Press, 2000. Translation of *Publis angelical* (Barcelona: Seix Barral, 1979).

————. *Tropical Night Falling*. Translated by Suzanne Jill Levine. New York: W.W. Norton, 1993. Translation of *Cae la noche tropical* (Barcelona: Seix Barral, 1988).

Quiroga, Eduardo. *On Foreign Ground: A Novel*. London: André Deutsch, 1986.

Rabanal, Rodolfo. *El apartado*. Buenos Aires: Editorial Sudamericana, 1975.

————. *En otra parte*. Madrid: Legasa Literaria, 1981.

————. *El pasajero*. Buenos Aires: Emecé Editores, 1984.

Rivabella, Omar. *Requiem for a Woman's Soul*. Translated by Paul Riviera and Omar Rivabella. New York: Random House, 1986. Translation of *Requiem por el alma de una mujer*.

Rivera, Andrés. *Los vencedores no dudan*. Buenos Aires: Grupo Editorial Latinoamericano, 1989.

Roffé, Reina. *La rompiente*. Xalapa, Mexico: Universidad Veracruzana, 1987.

Sábato, Ernesto. *The Angel of Darkness*. Translated by Andrew Hurley. New York: Ballantine Books, 1991. Translation of *Abaddón, el exterminador* (Buenos Aires: Editorial Sudamericana, 1974).

Saer, Juan José. *The Event*. Translated by Helen R. Lane. London: Serpent's Tail, 1995. Translation of *La ocasión* (Barcelona: Ediciones

Destino, 1988).

———. *Glosa*. Buenos Aires: Alianza Editorial, 1986.

———. *Lo imborrable*. Buenos Aires: Alianza, 1993.

———. *Nobody Nothing Never*. Translated by Helen R. Lane. London: Serpent's Tail, 1993. Translation of *Nadie nada nunca* (Mexico City: Siglo XXI, 1980).

Shua, Ana María. *Patient*. Translated by David William Foster. Translation of *Soy paciente* (Buenos Aires: Editorial Losada, 1980).

Slaughter, Charles H. *The Dirty War*. New York: Walker and Company, 1994. Young adult fiction.

Soriano, Osvaldo. *A Funny Dirty Little War*. Translated by Nick Caistor. New York: Readers International, 1986. Translation of *No habrá más penas ni olvido* (Barcelona: Grupo Editorial Norma, 1974). The basis of the film *No habrá más penas ni olvido* (*Funny Dirty Little War*).

———. *Winter Quarters: A Novel of Argentina*. Translated by Nick Caistor. London: Readers International, 1989. Translation of *Cuarteles de invierno* (Barcelona: Bruguera, 1982). The basis of the film *Cuarteles de invierno* (*Winter Quarters*).

Thornton, Lawrence. *Imagining Argentina*. New York: Doubleday, 1987.

———. *Naming the Spirits*. 1995. New York: Doubleday, 1995.

———. *Tales from the Blue Archives*. New York: Doubleday, 1997.

Tizón, Héctor. *La casa y el viento*. Buenos Aires: Editorial Legasa, 1984.

Torchelli, Américo Alfredo. *Bosta de paloma: Novela*. Buenos Aires: El Cid Editor, 1983.

Torre, Javier. *Las noches del Maco*. Buenos Aires: Editorial Legasa, 1986.

———. *Quemar las naves*. Buenos Aires: Legasa Literaria, 1983.

———. *Rubita*. Buenos Aires: Ediciones Corregidor, 1975.

Torres Molina, Susana. *Y a otra cosa mariposa*. Buenos Aires: Ediciones Búsqueda, 1988.

Traba, Marta. *En cualquier lugar*. Bogotá: Siglo Veintiuno Editores, 1984.

———. *Mothers and Shadows*. Translated by Jo Labanyi. London: Readers International, 1985. Translation of *Conversación al sur* (Mexico City: Siglo Veintiuno Editores, 1981).

Valenzuela, Luisa. *Bedside Manners*. Translated by Margaret Jull Acosta. London: Serpent's Tail/High Risk Books, 1995. Translation of *Realidad nacional desde la cama* (Buenos Aires: Grupo Editor Latinoamericano, 1990).

———. *Black Novel with Argentines*. Translated by Toby Talbot. New York: Simon and Schuster, 1992. Translation of *Novela negra con argentinos* (Barcelona: Plaza & Janés, 1990).

————. *He Who Searches.* Translated by Helen R. Lane. Elmwood Park, Ill: Dalkey Archives Press, 1996. Translation of *Como en la guerra* (Buenos Aires: Editorial Sudamericana, 1977).

————. *The Lizard's Tail.* Translated by Gregory Rabassa. London: Serpent's Tail, 1987. Translation of *Cola de lagartija* (Buenos Aires: Bruguera, 1983).

————. *Other Weapons.* Translated by Deborah Bonner. Hanover, N.H.: Ediciones del Norte, 1988. Translation of *Cambio de armas* (Hanover, N.H.: Ediciones del Norte, 1982).

————. *Strange Things Happen Here: Twenty-Six Short Stories and a Novel.* Translated by Helen R. Lane. New York: Harcourt Brace Jovanovich, 1979. Translation of *Aquí pasan cosas raras* (Buenos Aires: Ediciones de la Flor, 1975).

————. *Symmetries: Stories.* Translated by Margaret Jull Costa. London: Serpent's Tail, 1998. Translation of *Simetrías* (Buenos Aires: Sudamericana, 1993).

Vázquez, María Carmela. *Luna sangrienta = Quilla Yaár.* N.p.: Editorial Diaguita, 1984.

Vázquez Rial, Horacio. *Triste's History.* Translated by Jo Labanyi. London: Readers International, 1990. Translation of *Historia del Triste* (Barcelona: Destino, 1987).

Viñas, David. *Cuerpo a cuerpo.* Mexico City: Siglo XXI, 1979.

Zamora, Francisco. *Bisiesto viene de golpe.* Buenos Aires: Bruguera, 1983.

Films and Documentaries

Algunas mujeres (Some Women). Produced by Leonor Schlimovich. 14 minutes. El Ojo Avisor, 1992.

Amiga, La (The Girlfriend). Directed by Jeanine Meerapfel. 115 minutes. Jorge Estrada Mora, 1987.

Amor es un mujer gorda, El (Love is a Fat Woman). Directed by Alejandro Agresti. 75 minutes. 1987.

Beso del olvido, El. Directed by Claudio Campo. 80 minutes. Tea Imagen, 1997.

Boda secreta (Secret Wedding). Directed by Alejandro Agresti. 95 minutes. 1989.

Botín de guerra (Spoils of War). Directed by David Blaustein. 116 minutes. INCAA, 1999.

Buenos Aires Viceversa. Directed by Alejandro Agresti. 100 minutes. Agresti Harding Films, 1996.

Camila. Directed by María Luisa Bemberg. 105 minutes. GEA Cinematográfica, 1984.

Chicos de la guerra, Los. Directed by Bebe Kamin. 1987. Based on the book *Los chicos de la guerra: hablan los soldados que estuvieron en Malvinas* (*The Boys of the War*) by Daniel Kon.

Colours of Hope. 20 minutes. David Grubin Productions, 1985.

Cuarteles de invierno (*Winter Barracks*). Directed by Lautaro Murúa. Produced by Guillermo Smith. 116 minutes. 1984. Based on the novel by Osvaldo Soriano.

De eso no se habla (*I Don't Want to Talk about It*). Directed by María-Luisa Bemberg. 102 minutes. Mojame S.A., Oscar Kramer S.A., Aura Films S.R.L., 1993.

Despertar del L., El. Directed by Poli Nardi. 86 minutes. Aleph Media, 2001.

Dueños del silencio, Los. Directed by Carlos Lemos. 90 minutes. Instituto Nacional de Cinematográfica de Suecia, Crescendo Film-Suecia, and G.C. Producciones-Argentina, 1987.

En retirada (*Bloody Retreat*). Directed by Juan Carlos Desanzo.

Figli/Hijos (*Sons and Daughters*). Directed by Marco Bechis. 100 minutes. Cecchi Gori Group Tiger Cinematográfica, 2001.

Garage Olimpo (*Garage Olimpo*). Directed by Marco Bechis. 98 minutes. Classic-Nisarga-Paradis Film, 1999.

Graffiti. Directed by Matthew Patrick. 28 minutes. Produced by Dianna Costello. The American Film Institute, 1985.

Historia oficial, La (*The Official Story*). Directed by Luis Puenzo. 112 minutes. Almi Pictures, 1985.

Hombre mirando al sudeste (*Man Facing Southeast*). Directed by Eliseo Subiela. 105 minutes. Cinequanon, 1986.

Jacobo Timerman: Prisoner without a Name, Cell without a Number. Produced and directed by Linda Yellen. 97 minuets. 1983.

Kiss of the Spider Woman. Directed by Hector Babenco. 119 minutes. H.B. Filmes, 1986. Based on the novel of the same title by Manuel Puig.

Líneas de teléfonos. Directed by Marcelo Brigante. 18 minutes. Instituto Nacional de Cine y Artes Audiovisuales (INCAA), 1996.

Lo que vendrá (*Times to Come*). Directed by Gustavo Mosquera. 98 minutes. Tripiquicios Sociedad de Capitol e Industria, 1988.

Madres de la Plaza de Mayo, Las (*The Mothers of the Plaza de Mayo*). Produced and directed by Susana Muñoz and Lourdes Portillo. 64 minutes. 1985.

Malajunta (*Bad Company*). Directed by Eduardo Aliverti, Pablo Milstein and Javier Rubel. 57 minutes. CREARS Producciones, 1996.

Miss Mary. Directed by María Luisa Bemberg. 100 minutes. GEA Cinematográfica and New World Pictures, 1986.

Muro del silencio, Un. Directed by Lita Stantic. 107 minutes. Aleph Producciones, Instituto Mexicano de Cinematografía, Channel 4 (Great Britain), 1993.

No al punto final. Directed by Jorge Denti. 24 minutes. 1986.

No habrá más penas ni olvido (Funny Dirty Little War). Directed by Hector Olivera. 80 minutes. Connoisseur Video Collection, Aires Cinematográfica Argentina, 1983. Based on the novel by Osvaldo Soriano.

No te metas (Don't Get Involved). Directed by Jorge Weller. 29 minutes. Ellipsis Film & TV, 1988.

Noche de los lápices, La (The Night of the Pencils). Directed by Hector Olivera. 101 minutes. Aries Cinematográfica, 1986. Based on the book of the same title by María Seoane and Hector Ruíz Núñez.

Pampa del infierno. Directed by Jorge Denti. 25 minutes. 1986.

Por esos ojos (For These Eyes). Directed by Gonzalo Arijón and Virginia Martínez. 52 minutes. France 2 Cinéma, Point du Jour, Télé Europe, 1997.

Prohibido. Directed by Andres di Tella. 105 minutes. Patagonik Film Group, 1997.

The Quest for Truth. 49 minutes. 1997.

Razón de la memoria (Reason of Memory). Directed by Myuca Lorens and Dimas Games. 18 minutes. Taller Julio Cortázar, 1995.

Redada, La (The Raid). Directed by Rolando Pardo. 97 minutes. Pablo Rovito, 1991.

The Search for the Disappeared. 58 minutes. Nova Series. WGBH-TV, 1987.

Ser periodista bajo el culto del miedo y de la muerte. Directed by Suzanne Bilello and Daniela Blanco. 30 minutes. 1999.

Sur (South). Directed by Fernando Solanas. Envar El Kadri/Cinesur, 1987.

Tango Bar. Directed by Marcos Zurinaga. 90 minutes. Beco Films/Zaga Films, 1989.

Tangos: el exilio de Gardel (Tangos: the exile of Gardel). Directed by Fernando Solanas. 125 minutes. Terciné, Cinesur, 1985.

Tiempo de revancha (Time for Revenge). Directed by Adolfo Aristarain. 112 minutes. Aries Cinematográfica, 1983.

Timerman: The News from Argentina. Hosted by Hodding Carter. 29 minutes. Press and the Public Project, Inc. (PREPPI), 1984.

Venda, La. Directed by Gloria Camiruaga. 30 minutes. 2000.

Vidas privadas. Directed by Fito Páez. Mate Producciones y Circo Beat, 2001.

Voz de los pañuelos, La (*The Voice of the Shawls*). Directed by Carmen Guarini and Marcelo Cespedes. 45 minutes. Asociación Madres de Plaza de Mayo, Cine Ojo, 1992.

The Aftermath of the "Dirty War"

Acuña, Carlos H., and Catalina Smulovitz. *Ni olvido ni perdón: Derechos humanos y tensiones civico-militares en la transición argentina.* Documento CEDES, no. 69. Buenos Aires: CEDES, 1991.

Alfonsín, Raúl. "The Transition toward Democracy in a Developing Country: The Case of Argentina." In *After Authoritarianism: Democracy or Disorder,* edited by Daniel N. Nelson, 17–30. Westport, Conn.: Greenwood Press, 1995.

Amnesty International. *Argentina: The Military Juntas and Human Rights: Report of the Trial of the Former Junta Members, 1985.* London: Amnesty International, 1987.

Argentina. Comisión Nacional sobre la Desaparición de Personas. *Anexos del informe de la Comisión Nacional sobre la Desaparición de Personas.* Buenos Aires: EUDEBA, 1994.

———. *Nunca Más [Never Again]: The Report of the Argentine National Commission on the Disappeared.* New York: Farrar, Straus, and Giroux, 1986. Translation of *Nunca más: informe de la Comisión Nacional Sobre la Desaparición de Personas* (Buenos Aires: EUDEBA, 1984).

Argentina: Juicio a los militares: Documentos secretos, decretos-leyes, jurisprudencia. Cuadernos de la Asociación Americana de Juristas, no. 4. Buenos Aires: Rama Argentina de la Asociación de Juristas, 1988.

"Argentina's 'Dirty War' Trial, 1985." In *Great World Trials,* edited by Edward W. Knappman, 411–15. Detroit: Gale, 1994.

"Argentine Political Crimes: Closing in." *Economist* (6 November 1999): 34.

Asociación de Abuelas de Plaza de Mayo. *Culpables para la sociedad, impunes por la ley.* Buenos Aires: M.T. Piñero, 1988.

Avellaneda, Andrés. *Censura, autoritarismo y cultura: Argentina, 1960–1983.* Buenos Aires: Centro Editor América Latina, 1986.

Baloyra, Enrique. "Argentina: Transición o disolución." In *Para vivir la democracia: dilemas de su consolidación,* compiled by Carlos Huneeus, 87–136. Santiago, Chile: Academia Humanismo Cristiano, 1987.

Bermúdez, Norberto, and Juan Gasparini. *El testigo secreto.* Buenos Aires: Javier Vergara, 1999.

Brysk, Alison. *Politics of Human Rights in Argentina: Protest, Change, and Democratization.* Stanford, Calif.: Stanford University Press, 1994.

———. "The Politics of Measurement: The Contested Count of the Disappeared in Argentina." *Human Rights Quarterly* 16, no. 4 (1994): 676–92.

Burns, Jimmy. *The Land That Lost Its Heroes: The Falklands, the Post-War and Alfonsín.* London: Bloomsbury, 1987.

Carlson, Eric Stener. *I Remember Julia: Voices of the Disappeared.* Philadelphia: Temple University Press, 1996.

Centro de Estudios Legales y Sociales. *Terrorismo de estado: 692 responsables: programa de documentación, estudios y publicaciones.* Buenos Aires: Centro de Estudios Legales y Sociales, 1986.

Cerruti, Gabriela. "A Dirty Warrior in Repose" [Interview with Alfredo Astiz]. Translated by Marko Miletich. *Harper's* (April 1998): 25–27.

Ciancaglini, Sergio. *Nada más que la verdad: El juicio a las juntas.* Buenos Aires: Planeta, 1995.

Colás, Santiago. *Postmodernity in Latin America: The Argentine Paradigm.* Durham, N.C.: Duke University Press, 1994.

Corbatta, Jorgelina. *Narrativas de la guerra sucia en Argentina: Piglia, Saer, Valenzuela, Puig.* Buenos Aires: Ediciones Corregidor, 1999.

Corradi, Juan. *The Fitful Republic: Economy, Society and Politics in Argentina.* Boulder, Colo.: Westview Press, 1985.

Democracia vigilada/fotógrafos argentinos. Mexico City: Fondo de Cultura Económica, 1988.

Diana, Marta. *Mujeres guerrilleras: La militancia de los setenta en el testimonio de sus protagonistas femeninas.* Buenos Aires: Planeta, 1996.

España, Claudio, comp. *Cine argentino en democracia, 1983–1993.* Buenos Aires: Fondo Nacional de las Artes, 1994.

Evangelista, Liria. *Voices of the Survivors: Testimony, Mourning, and Memory in Post-Dictatorship Argentina (1983–1995).* Translated by Renzo Llorente. Garland Reference Library of the Humanities. Latin American Studies, vol. 13. New York: Garland, 1998.

Feitlowitz, Marguerite. *A Lexicon of Terror: Argentina and the Legacies of Torture.* New York: Oxford University Press, 1998.

Fernández Meijide, Graciela. *Las cifras de la guerra sucia.* Buenos Aires: Asamblea Permanente por los Derechos Humanos, 1988.

"Former Dictator Arrested for Stealing Children during Dirty War" [Case of Jorge Videla]. *NACLA Report on the Americas* 32, no. 1 (July/August 1998): 1.

Foro de Estudios sobre la Administración de Justicia. *Definativamente—Nunca más: la otra care del informe de la CONADEP.* Buenos Aires:

Foro de Estudios sobre la Administración de Justicia, 1985.

Foster, David William, ed. *The Redemocratization of Argentine Culture, 1983 and Beyond: An International Research Symposium at Arizona State University, February 16–17, 1987: Proceedings*. Trans. Juliette Spence. Tempe: Center for Latin American Studies, Arizona State University, 1989.

"From Military Rule in Argentina and Brazil." In *Authoritarian Regimes in Transition*, edited by Hans Binnendijk with Peggy Nalle and Diane Bendahmane, 223–74. Washington, D.C.: Foreign Service Institute, U.S. Dept. of State, 1997.

Halperín Donghi, Tulio. "Argentina's Unmastered Past." *Latin American Research Review* 23, no. 2 (1988): 3–24.

Herrera, Matilde, and Ernesto Tenembaum. *Identidad, despojo y restitución*. Buenos Aires: Editorial Contrapunto, 1989.

Joyce, Christopher, and Eric Stover. *Witnesses from the Grave: The Stories Bones Tell*. Boston: Little, Brown and Company, 1991.

Labrune, Noemi. *Buscados: represores del Alto Valle y Neuquén*. Buenos Aires: Asamblea Permanente por los Derechos Humanos, Delegación Neuquén: Centro Editor de América Latina, 1988.

López, Ernesto. *Ni la ceniza ni la gloria: Actores, sistema político y cuestión militar en los años de Alfonsín*. Buenos Aires: Universidad Nacional de Quilmes, 1994.

López Laval, Hilda. *Autoritarismo y cultura: Argentina, 1976–1983*. Madrid: Fundamentos, 1995.

McSherry, J. Patrice. *Incomplete Transition: Military Power and Democracy in Argentina*. New York: St. Martin's Press, 1997.

Malamud Goti, Jaime E. *Game without End: State Terror and the Politics of Justice*. Norman: University of Oklahoma Press, 1996.

Mignone, Emilio Fermín, Cynthia L. Estlund, and Samuel Issacharoff. "Dictatorship on Trial: Prosecution of Human Rights Violations in Argentina." *Yale Journal of International Law* 10 (Fall 1984): 118–50.

"A National Exorcism." *Time* (27 May 1985): 44.

Nino, Carlos Santiago. "The Human Rights Policy of the Argentine Constitutional Government: A Reply." *Yale Journal of International Law* 11 (Fall 1985): 217–30. (Discussion of "Dictatorship on Trial: Prosecution of Human Rights Violations in Argentina." Emilio Fermín Mignone, Cynthia L. Estlund, and Samuel Issacharoff. *Yale Journal of International Law* 10 (Fall 1984): 118–50.)

———. *Radical Evil on Trial*. New Haven, Conn.: Yale University Press, 1996.

Norden, Deborah L. *Military Rebellion in Argentina: Between Coups and Consolidation*. Lincoln: University of Nebraska Press, 1996.

Ocampo, Luis Moreno. "Beyond Punishment: Justice in the Wake of Massive Crimes in Argentina." *Journal of International Affairs* 52, no. 2 (Spring 1999): 669–89.

Osiel, Mark. *Mass Atrocity, Ordinary Evil, and Hannah Arendt: Criminal Consciousness in Argentina's Dirty War*. New Haven, Conn.: Yale University Press, 2001.

Peralta-Ramos, Mónica, and Carlos H. Waisman. *From Military Rule to Liberal Democracy in Argentina*. Boulder, Colo.: Westview, 1987.

Perelli, Carina. "Settling Accounts with Blood Memory: The Case of Argentina." *Social Research* 59, no. 2 (Summer 1992): 415–51.

Pion-Berlin, David. *Through Corridors of Power: Institutions and Civil-Military Relations in Argentina*. University Park: Pennsylvania State University Press, 1997.

Poneman, Daniel. *Argentina: Democracy on Trial*. New York: Paragon House, 1987.

Reati, Fernando O. *Nombrar lo innombrable: Violencia política y novela argentina, 1975–1985*. Buenos Aires: Editorial Legasa, 1992.

Sancinetti, Marcelo A. *Derechos humanos en la Argentina postdictatorial: juicio a los ex comandantes, Punto Final, obediencia debida, apéndice documental*. Buenos Aires: Lerner Editores Asociados, 1988.

Sosnowski, Saúl, comp. *Represión y reconstrucción de una cultura: el caso argentino*. Buenos Aires: Eudeba, 1985.

Stevenson, Matthew. "Cleaning Up after a Dirty War." *American Spectator* (June 1998): 38–41.

Valenzuela, Luisa. "A Legacy of Poets and Cannibals: Literature Revives in Argentina." In *Lives on the Line: The Testimony of Contemporary Latin American Authors*, edited and with an introduction by Doris Meyer, 292–7. Berkeley: University of California Press, 1988.

Veiga, Raúl. *Las organizaciones de derechos humanos*. Buenos Aires: Centro Editor de América Latina, 1985.

Veinte años: 361 imágines contra los crímenes de ayer y de hoy (art exhibition). Buenos Aires: s.n., 1996.

Verbitsky, Horacio. *Civiles y militares: Memoria secreta de la transición*. 2d ed. Colección Memoria y presente. Buenos Aires: Editorial Contrapunto, 1997.

———. *La posguerra sucia: un análisis de la transición*. Buenos Aires: Legasa, 1985.

Vidal, Hernán, ed. *Fascismo y experiencia literaria: reflexiones para una recanonización*. Minneapolis, Minn.: Institute for the Study of Ideologies and Literature, 1985.

Chile

Background to the "Dirty War"

Allende Gossens, Salvador. *Chile's Road to Socialism*. Edited by Joan E. Garces. Translated by J. Darling. Baltimore: Penguin Books, 1973.
———. *The Salvador Allende Reader: Chile's Voice of Democracy*. Edited by James D. Cockcroft. Translated by Moisés Espinoza and Nancy Nuñez. Melbourne, Vic., Australia: Ocean Press, 2000.
Boorstein, Edward. *Allende's Chile: An Inside View*. New York: International, 1977.
Davis, Nathaniel. *The Last Two Years of Salvador Allende*. Ithaca, N.Y.: Cornell University Press, 1985.
Davis, William Columbus. "Chile: Democracy That Was." Chap. 4 in *Warnings from the Far South: Democracy versus Dictatorship in Uruguay, Argentina, and Chile*, 151–216. Westport, Conn.: Praeger, 1995.
Evans, Leslie, ed. *Disaster in Chile: Allende's Strategy and Why It Failed*. New York: Pathfinder, 1974.
Kaufman, Edy. *Crisis in Allende's Chile: New Perspectives*. New York: Praeger, 1988.
Morris, David J. *We Must Make Haste—Slowly: The Process of Revolution in Chile*. New York: Random House, 1973.
Pinochet Ugarte, Augusto. *The Crucial Day, September 11, 1973*. Translated by María Teresa Escobar. Santiago de Chile: Editorial Renacimiento, 1982. Translation of *El día decisivo, 11 de septiembre de 1973* (Santiago: Editorial Andrés Bello, 1979).
Power, Margaret. *Right-Wing Women in Chile: Feminine Power and the Struggle against Allende*. University Park: Pennsylvania State University Press, 2002.
Rojas, Róbinson. *The Murder of Allende and the End of the Chilean Way to Socialism*. New York: Harper & Row, 1976. Translated by Andrée Conrad. Translation of *Estos mataron a Allende: Reportaje a la masacre de un pueblo* (Barcelona: Martínez Roca, 1974).
Sigmund, Paul E. *The Overthrow of Allende and the Politics of Chile, 1964–1976*. Pittsburgh: University of Pittsburgh Press, 1977.

United States. Congress. Senate. Select Committee to Study Governmental Operations with Respect to Intelligence Activities. *Covert Action in Chile.* Washington, D.C.: U.S. Government Printing Office, 1975.

Valenzuela, J. Samuel, and Arturo Valenzuela. "Chile and the Breakdown of Democracy." In *Latin American Politics and Development,* 2d ed., edited by Howard J. Wiarda and Howard F. Kline, 212–48. Boulder, Colo.: Westview Press, 1985.

The "Dirty War," 1973–1990

Nonfiction and Testimonios

Agger, Inger, and Søren Buus Jensen. *Trauma and Healing under State Terrorism.* London: Zed Books, 1996. Translation of *Trauma y cura en situaciones de terrorismo de estado: derechos humanos y salud mental in Chile bajo la dictadura militar.* Santiago: CESOC, Ediciones Chile-América, 1996.

Agosin, Marjorie. *The Alphabet in My Hands: A Writing Life.* Translated by Nancy Abraham Hall. New Brunswick, N.J.: Rutgers University Press, 2000.

———. *Tapestries of Hope, Threads of Love: The Arpillera Movement in Chile, 1974–1994.* Translated by Celeste Kostopulos-Cooperman. Albuquerque: University of New Mexico Press, 1998.

Ahumada, Eugenio, and Rodrigo Atria. *Chile, la memoria prohibida: las violaciones a los derechos humanos, 1973–1983.* 3 vols. Santiago: Pehuén, 1989.

Amnesty International. *Chile: An Amnesty International Report.* London: Amnesty International Publications, 1974.

———. *Chile: An Amnesty International Report.* London: Amnesty International Publications, 1983.

Arriagada Herrera, Genaro. *Pinochet: The Politics of Power.* Translated by Nancy Morris, Vincent Ercolano, and Kristin Whitney. Boston: Allen & Unwin, 1988. Translation of *La política militar de Pinochet* (Chile: G. Arriagada Herrera, 1985).

———. *Por la razón o la fuerza: Chile bajo Pinochet.* Santiago: Editorial Sudamericana, 1998.

Axelsson, Sun, Birgitta Leander, and Raúl Silva C. *Evidence on the Terror in Chile.* Translated from the Swedish by Brian McBeth. London: Merlin Press, 1974. Translation of *Terrorn i Chile* (1974).

Bitar, Sergio. *Isla 10.* 2d ed. Santiago: Pehuén, 1988.

Blixen, Samuel. *El vientre del cóndor: del archivo del terror al caso Ber-*

ríos. Montevideo: Brecha, 1994.

Branch, Taylor, and Eugene M. Propper. *Labyrinth* [the assassination of Orlando Letelier]. New York: Viking Press, 1982.

Buschmann, Sergio. *Así me fugué: testimonio de un combatiente del FPMR fugado de una cárcel de Pinochet.* Santiago: Frente Patriótico Manuel Rodríguez, 1988.

Cabieses, Manuel. *Chile: 11808* [i.e., once mil ochocientos y ocho] *horas en campos de concentración.* Caracas: Fondo Editorial Salvador de la Plaza, 1975.

Carrasco, Rolando. *Chile's Prisoners of War.* Moscow: Novosti Press Agency Pub. House, 1977.

Cassidy, Sheila. *Audacity to Believe.* London: Collins, 1977.

Castillo, Carmen. *Un día de octubre en Santiago.* Mexico City: Ediciones Era, 1982. Translation of *Un jour d'octubre à Santiago* (Paris: Stock, 1980).

Castillo Yáñez, Pedro. *Perito en cárceles: relato de cadenas, encierros y antifaces.* Santiago: Imprenta La Unión, 1989.

Cavanaugh, William T. *Torture and Eucharist: Theology, Politics and the Body of Christ.* Oxford: Blackwell, 1998.

Cayuela, José, comp. *Chile, la masacre de un pueblo: testimonios de nueve venezolanos víctimas del golpe militar chileno.* Caracas: Sintesis Dosmil, 1974.

Centro de Estudios y Publicaciones. *Chile:* [*con documentos inéditos*]. Lima: CEP, 1974.

Chuchryk, Patricia. "Subversive Mothers: The Opposition to the Military Regime in Chile." In *Surviving beyond Fear: Women, Children, and Human Rights in Latin America,* edited by Marjorie Agosin and Monica Bruno, 86–97. Fredonia, N.Y.: White Pine Press, 1993.

Comité Chileno de Solidaridid con la Resistancia Antifascista de La Habana. *Presos políticos desaparecidos en Chile.* Mexico City: Casa de Chile en México, 1977.

Constable, Pamela, and Arturo Valenzuela. *A Nation of Enemies: Chile Under Pinochet.* New York: Norton, 1991.

Cooper, Marc. *Pinochet and Me: A Chilean Anti-Memoir.* New York: Verso, 2001.

Dinges, John, and Saul Landau. *Assassination on Embassy Row* [the assassination of Orlando Letelier]. New York: Pantheon, 1980.

Dorfman, Ariel. *Heading South, Looking North: A Bilingual Journey.* New York: Farrar, Straus, and Giroux, 1998. Published in Spanish as *Rumbo al sur, deseando el norte: un romance bilingüe.* Translated by the author (Barcelona: Planeta, 1998).

Ensalaco, Mark. *Chile Under Pinochet: Uncovering the Truth.* Philadelphia: University of Pennsylvania, 2000.

Falcoff, Mark. *Modern Chile, 1970–1989: A Critical History.* New Brunswick, N.J.: Transaction Books, 1989.

Free, Donald. *Death in Washington: The Murder of Orlando Letelier.* Westport, Conn.: Lawrence Hill, 1980.

Fuerzas armadas chilenas, cómo son y cómo actuan. N.p.: Editora y Distribuidora Runamarka, [1978].

García Villegas, René. *Soy testigo: dictadura, tortura, injusticia.* Santiago: Amerinda, 1990.

Garretón, Manuel Antonio. "The Political Evolution of the Chilean Military Regime and Problems in the Transition to Democracy." In *Transitions from Authoritarian Rule: Latin America,* edited by Guillermo O'Donnell, Philippe C. Schmitter, and Laurence Whitehead, 95–122. Baltimore: Johns Hopkins University Press, 1986.

González, Ruth. *Generación perdida de Paz Rodríguez.* Nuñoa, Chile: Editorial Mosquito Comunicaciones, 1991.

Guzmán J., Nancy. *Un grito desde el silencio: detención, asesinato y desaparición de Bautista van Schouwen y Patricio Munita.* Santiago: Lom Ediciones, 1998.

———. *Romo: confesiones de un torturador.* Santiago: Planeta, 2000.

Hauser, Thomas. *Missing.* New York: Avon, 1982. Originally published as *The Execution of Charles Horman* (New York: Harcourt Brace Jovanovich, 1978). The basis of the film *Missing.*

Hickman, John. *News from the End of the Earth: A Portrait of Chile.* New York: St. Martin's Press, 1998.

International Commission of Enquiry into the Crimes of the Military Junta in Chile. *Denuncia y testimonio: Tercera Sesión de la Comisión Internacional de Investigación de los Crímenes de la Junta Militar en Chile, Ciudad de México, 18–21 de febrero de 1975.* Helsinki: The Commission, 1975.

International Commission of Jurists. *Arrests and Detentions and Freedom of Information in Chile, September 1976: A Supplement to the Report of the ICJ Mission to Chile, April 1974.* Geneva, Switzerland: International Commission of Jurists, 1976.

———. *Final Report of Mission to Chile, April 1974, to Study the Legal System and the Protection of Human Rights.* Geneva, Switzerland: International Commission of Jurists, 1974.

———. *Supplement to Final Report of International Commission of Jurists' Mission to Chile.* Geneva, Switzerland: International Commission of Jurists, 1975.

Jara, Joan. *An Unfinished Song: The Life of Victor Jara.* New York: Ticknor & Fields, 1984. Originally published as *Victor: An Unfinished Song* (London: Jonathan Cape, 1983).

Ladrón de Guevara, Matilde, and Gabriel Egaña. *Pacto sublime.* Santiago: Editorial La Noria, 1992.

Martín de Pozuelo, Eduardo, and Santiago Tarín. *España acusa.* Barcelona: Plaza & Janés, 1999.

Merino Vega, Marcia Alejandra. *Mi verdad: "Más allá del horror, yo acuso . . . ."* Santiago: M. Merino Vega, 1993.

National Chile Center. *The Chilean Junta: Vandals in the University.* New York: National Chile Center, 1978.

Organization of American States. Inter-American Commission on Human Rights. *Report on the Status of Human Rights in Chile: Findings of "on the Spot" Observations in the Republic of Chile, July 22–August 2, 1974: Approved by the Commission at its 42nd Meeting, Held October 24, 1974.* Washington, D.C.: General Secretariat of the Organization of American States, 1974. Published in Spanish as *Informe sobre la situación de los derechos humanos in Chile: resultado de la observación "in loco" practicada en la República de Chile del 22 de Julio al 2 de agosto de 1974* (Washington, D.C.: Secretaría General de la Organización de los Estados Americanos, 1974).

———. *Third Report on the Situation of Human Rights in Chile.* Washington, D.C.: General Secretariat of the Organization of American States, 1977. Published in Spanish as *Tercer informe sobre la situación de los derechos humanos en Chile* (Washington, D.C.: Secretaría General de la Organización de los Estados Americanos, 1977).

O'Shaughnessy, Hugh. *Pinochet, the Politics of Torture.* New York: New York University Press, 2000.

Peña, Ana Verónica. *Fuga al anochecer.* Santiago: Editorial Los Andes, 1990.

Politzer, Patricia. *Fear in Chile: Lives under Pinochet.* New York: Pantheon, 1989.

———. *La ira de Pedro y los otros.* Santiago: Planeta, 1988.

Prieto F., Luis B. *Los crímenes fascistas de la Junta Militar Chilena: informe de la Comisión Internacional Investigadora de los Crímenes de la Junta Militar en Chile.* Caracas: Ediciones Centauro, 1976.

Quigley, Thomas. "The Chilean Coup, the Church and the Human Rights Movement." *America* (11 February 2002): 12–14.

Quijada Cerda, Aníbal. *Cerca de púas.* Havana: Casa de las Américas, 1977.

Quinteros, Heroldo. *Diario de un preso politico chileno.* Madrid: Ediciones de la Torre, 1979.

Rojas, Carmen. *Recuerdos de una mirista.* Montevideo: Deltaller, 1988.

Scherer García, Julio. *Pinochet: Vivir matando.* Mexico City: Nuevo Siglo, 2000.

Schirmer, Jennifer G. "Chile: The Loss of Childhood." In *Surviving beyond Fear: Women, Children, and Human Rights in Latin America,* edited by Marjorie Agosin and Monica Bruno, 162–7. Fredonia, N.Y.: White Pine Press, 1993.

Schnake, Erich. *De improviso la nada: testimonio de prisión y exilio.* Santiago: Ediciones Documentas, 1988.

Sepúlveda Pulvirenti, Emma, ed. *We, Chile: Personal Testimonies of the Chilean arpilleristas.* Translated by Bridget Morgan. Falls Church, Va.: Azul Editions, 1996.

Simón Rivas, Francisco. *Traición a Hipócrates: médicos en el aparato represivo de la dictadura.* Santiago: Ediciones ChileAmérica, 1990.

Spooner, Mary Helen. *Soldiers in a Narrow Land: The Pinochet Regime in Chile.* Berkeley: University of California, 1994.

Stover, Eric. *The Open Secret: Torture and the Medical Profession in Chile.* Washington, D.C.: Committee on Scientific Freedom and Responsibility, American Association for the Advancement of Science, 1987.

Teitelboim Volosky, Sergio. *Derechos humanos y soberanía popular.* Santiago: Ediciones "Instituto de Ciencias Alejandro Lipschutz, 1985.

Timerman, Jacobo. *Chile: Death in the South.* Translated by Robert Cox. New York: Knopf, 1987. Translation of *Chile: el galope muerto* (Madrid: Ediciones El País, 1987).

United States. Congress. Senate. Committee on the Judiciary Subcommittee to Investigate Problems Connected with Refugees and Escapees. *Refugee and Humanitarian Problems in Chile. Hearing[s] Ninety-Third Congress, first session–Ninety-Fourth Congress, first session.* Washington, D.C.: United States Government Printing Office, 1973– .

Valdés, Hernán. *Tejas Verdes: diario de un campo de concentración en Chile.* Esplugues de Llobregat, Spain: Editorial Ariel, 1974.

Valdés, Juan Gabriel. *Pinochet's Economists: The Chicago School in Chile.* Cambridge, England: Cambridge University Press, 1995.

Valenzuela, Arturo, and Samuel J. Valenzuela, eds. *Chile: Politics and Society.* New Brunswick, N.J.: Transaction Books, 1976.

Valenzuela, J. Samuel, and Arturo Valenzuela, eds. *Military Rule in Chile: Dictatorship and Oppositions.* Baltimore: Johns Hopkins University Press, 1986.

Valle, Juan del. *Campos de concentración en Chile, 1973–1976*. Santiago: Mosquito Comunicaciones, 1977.

Verdugo, Patricia. *Bucarest 187*. Santiago: Editorial Sudamericana, 1999.

———. *Chile, Pinochet, and the Caravan of Death*. Translated by Marcelo Montecino. Coral Gables, Fla.: North-South Center Press, 2001. Translation of *Caso Arellano: Los zarpazos del puma* (Santiago: CESOC, Ediciones ChileAmérica, 1989).

———. *Interferencia secreta*. Santiago: Editorial Sudamericana, 1998.

Vidal, Hernán. *El Movimiento Contra la Tortura "Sebastián Acevedo": derechos humanos y la producción de símbolos nacionales bajo el fascismo chileno*. Minneapolis, Minn.: Institute for the Study of Ideologies and Literature, 1996.

Villegas, Sergio. *El estadio: once de septiembre en el país del Edén*. Santiago: Emisión, 1990.

Vuskovic Rojo, Sergio. *Dawson*. Madrid: Ediciones Michay, 1984.

Weitzel, Ruby. *Tumbas de cristal: libro testimonio de la Vicaría de la Solidaridad del Arzobispado de Santiago*. Santiago: FASIC: Interamericana, 1987.

Witker Velásquez, Alejandro. *Prisión en Chile*. Mexico City: Fondo de Cultura Económica, 1975.

Wright, Thomas, and Rody Oñate. *Flight from Chile: Voices of Exile*. Albuquerque: University of New Mexico Press, 1998.

Ya te vimos, Pinochet [caricatures and political cartoons]. Selection and prologue by Rius. Mexico City: Editorial Posada, 1974.

Literature

Agosin, Marjorie. *An Absence of Shadows: Poems*. Translated by Celeste Kostopulos-Cooperman, Cola Franzen, and Mary G. Berg. Fredonia, N.Y.: White Pine Press, 1998.

Agosin, Marjorie, and others. *What Is Secret: Stories by Chilean Women*. Fredonia, N.Y.: White Pine Press, 1995.

Alegría, Fernando. *Allende: A Novel*. Translated by Frank Janney. Stanford: Stanford University Press, 1993. Translation of *Allende: Mi vecino el presidente* (Santiago: Planeta, 1989).

———. *The Chilean Spring*. Translated by Stephen Fredman. Pittsburgh, Pa.: Latin American Literary Review Press, 1980.

———, ed. *Chilean Writers in Exile: Eight Short Novels*. Trumansburg, N.Y.: Crossing Press, 1982.

Allende, Isabel. *House of the Spirits.* Translated by Magda Bogin. New York: Knopf, 1985. Translation of *La casa de los espíritus* (Barcelona: Plaza & Janés, 1982). The basis of a film of the same title.

————. *Of Love and Shadows.* Translated by Magda Bogin. New York: Knopf, 1987. Translation of *De amor y de sombra* (Barcelona: Plaza & Janés, 1984). The basis of a film of the same title.

————. *Portrait in Sepia: A Novel.* Translated by Margaret Sayers Peden. New York: HarperCollins, 2001. Translation of *Retrato en sepia: novela.* (New York: Rayo, 2001).

Benavente, David. *Pedro, Juan y Diego: Tres Marías y una rosa; Ensayo "Ave Felix," teatro chileno post-golpe.* Santiago: CESOC, Ediciones ChileAmérica, 1989.

Donoso, José. *Curfew: A Novel.* Translated by Alfred MacAdam. New York: Weidenfeld & Nicolson, 1988. Translation of *La desesperanza* (Barcelona: Seix Barrarl, 1986).

————. *The Garden Next Door.* Translated by Hardie St. Martin. New York: Grove Press, 1992. Translation of *El jardín de al lado* (Barcelona: Seix Barral, 1981).

————. *A House in the Country.* Translated by David Pritchard with Suzanne Jill Levine. New York: Knopf, 1984. Translation of *Casa de campo* (Barcelona: Seix Barral, 1978).

Dorfman, Ariel. *Death and the Maiden* [A Play in Three Acts]. New York: Penguin Books, 1992. Translation of *La muerte y la doncella* (Buenos Aires: Ediciones de la Flor, 1992).

————. *Hard Rain.* Translated by George Shivers with the author. Columbia, La.: Readers International, 1990. Translation of *Moros en la costa* (Buenos Aires: Editorial Sudamericana, 1973).

————. *Last Waltz in Santiago.* Translated by Edith Grossman and the author. New York: Viking, 1988. Translation of *Pastel de choclo* (Santiago: Sinfronteras, 1986).

————. *Missing: Poems.* Translated by Edie Grossman. London: Amnesty International British Section, 1981.

————. *Widows.* Translated by Stephen Kessler. New York: Pantheon, 1983. Translation of *Viudas* (Mexico City: Siglo XXI, 1981).

Fuguet, Alberto. *Bad Vibes.* Translated by Kristina Cordero. New York: St. Martin's Press, 1997. Translation of *Mala onda* (Santiago: Aguilar Chilena de Ediciones, 1996).

Hazuka, Tom. *In the City of the Disappeared.* Bridgehampton, N.Y.: Bridgeworks, 2000.

Marras, Sergio. *Carta apócrifa de Pinochet a un siquiatra chileno.* Santiago: Demens Sapiens, 1998.

Muñoz Morales, Nelson. *Caballo bermejo: lejos ya, les sacarán las vendas y verán nuevamente el mar.* Santiago: Lom Ediciones, 2000.

Parra, Marco Antonio de la. *The Secret Holy War of Santiago de Chile.* Translated by Charles Philip Thomas. New York: Interlink Books, 1994. Translation of *La secreta guerra santa de Santiago de Chile.* (Santiago: Planeta, 1989).

―――. *Teatro: lo crudo, lo cocido, lo podrido; matatangos (disparen sobre el zorzal).* Santiago: Editorial Nascimento, 1983.

Richards, Caroline. *Sweet Country.* New York: Harcourt Brace Jovanovich, 1979. The basis of the film *Sweet Country (Dulce país).*

Sepúlveda, Luis. *The Name of the Bullfighter.* Translated by Suzanne Ruta. New York: Harcourt Brace, 1996. Translation of *Nombre de torero* (Barcelona: Tusquets Editores, 1994).

Skármeta, Antonio. *Burning Patience.* Translated by Katherine Silver. New York: Pantheon, 1987. Translation of *Ardiente paciencia* (Buenos Aires: Editorial Sudamericana, 1985). The basis of the film *Il postino.*

―――. *The Composition.* Translated by Elisa Amado and illustrated by Alfonso Ruano. Toronto: Groundwood Books, 2000. Translation of *La composición* (Caracas: Ediciones Ekaré, 2000). Juvenile fiction. This story is included in *Watch Where the Wolf Is Going: Stories,* translated by Donald L. Schmidt and Federico Cordovez (Columbia, La.: Readers International, 1991).

―――. *I Dreamt the Snow Was Burning.* Translated by Malcolm Coad. London: Readers International, 1985. Translation of *Soñé que la nieve ardía* (Barcelona: Planeta, 1975).

―――. *Tiro libre* [short stories]. Buenos Aires: Siglo Veintiuno Argentina, 1973. These stories are included in *Watch Where the Wolf Is Going: Stories,* translated by Donald L. Schmidt and Federico Cordovez (Columbia, La.: Readers International, 1991).

Watson, James. *Talking in Whispers.* New York: Knopf, 1983. Young adult fiction.

Films and Documentaries

Actas de Marusia. Directed by Miguel Littin. 90 minutes. Conacine, 1985.

Amnesia. Directed by Gonzalo Justiniano. 90 minutes. Arca, 1994.

Angeles (Angels). Directed by Tatiana Gaviola. Ictus, 1988.

Armas de la paz, Las (The Arms of Peace). Directed by Augusto Gongoa. 39 minutes. Nueva Imagen, 1989.

Batalla de Chile: la lucha de un pueblo sin armas, La. 1. La insurrección de la burguesía (The Battle of Chile: The Struggle of an Unarmed Peo-

ple. 1. The Insurrection of the Bourgeoisie). Produced and directed by Patricio Guzmán. 96 minutes. 1975.

Batalla de Chile: la lucha de un pueblo sin armas, La. 2. El golpe del estado (The Battle of Chile: The Struggle of an Unarmed People. 2. The Coup). Produced and directed by Patricio Guzmán. 96 minutes. 1976.

Batalla de Chile: la lucha de un pueblo sin armas, La. 3. La fuerza del pueblo (The Battle of Chile: The Struggle of an Unarmed People. 3. The Power of the People). Produced and directed by Patricio Guzmán. 78 minutes. 1978.

Cas Pinochet, Le (El caso Pinochet; The Pinochet Case). Directed by Patricio Guzman. 110 minutes. 2001.

Chile: A History in Exile. Directed by Cecilia Araneda. 26 minutes. Cine al Azar, Winnepeg, with the assistance of the Canada Council: Media Arts and the National Film Board of Canada, 1998.

Chile: Defeat of a Dictator. Written, produced, and directed by Steve York. 34 minutes. York, Zimmerman, Inc.; WETA TV, 2000.

Chile en transición (Chile in Transition). Directed by Gaston Ancelovici and Frank Diamond. 73 minutes. Films Transit, 1991.

Chile: ¿Hasta cuando? Produced and directed by David Bradbury. 58 minutes. 1985.

Chile: No invoco tu nombre en vano (Chile, I Don't Take Your Name in Vain. 36 minutes. Colectivo Cine-OJO, 1984.

Chile: The New Victims. 20 minutes. Amnesty International [1986?].

Chile: Torture as a Political Instrument. Directed by Hernán Castro. 28 minutes. Centre Productions, 1988.

Chile: una historia de exilio (Chile: A History in Exile). Directed by Cecilia Araneda. 26 minutes. Cine al Azar, 1998.

Dance of Hope. Directed by Deborah Shaffer and Lavonne Poteet. 78 minutes. Produced by Deborah Shaffer and Lavonne Poteet. 1989.

Dead Line. Directed by Alexander Marengo. 26 minutes. Platinum Film and Television, 1998.

Death and the Maiden. Directed by Roman Polanski. 103 minutes. Fine Line Features; Capitol Films, 1995.

Dulce patria (Sweet Country). Directed by Juan Andres Racy. Produced by Barbara Margolis and Juan Andres Racy. 57 minutes. 1985.

En nombre de Dios. Directed by Patricio Guzman. 90 minutes. 1987.

Estación del regreso, La. (The Season of Our Return). Directed by Leonardo Knocking. 84 minutes. Produced by Cristián Kaulen and Guillermo Palma. 1987.

Fernando ha vuelto (Fernando Is Back). Directed by Silvio Caiozzi. 31

minutes. Andrea Films, 1998.

Frontera, La (*The Frontier*). Directed by Ricardo Larrain. 113 minutes. Cine XXI, 1991.

General Pinochet. Directed by Rosalind Bain and Jenny Barraclough. 57 minutes. Mentorn Barraclough Carey for Channel 4, 1998.

Gringuito (*Little Gringo*). Directed by Sergio Castilla. 90 minutes. 1998.

Hijos de la guerra fría (*Children of the Cold War*). Directed by Gonzalo Justiniano. 76 minutes. 1985.

Historias de Lagartos (*Lizards' Tale*). Directed by Juan Carlos Bustamante. 80 minutes. Bustamante Producciones, 1988.

The House of the Spirits. Directed by Neue Constantin. Miramax, 1993. Based on the novel of the same title by Isabel Allende.

Imagen latente (*Latent Image*). Directed by Pablo Perelman. 92 minutes. 1987.

In a Time of Betrayal. Directed by Carmen Castillo. 60 minutes. INA, 1994.

Inside Pinochet's Prisons. 30 minutes. Journeyman Pictures, 1973.

Memoirs of an Everyday War. Directed by Gaston Ancelovici. 30 minutes. Comisión Chileana de Derechos Humanos; Cinemateca Chilena, 1986.

Missing. Directed by Costa-Gavras. Universal Pictures, 1982. Based on the book *Missing*, by Thomas Hauser, which was originally published as *The Execution of Charles Horman.*

My House Is on Fire. Directed by Rodrigo and Ariel Dorfman. 19 minutes. Dorfsky Brothers, 1997.

No me amenaces (*Don't Threaten Me*). Directed by Juan Andres Racz. 52 minutes. La Mar Films, 1990.

No me olvides (*Don't Forget Me*). Directed by Tatiana Gaviola. 13 minutes. Institut culturel et technique d'utilité sociale (ICTUS), 1988.

Of Love and Shadows. Directed by Betty Kaplan. 104 minutes. Miramax, 1996. Based on the novel of the same title by Isabel Allende.

Padre santo y la Gloria (*Holy Father and Gloria*). Produced and directed by Estela Bravo. 43 minutes. 1987.

Patio 29: Historias de silencio (*Patio 29: Stories of Silence*). Directed by Esteban Larrain. 84 minutes. Fondo para del Desarrollo de las Artes y la Cultura, 1998.

Pleut sur Santiago, Il (*It's Raining on Santiago*). Directed by Helvio Soto. 109 minutes. 1977.

Postino, Il (*The Postman*). Directed by Michael Radford. 112 minutes. Cecchi Gori Group, 1995. Based on the novel *Ardiente Paciencia*, by Antonio Skármeta.

September 11, 1973: The Last Stand of Salvador Allende. Directed by Patricio Henríquez. 58 minutes. Macumba International, 1998.

Solidaridad: Faith, Hope and Haven. Directed by Edgardo Reyes and Gillian Brown. 57 minutes. Insite Video, 1989.

Somos más (Somos+, Somos, We Are More). Directed by Pablo Salas and Pedro Chaskel. 15 minutes. Antu, 1985.

Steel Blues (Jours de fer). Directed by Jorge Fajardo. 34 minutes. Canada, 1976. A segment of *Il n'y a pas d'oubli,* directed by Jorge Fajardo, Marilú Mallet, and Rodrigo González (Canada, 1976).

Sweet Country (Dulce país). Produced and Directed by Michael Cacoyannis. 120 minutes. 1985. Based on the novel of the same title by Caroline Richards.

Threads of Hope. Produced by Les Harris. 50 minutes. TVOntario, CKVR TV, and Vision TV, 1996.

Tyrants Will Rise from My Tomb, Chile. 30 minutes. Australian Broadcasting Corporation, 1986.

Vecino, El. Directed by Juan Carlos Bustamante. 90 minutes. Bustamante Productions, 1998.

Verdadera historia de Johnny Good, La. Directed by Pablo Tupper and Patricia del Rio. 36 minutes. Grupo Proceso, 1990.

The Aftermath of the "Dirty War"

Allen, Paula. *Flores en el desierto* [pictorial works]. Prologue by Isabel Allende. Introduction by Patricia Verdugo. Santiago: Editorial Cuarto Propio, 1999.

Amnesty International. *Pinochet Case: Universal Jurisdiction and the Absence of Immunity for Crimes against Humanity.* London: Amnesty International, International Secretariat, 1999.

Avelar, Idelber. *The Untimely Present: Postdictatorial Latin American Fiction and the Task of Mourning.* Durham, N.C.: Duke University Press, 1999.

Bermúdez, Norberto, and Juan Gasparini. *El testigo secreto.* Buenos Aires: Javier Vergara, 1999.

Cánovas, Rodrigo. *Lihn, Zurita, Ictus, Radrigán: literatura chilena y experiencia autoritaria.* Santiago: Facultad Latinoamericana de Ciencias Sociales, 1986.

Caucoto Pereira, Nelson, and Héctor Salazar Ardiles. *Un verde manto de impunidad.* Santiago: Edicones Academia, Universidad Academia de Humanismo Cristiano: Fundación de Ayuda Social de las Iglesias Cristianas, 1994.

Chile. Comisión Chilena de Derechos Humanos. *Nunca más en Chile: síntesis corregida y actualizada del informe Rettig.* 2d ed. Santiago: Lom Ediciones: Comisión Chilena de Derechos Humanos: Fundación Ideas, 1999.

Chile. Comisión Nacional de Verdad y Reconciliación. *Report of the Chilean National Commission on Truth and Reconciliation.* 2 vols. Translated by Phillip E. Berryman. Notre Dame, Ind.: University of Notre Dame Press, 1993.

Chile from Within, 1973–1988 [documentary photography]. New York: Norton, 1990.

Drago, Tito. *El retorno de la ilusion: Pinochet, el fin de la impunidad.* Barcelona: RBA, 1999.

Drake, Paul W., and Iván Jaksic, eds. *The Struggle for Democracy in Chile.* Rev. ed. Lincoln: University of Nebraska Press, 1995.

España, Aristóteles. *El sur de la memoria.* Punta Arenas, Chile: Divina Ediciones; Copenhagen, Denmark: Rehabilitation Centre for Torture Victims, 1992.

García Villegas, René. *¡Pisagua! Cain, ¿qué has hecho de tu hermano?* Santiago: Editorial Periodística Emisión, 1990.

Gómez Araneda, León. *Tras la huella de los desaparecidos.* Santiago: Ediciones Caleuche, 1990.

Guerra-Cunningham, Lucía. *Texto e ideología en la narrativa chilena.* Minneapolis, Minn.: Institute for the Study of Ideologies and Literatures: Prisma Institute, 1987.

Hitchens, Christopher. *The Trial of Henry Kissinger.* London: Verso, 2001.

Jara, René. *Los límites de la representación: la novela chilena del golpe.* Valencia, Spain: Fundación Instituto Shakespeare: Instituto de Cine y Radio-Televisión, 1985.

Lepeley, Oscar. "Autoritarismo y discurso literario: teatro contestario chileno post-golpe." Ph.D. diss., University of Illinois, Urbana-Champaign, 1994.

Montoya, Roberto, and Daniel Pereyra. *El caso Pinochet y la impunidad en América Latina.* La Rioja, Argentina: Editorial Pandemia, 2000.

Padilla Ballesteros, Elías. *La memoria y el ovido: detenidos desaparecidos en Chile.* Santiago: Ediciones Orígenes, 1995.

Parodi Pinedo, Patricio C. *El secuestro del general.* [Chile?]: P.C. Parodi Pinedo, 1999.

Pinochet Ugarte, Augusto, and María Eugenia Oyarzún. *Augusto Pinochet: diálogos con su historia: conversaciones inéditas.* Providencia, Chile: Editorial Sudamericana, 1999.

Pratt, Mary Louise. "Overwriting Pinochet: Undoing the Culture of Fear in Chile." *Modern Language Quarterly* 57, no. 2 (1996): 151–63. Reprinted in *The Places of History: Regionalism Revisited in Latin America*, edited by Doris Sommer, 21–33. Durham, N.C.: Duke University Press, 1999.

Ramos Arellano, Marcela, and Juan Andrés Guzmán de Luigi. *La extraña muerte de un soldado en tiempos de paz: el caso de Pedro Soto Tapia*. Santiago: Lom Ediciones, 1998.

Richard, Nelly, ed. *Políticas y estéticas de la memoria*. Coloquio "Políticas y Estéticas de la Memoria," Universidad de Chile, 1999. Providencia, Santiago: Editorial Cuarto Propio, 2000.

Rodley, Nigel S. *Report of the Special Rapporteur, Mr. Nigel S. Rodley, Submitted Pursuant to Commission on Human Rights Resolution 1995/37: Addendum: Visit by the Special Rapporteur to Chile*. Geneva, Switzerland: United Nations, 1996.

Rojas B., Paz. *Persona, estado, poder: estudios sobre salud mental*. 2 vols. Santiago: Comité de Defensa de los Derechos del Pueblo, CODEPU, 1989–1996.

———. *Tarda pero llega: Pinochet ante la justicia española*. Santiago: Lom Ediciones: CODEPU, 1998.

Salinas, Luis Alejandro. *The London Clinic*. Santiago: Lom Ediciones, 1999.

Schemo, Diana Jean. "U.S. Victims of Chile's Coup: The Uncensored File." *New York Times*, 13 February 2000, late edition (East Coast).

Sigmund, Paul E. *The United States and Democracy in Chile*. Baltimore: Johns Hopkins University Press, 1993.

Spero, Nancy. "Torture of Women" [selected panels]. In *Leon Golub and Nancy Spero: War and Memory* [exhibition catalog], 39–40, 72–3. Cambridge, Mass.: MIT List Visual Arts Center, 1994.

Uribe Arce, Armando, and Miguel Vicuña Navarro. *El accidente Pinochet*. Santiago: Editorial Sudamericana, 1999.

Vidal, Hernán. *Cultura nacional chilena, crítica literaria y derechos humanos*. Series Literature and Human Rights, no. 5. Minneapolis, Minn.: Institute for the Study of Ideologies and Literatures, 1989.

Vitale, Luis [et al.]. *Para recuperar la memoria histórica: Frei, Allende y Pinochet*. Santiago: CESOC: Ediciones ChileAmérica, 1999.

Wright, Thomas C. "Legacy of Dictatorship: Works on the Chilean Diaspora." *Latin American Research Review* 30, no. 3 (1995): 198–209.

Uruguay

Background to the "Dirty War"

Davis, William Columbus. "Uruguay: Lost Utopia." Chap. 2 in *Warnings from the Far South: Democracy versus Dictatorship in Uruguay, Argentina, and Chile,* 17–69. Westport, Conn.: Praeger, 1995.

Gilio, María Esther. *The Tupamaro Guerrillas.* Translated by Anne Edmondson. New York: Saturday Review Press, 1972. Translation of *La guerrilla tupamara* (Havana: Casa de las Américas, 1970).

Jackson, Sir Geoffrey. *Surviving the Long Night.* New York: Vanguard, 1974. Published in 1973 under the title *People's Prison* (London: Faber). Published in Spanish under the title *Secuestrado por el pueblo* (Barcelona: Pomaire, 1974).

Kaufman, Edy. *Uruguay in Transition: From Civilian to Military Rule.* New Brunswick, N.J.: Transaction Books, 1979.

Labrousse, Alain. *The Tupamaros.* New York: Penguin Books, 1973.

Nuñez, Carlos. "The Tupamaros: Armed Vanguard in Uruguay." *Red Sky/Blue Sky,* no. 2 (April 1970): 1–4.

Porzecanski, Arturo C. *Uruguay's Tupamaros: The Urban Guerrilla.* New York: Praeger, 1973.

Taylor, Philip B., Jr. "Uruguay: The Costs of Inept Political Corporatism." In *Latin American Politics and Development,* 2d. ed., edited by Howard J. Wiarda and Harvey F. Kline, 317–40. Boulder, Colo.: Westview Press, 1985.

Weinstein, Martin. *Uruguay: The Politics of Failure.* Westport, Conn.: Greenwood Press, 1975.

Wilson, Carlos. *The Tupamaros: The Unmentionables.* Boston: Branden Press, 1974.

The "Dirty War," 1973–1985

Nonfiction and Testimonios

Bloche, Maxwell G. "Uruguay's Military Physicians: Cogs in a System of State Terror." *JAMA: the Journal of the American Medical Association* 255, no. 20 (1986): 2788–93.

González Bermejo, Ernesto. *Las manos en el fuego.* 3 vols. Montevideo: Ediciones de la Banda Oriental, 1985.

LaBarthe, J. F. "In Libertad Prison." *New York Review of Books* 28 (19 November 1981): 38–39.

Organization of American States. Inter-American Commission on Human Rights. *Report on the Situation of Human Rights in Uruguay.* Washington, D.C.: Secretary General of the Organization of American States, 1978. Published in Spanish as *Informe sobre la situación de los derechos humanos en Uruguay* (Washington, D.C.: Comisión Interamericana de Derechos Humanos, Secretaria General de la Organización de los Estados Americanos, 1978).

Rial Roade, Juan. *Partidos políticos, democracia y autoritarismo.* 2 vols. Montevideo: Centro de Informaciones y Estudios del Uruguay: Ediciones de la Banda Oriental, 1984.

Rosencof, Mauricio, and Eleuterio Fernández Huidobro. *Memorias del calabozo.* 3 vols. Montevideo: TAE Editorial, 1987.

Literature

Aínsa, Fernando. *Los naufragios de Malinow y otros relatos.* Montevideo: Editorial de La Plaza, 1988.

―――. *Las palomas de Rodrigo.* Montevideo: Monte Sexto, 1988.

Arregui, Mario. *La escoba de la bruja.* Montevideo: Acali Editorial, 1979.

―――. *Ramos generales.* Montevideo: Arca, 1985.

Banchero, Anderssen. *Ojos en la noche.* Montevideo: Ediciones de la Banda Oriental, 1985.

―――. *Las orillas del mundo.* Montevideo: Ediciones de la Banda Oriental, 1980.

―――. *Los regresos.* Montevideo: Ediciones de la Banda Oriental, 1989.

―――. *Triste de la calle cortada.* Montevideo: Ediciones de la Banda Oriental, 1975.

Benedetti, Mario. *Articulario: Desexilio y perplejidades: Reflexiones desde el sur.* Madrid: El País/Aguilar, 1994.

―――. *Con o sin nostalgia.* Mexico City: Siglo XXI, 1977.

―――. *Cotidianas.* Mexico City: Siglo XXI, 1979.

―――. *El desexilio y otras conjeturas.* Madrid: Ediciones El País, 1984.

―――. *Geografías.* Madrid: Alfaguara, 1984.

―――. *Pedro y el capitán: Pieza en cuatro actos.* Mexico City: Editorial Nueva Imagen, 1979.

―――. *Primavera con una esquina rota.* Madrid: Alfaguara, 1983.

―――. *Recuerdos olvidados.* Montevideo: Ediciones Trilce, 1988.

Bianqui, Matilde. *A la gran muñeca: Una novela y dos historias que nunca se contaron.* Montevideo: Tupac Amaru Editorial, 1988.

Bridal, Tessa. *The Tree of Red Stars.* Minneapolis, Minn.: Milkweed Editions, 1997.

Butazzoni, Fernando. *El tigre y la nieve.* Montevideo: Ediciones de la Banda Oriental, 1986.

Concurso Nacional de Cuentos de AEBU. *Catorce cuentos por nueve autores.* Montevideo: Arca, 1988.

Eyherabide, Gley. *En el zoo.* Montevideo: TAE Editorial, 1988.

Fernández Sastre, Roberto. *El turismo infame.* Barcelona: Anagrama, 1987.

Galeano, Eduardo H. *La canción de nosotros.* Buenos Aires: Editorial Sudamericana, 1975.

———. *Days and Nights of Love and War.* Translated by Bobby S. Ortiz. New York: Monthly Review Press, 1983. Translation of *Días y noches de amor y de guerra* (Barcelona: Editorial Laia, 1978).

Harari, Leo. *La nostalgia tiene bolsillo.* Montevideo: Editorial MZ, 1985.

Maia, Circe. *Un viaje a Salto.* Montevideo: Ediciones del Nuevo Mundo, 1988.

Marra, Nelson. *Cenicienta antes del parto.* Montevideo: Yoea Editorial, 1993.

———. *De cabreos y nostalgias.* Madrid: La Palma, 1995,

———. *El guardaespaldas y otros cuentos.* Stockholm: Nordam, 1980.

Martínez Moreno, Carlos. *Animal de palabras.* Montevideo: Arca, 1987.

———. *De vida o muerte.* Buenos Aires: Siglo XXI Argentina Editores, 1971.

———. *El infierno* [English]. Translated by Ann Wright. London: Readers International, 1988. Translation of *El color que el infierno me escondiera* (Mexico City: Editorial Nueva Imagen, 1981).

———. *Tierra en la boca.* Buenos Aires: Editorial Losada, 1974.

Musto, Jorge. *El pasajero.* Havana: Casa de las Americas, 1977.

Onetti, Juan Carlos. *Cuando entonces.* Madrid: Mondadori, 1987.

———. *Let the Wind Speak.* Translated by Helen Lane. London: Serpent's Tail, 1996. Translation of *Dejemos hablar al viento* (Barcelona: Bruguera, 1979).

———. *Presencia y otros cuentos.* Madrid: Almarubu, 1986.

Peri Rossi, Cristina. *Cosmoagonías.* Barcelona: Editorial Laia, 1988.

———. *A Forbidden Passion: Stories.* Translated by Jane Treacy. Pittsburgh: Cleis Press, 1993. Translation of *Una pasión prohibida* (Barcelona: Seix Barral, 1986).

———. *El museo de los esfuerzos inútiles.* Barcelona: Seix Barral, 1983.

———. *The Ship of Fools.* Translated by Psiche Hughes. Columbia, La.: Readers International, 1989. Translation of *La nave de los locos* (Barcelona: Seix Barral, 1984).

―――. *Solitaire of Love*. Translated by Robert S. Rudder and Gloria Arjona. Durham, N.C.: Duke University Press, 2000. Translation of *Solitario de amor* (Barcelona: Grijalbo, 1988).

Prego, Omar. *Sólo para exiliados*. Montevideo: Arca, 1987.

Rein, Mercedes. *Bocas de tormenta*. Montevideo: Arca, 1987.

―――. *Casa vacía*. Montevideo: Arca, 1983.

Solinas, Franco. *State of Siege*. Translated by Brooke Leveque. New York: Ballantine Books, 1973. Translation of *Estado de Sitio*. (Buenos Aires: Shapire, 1973). The screenplay for a film of the same title.

Vierci, Pablo. *Detrás de los árboles*. Montevideo: Editorial Proyección, 1987.

Films and Documentaries

Escondites del sol, Los (*Hideaways of the Sun*). Directed by Walter Tournier. 37 minutes. Imágenes, 1991.

Por esos ojos (*For These Eyes*). Directed by Gonzalo Arijón and Virginia Martínez. 52 minutes. France 2 Cinéma, Point du Jour, Télé Europe, 1997.

State of Siege. Directed by Costa-Gavras. Columbia, 1973. Based on the screenplay of the same title by Franco Solinas.

Tupamaros. Directed by Heidi Specogna and Rainer Hoffmann. 95 minutes. Specogna Film, 1996.

Welcome to Uruguay. Produced and directed by Gabriel Auer. 20 minutes. 1980.

Yeux des oiseaux, Les (*The Eyes of the Bird*). Directed by Gabriel Auer. 82 minutes. Antenne 2 et al., 1982.

The Aftermath of the "Dirty War"

Delgado, María. "Truth and Justice in Uruguay." *NACLA Report on the Americas* 34, no. 1 (July/August 2000): 37–39.

Gillespie, Charles G. "Uruguay's Transition from Collegial Military-Technocratic Rule." In *Transitions from Authoritarian Rule: Latin America*, edited by Guillermo O'Donnell, Philippe C. Schmitter, and Laurence Whitehead, 173–95. Baltimore: Johns Hopkins University Press, 1986.

Gonzalez, Luis E. *Political Structures and Democracy in Uruguay*. Notre Dame, Ind.: University of Notre Dame Press, 1991.

Ruffinelli, Jorge. "Uruguay: Dictadura y re-democratización: Un informe sobre la literatura, 1973–1989." *Nuevo texto crítico* 3, no. 5 (1990): 37–66.

Servicio Paz y Justicia, Uruguay. *Uruguay Nunca Más: Human Rights Violations, 1972–1985.* Translated by Elizabeth Hampsten. Philadelphia: Temple University Press, 1992. Translation of *Uruguay nunca más: Informe sobre la violación a los derechos humanos, 1972–1985* (Montevideo: Servicio Paz y Justicia, Uruguay, 1989).

Sosnowski, Saúl, compiler. *Represión, exilio, y democracia: La cultura uruguaya.* Montevideo: Ediciones de la Banda Oriental, 1987.

Stone, Kenton V. *Utopia Undone: The Fall of Uruguay in the Novels of Carlos Martínez Moreno.* Lewisburg, Pa.: Bucknell University Press, 1994.

Trigo, Abril. "Candombe and the Reterritorialization of Culture." *Callaloo* 16, no. 3 (1993): 716–28.

Weinstein, Martin. *Uruguay: Democracy at the Crossroads.* Boulder, Colo.: Westview Press, 1988.

Weschler, Lawrence. *A Miracle, a Universe: Settling Accounts with Torturers.* Chicago, Ill.: University of Chicago Press, 1998.

About the Authors

DAVID KOHUT (B.A. State University of New York at Binghamton; M.A., anthropology, State University of New York at Binghamton; M.L.S. State University of New York at Albany) is associate librarian in Byrne Memorial Library, Saint Xavier University, Chicago. He has published articles in library-science journals and contributed to reference works. He is coauthor of *Women Authors of Modern Hispanic South America: A Bibliography of Literary Criticism and Interpretation*, published by Scarecrow Press in 1989. He is a member of Amnesty International.

OLGA VILELLA (A.B. Vassar College; M.S.J. Columbia University; Ph.D. University of Chicago) is associate professor in the Department of English and Foreign Languages, Saint Xavier University, Chicago, specializing in Latin American literatures of the 19th and 20th centuries. Dr. Vilella also directs the Oaxaca Project, a language-and-service study program based in Oaxaca, Mexico, and sponsored by Saint Xavier University. Her research interests include Latin American *modernismo* and literary responses to dictatorship in 20th-century Latin America. She is a member of Amnesty International.

BEATRICE JULIAN (B.A. Loyola University, Chicago; M.S. University of Illinois at Urbana-Champaign) is assistant librarian in Byrne Memorial Library, Saint Xavier University, Chicago. In addition to working as a librarian in both public and academic libraries, she has served as an adult literacy coordinator and a public policy research analyst. A published writer and professional storyteller, she is interested in researching and documenting traditional forms of cultural expression. Her varied freelance writing and research assignments have resulted in magazine and newspaper articles, essays, elementary school textbook units, and poetry.